Evangelical Sermons of Our Day

Evangelical Sermons of Our Day

Thirty-seven Foremost Examples of Bible Preaching, compiled and edited with special annotations by

ANDREW W. BLACKWOOD

A CHANNEL PRESS BOOK

Harper & Brothers, New York

Dedicated
to Every One Who Preaches
the Faith of Our Fathers
for the Glory of Our God
and the Redemption of Our Sons

Library of Congress Catalog Card Number: 59-10752

FOREWORD

THE PUBLISHERS have asked me to prepare a volume of sermons representing the evangelical pulpit today. According to impartial experts in "opinion research," seventy-five per cent of the ministers in the States regard themselves as evangelical. No doubt an equal proportion of our laymen would take the same stand. At present we may think of more than fifty per cent as strongly evangelical, both among clergy and laity. Any such label or estimate has to be loose and elastic. Sometimes our labels sound like libels, and our estimates seem extreme, if not unkind and divisive. Any such attitude or spirit would be foreign to the design and character of this volume.

This book seeks to present examples of pulpit work from evangelicals, but does not presume to pass on the orthodoxy of others. The larger the number of evangelicals, the more heartily should we rejoice. Among evangelicals the majority belong to "older denominations." So do I, the editor; and so do most of the contributors, but by no means all. In order to secure the names of evangelical preachers, I sought the aid of leaders in various denominations, in "newer churches," and in other groups of evangelicals. From these varied sources I received hundreds of names, including some of men overseas. I initiated few nominations, and I ignored none.

Practically all the men who received my invitations replied. As a rule they commended the project, and none threw cold water. Many agreed to send a manuscript, often more than one. Not long after their sermons had been received, two well-known church leaders went home to God.

Others, overworked and weary, reluctantly declined. A few men of renown did not even acknowledge the invitation. Doubtless each of them has a secretary who screens incoming mail and discards appeals from ecclesiastical beggars.

The correspondence led to fellowship with many choice spirits. Even from afar these men strengthened my faith in the Evangel and increased my hopes for the morrow. The thirty-seven sermons chosen, like all the others, show variety of outlook and emphasis. For instance, Wesley's followers often think and preach in ways that differ from those of Calvin's disciples. But we all love the same Lord, and preach the same Gospel. Out of the many sermons that do not now appear I could have assembled another volume of equal size, different in outlook and emphasis, but equally evangelical.

Not all of the thirty-seven seem to me "great," or to come from "great preachers." If they did, whom would they represent? Personally, I know few men whom I deem to be "great," and fewer still among ministers. After having read countless sermons from our own time, I do not recall one since 1930 that I consider "great." But who am I to judge? I cannot even certify that I have chosen the best of the many good sermons now in my hands. Ideally, we should think of sermons, not as great and famous, but as "good and faithful." Indeed, we should often hear the Master saying, "Welcome, thou good and faithful sermon!"

"Good" here means helpful to those who hear; "faithful" means in accord with the revealed will of God. As for "greatness" in written work, the foremost university professors of literature say that the test can come only after the lapse of time. As with Homer's *Iliad* or Dante's *Inferno*, greatness means literary excellence and influence that continue and increase after the conditions that produced the writing have passed away. From this point of view, how can any editor appraise a contemporary preacher as "great," and a sermon as "best"? Who can know, except God?

For the recent fashion of labeling sermons "great" and "best" we who teach and write must bear the chief blame. Have we not led eager young learners to fall down and do obeisance to departed preachers, most of whom would have refused to accept homage that should go only to God? As elsewhere in writing, I am finding fault with no one more than myself. Only gradually have I learned that the Lord looks on our pulpit work, ideally, not as "great" but "good," because full of grace and truth.

In selecting these sermons I have needed wisdom higher than my own. Still I thank God for the privilege. I feel grateful to the publishers for the project, and to other publishers for setting me free; to librarians near and far for expert and painstaking counsel; to busy divines for submitting lists of nominees; and especially to those who sent me manuscripts. On the basis of all these materials I have dared to appraise the evangelical preaching of today, and I have gradually envisioned the pattern of this volume.

I hope that the book will go into the hands of countless ministers and laymen. I believe that the sermons will encourage the ministerial reader to prepare nothing but "good and faithful" evangelical messages; and that they will hearten the lay reader to uphold his pastor in delivering evangelical sermons—to the end that he may help every brother in the pew, whether that brother be unsaved or unchurched, untaught or unsanctified, unready or untrained for heroic service in the Kingdom.

I also hope that these sermons will help students of divinity in classes and in private reading. Before any one of them goes out into the pastorate, or the mission field—the most important work in the world today, and the most difficult—I hope that he will give himself completely into the keeping of the hands that were pierced. Then he will resolve never to preach anything but "good and faithful" sermons. Thus he will hold true to the faith of our evangelical fathers and mothers. He will ever strive to meet the spiritual needs of his flock, men and women, as well as boys and girls, all of them dear to the heart of God.

II CORINTHIANS 4:5-7   ANDREW W. BLACKWOOD

CONTENTS

III. With Christ Near His End

IV. With Christ After the Ascension

V. With Christ in Later Epistles

VI. With Christ in the Unknown Future

INTRODUCTION

THESE THIRTY-SEVEN sermons represent a variety of evangelical preaching today. "Evangelical preaching" here refers to what the fathers used to call "Gospel sermons." But that term might cause readers to expect messages intended only to save souls. Hence we may think of evangelical preachers as those who gladly follow in the train of the Prophets and the Apostles, not to speak of their Lord. Among present-day scholars the core of Bible preaching about Christ has become known as the *kerygma,* the transliteration of a Greek term, "preaching the Gospel." Through the ages since Christ most evangelical preachers have given a smaller place to the *didache,* another Greek term that means, approximately, "teaching the truths of God to believers."

Instead of trying further to define the word evangelical, let us think about it in terms of leading exemplars from other days. Evangelical preachers follow in the tradition of such contrasting personalities as Isaiah and Hosea, Peter and Paul, Augustine and Chrysostom, Bernard of Clairvaux and Francis of Assisi, Luther and Calvin, Bunyan and John Donne, Wesley and Whitefield, Spurgeon and Canon H. P. Liddon, Jonathan Edwards and Lyman Beecher, Dwight L. Moody and Bishop Matthew Simpson, Alexander Whyte and John Henry Jowett, G. Campbell Morgan and George W. Truett, with a host of more recent divines.

13

The preaching of those worthies differed as much as stars in the sky at midnight. "Where the Spirit of the Lord is, there is freedom" (II Cor. 3:17). But those men were all alike in sounding the message that we know as evangelical. Every one of them strove to meet the needs of his hearers by looking to God for a message, and presenting the truth of God in a fashion all his own. At least ideally, the same holds true of the thirty-seven sermons that follow. They sound the note that we term evangelical. As a key verse for the book we could take Ephesians 2:8, "By grace are ye saved through faith; and that not of yourselves: it is the gift of God." Hence the opening sermon has to do with the grace of God. After that the other thirty-six follow the order of the Bible texts. Each man chooses his own version of the Scriptures.

The sermons appear under six general headings, suggestive rather than exact. All of them point to Christ. On the basis of these sermons, as well as many others now in hand, I have formed certain conclusions about evangelical preaching today. Here I call attention to elements of strength, to signs of weakness, and to reasons for hope. Since many of these ideas seem self-evident, they call for limited discussion. To deal with them adequately would require a large book. If at times I cut across lots, and seem to be laying down the law, instead of holding up a light, I am trying to suggest lines of thought for the reader to follow in a way different from my own, which is never inspired nor infallible.

I. THE STRENGTH OF THE EVANGELICAL PULPIT

At its best, evangelical preaching carries out the ideals of the Reformation. They in turn go back to the Bible. As every reader knows, the Reformation had to do with preaching, as an all-important part of public worship, and with other vital matters that do not concern us in this book. As preachers, Luther, Calvin, and the other Reformers strove not to change and invent, but to restore and revive. In some respects they fell short. They did not sufficiently stress evangelism at home and missions abroad.

They did not always correctly apply Christian truth to moral problems of their day. But still they have given us ideals and traditions of evangelical preaching, for which we thank God. In many respects the evangelical pulpit of our day resembles that of the Reformers. As a rule these likenesses have to do with the substance and the spirit of preaching, rather than the structure and the style.

1. *The Dependence on Holy Scripture.* At its best, evangelical preaching bases everything on the written revelation of God's holy will. In the sermons that follow, the form may be largely textual or topical, expository or inspirational, with various blendings of these types. Such labels refer to different ways of preparing the strong meat of the Gospel, or the pure milk of the Word, so as to secure a wholesome variety of pulpit fare, and continued appeal to common people—such as those in Galilee who heard the Master gladly, and those in Wittenberg who heard Luther with delight. Thank God for such "popular preaching"!

In the States at present there seems to be more of pulpit dependence on the Bible than at any previous time in our century. Often before World War II the treatment appeared to be psychological, sociological, philosophic, pragmatic, or some other form not strongly Biblical. The stress often fell on human experience rather than divine power, and on human interest rather than divine revelation. Some of these emphases have a rightful place in the evangelical pulpit, but only as ways of setting forth truths that God has revealed in His written Word. In the present statement about evangelical preaching the element of Biblical quality comes first because it is the most important and the most distinctive characteristic. Just as a Roman Catholic in the puplit speaks with authority from his Church, so an evangelical Protestant speaks with the authority of Holy Scripture. For this reason he stands at the open Bible, as "the man behind the Book."

2. *The Custom of Preaching from a Text.* Preaching from the Bible means that the truth comes from God through his Holy Book, and as a rule from one portion in a sermon. A man learned in the Scriptures singles out a literary unit that deals with the subject of the coming sermon. Then he usually selects a key text,

fairly brief, which every hearer can recall, because it contains the
gist of the discourse. In preparing for a varsity debate at Yale or
Harvard the coach had one rule, from which no speaker dared to
depart: "Begin with a statement of the assigned subject, and be
sure to repeat it word for word." Popular preaching consists in
persuasion, rather than argument, but otherwise the analogy
holds. A wise minister starts a sermon by announcing his text,
as the most important thing he has to say. From time to time he
repeats the text, to make it memorable.

If chosen with skill and care, a preaching text serves as a gate-
way into a Biblical garden abounding with food for hungry
souls. As Beecher used to say, don't waste any time swinging
on the gate. When a man announces the text, he may at once
state the topic, which interprets the text, and also names the
sermon. Whatever the method—and it ought to vary—hearers
have a right to expect an intelligent, interesting discussion of the
dominant truth in the text, in the light of the immediate context,
and of that Bible book. Evangelical laymen have a right to expect
their minister to be learned in the Scriptures, and under the
guidance of the Spirit, to bring out Gospel truth that "speaks to
their condition" today.

A young seminary graduate may not yet know his Bible well
enough to preach this way. But he can settle down with an
important Bible book, to live with it and with commentaries
so long and lovingly that he can preach from any part of it
with assurance. "With joy shall ye draw water from the wells of
salvation" (Isa. 12:3). Ah, but what if a man has nothing to draw
with, for these Bible wells are deep! Even so, the way to learn
how to do this kind of evangelical preaching is to keep doing it
week after week. Spiritual and intellectual muscles grow through
proper use.

Intelligent use of a text helps to keep a sermon from scattering.
According to John Henry Newman in his *Idea of a University
Defined* (1873), the pulpit work of a minister at home ought as
a rule to be specific. This means that in each sermon he deals
with one large truth or duty, and that he repeats at intervals any
idea he wishes the hearers to carry home for meditation and later
action. Without a Bible text to keep the speaker "on the beam,"

he might "go everywhere preaching the Gospel." As for ways of dealing with a text, little do laymen know or care about our labels. Like a mother's way of identifying her jellies and jams, the ministerial son's labels ought never to appear in the presence of invited guests.

3. *The Preaching of Bible Doctrine.* In the past history of the evangelical pulpit, especially at the Reformation, Bible doctrine provided the warp of almost every sermon. According to the fathers, "Preach doctrine ethically, and ethics doctrinally." In other words, no sermon without its important doctrine, and no important doctrine without a yearly sermon. Often indirectly, God's local representative uses a Bible doctrine as the basis for a message intended to win souls; to cheer the hearts of believers; to help a person afflicted with doubt; or to guide in the performance of some difficult duty. For example, why should a believer stand ready to forgive a person who has inflicted a deadly wrong? Because the believer himself has received forgiveness from God, and he should be like his heavenly Father. A man's forgiveness of serious wrongs ought to be like God's forgiveness of deadly sins.

A wise minister also learns how to preach doctrine directly. The writer used to do so at the evening service. Thus he gained a good hearing at night, in three fields where the lay officers said it could never be done. In a doctrinal or teaching sermon, the didactic aim governs the choice of the text, the phrasing of the topic, the form of the introduction, and every succeeding part of the sermon. Everywhere the test is clarity, with human interest, and fidelity to the meaning and spirit of the Bible passage.

Better still, such a truth as "The Work of the Spirit in the Life of the Believer" may call for a number of consecutive sermons at the same hour on each Lord's Day. In a month with four or five Sundays there may be that many specific sermons, such as "The Holy Spirit As Your Teacher." In looking back over his pulpit ministry any preacher can see that he has accomplished more by specific sermons, which required him to dig, than by sweeping surveys, which usually called for little mental effort and no immediate mastery of a Bible passage.

4. *The Stress on Divine Grace.* In a typical evangelical pulpit

the main stress falls on the grace of God, though never apart
from His dealings with men. Grace here means the almighty
power and goodness of the Lord in meeting the needs of men's
hearts today, especially the needs arising from sin. Throughout
Christian history there have been two pulpit emphases: the one
on redemption from sin through the grace of Christ; the other
on men's search after God, and their endeavors to find ways of
growing more like Him.

One way of preaching calls on the hearer to look up, because
the day of his redemption draweth nigh; the other bids him
stand on his feet and make the most of all his manly powers. The
one is largely vertical; the other is mainly horizontal. In every
city you can hear the two sorts of pulpit work. The same holds
true in books about doctrine. Where Charles Hodge or William
G. T. Shedd began a treatise on theology with stress on God's
revelation of Himself, the ablest living American philosophical
theologian devotes one-third of his first volume to man and his
reason. Here too, however, the trend seems to be turning towards
giving the first place to the Biblical revelation of God's grace.

5. *The Emphasis on the Hereafter.* The preaching of doctrine,
Biblically, calls for a good deal of attention to what lies beyond.
Often the sermon has to do with the brighter aspects of the
hereafter. Much to his amazement, a young pastor discovers that
laymen relish intelligent preaching about heaven, but only if
he speaks about it with the human interest and warmth of a man
who knows the truths of the Book experientially. In a certain
congregation the pastor wished to interest young married people
in sermons to meet their heart needs. To his amazement, out of
all the suggested subjects that he put in their hands, they gave
the preference to these two: "What Are Theologians Teaching
Today?" and "What Is the Christian Meaning of Death?" Both
subjects doctrinal, and one of them eschatological! And that
among a group of more than a hundred young married folk, not
yet apparently much concerned about the things of God!

Sometimes the stress ought to fall on "the dark line in God's
face." In the Gospels our Lord says almost as much about hell
as about heaven. Also, He tells more than a little about the
Judgment Day. Strange as it may seem, in the first three Gospels

He is reported as appealing to fear more often than to any other emotion. Now that the peoples of the earth are shivering because of possible atomic warfare, they ought to learn both sides of what the Scriptures reveal about what lies beyond the Final Return of our Lord. Here too the trend now seems to be toward a more balanced preaching of Bible doctrine.

6. *The Stress on Pulpit Evangelism.* In the past the evangelical movement has usually given a worthy place to soul-winning sermons. Not only has it sent forth a succession of "professional evangelists," such as Dwight L. Moody and Billy Graham. The evangelical pastor, as a rule, has looked on himself as a local evangelist. For a time between our two World Wars many church leaders insisted that the day of group evangelism had departed, and that henceforth we must rely mainly on personal work. But now younger leaders have discovered that it still pleases God to save adult sinners through sermons intended to win souls. Meanwhile local churches that did not abandon such ways of preaching kept on growing by adult accessions from the world. Let us conclude that a non-evangelistic congregation cannot be strongly evangelical.

7. *The Nurture of Christian Souls.* The evangelical pulpit has always given a large place to the feeding and guidance of those who already believe in Christ. Such an evangelist as Moody held week-day meetings for church folk. There, with open Bible, he fed them with what we call "pastoral sermons." In the parish ministry Alexander Maclaren and John Henry Jowett looked with favor on soul-winning sermons by others, but gave themselves almost exclusively to messages that instructed and helped people who already belonged to Christ. Here again, there is need of balance. With some exceptions, as with Billy Graham, the Lord intends every minister to preach both sorts of sermons. Only in a church with more than one pastor do the facts locally call for a man who preaches only to the saints, or only to the unsaved and the unchurched.

8. *The Call for Pulpit Counseling.* In comparatively recent times the word "counseling" has come to the fore. In private by appointment the minister confers with a person in distress because of doubt or fear, despondency or marital infelicity. Often the

basic cause proves to be sin against God, resulting in strained relations with others, and strife within, like that in the early experience of Paul (Rom. 7:13-25). After a while a minister learns that without divulging the secrets of any broken heart he can engage in pastoral counseling from the pulpit, as a sort of spiritual prophylactic. How otherwise could he deal honestly with a psalm about God's cure for discouragement (42,43), or doubt (73), or fear (27)? If he begins to feel that he has been doing something new and strange, he may find that evangelical preachers such as John Bunyan and Richard Baxter long ago excelled in group counseling, and so did our Lord, though not with present-day labels, and seldom without relying on Holy Writ to provide the healing balm for broken hearts (Jer. 8:22).

9. *The Message with Divine Authority.* In some of their forms so far the ways of evangelical preachers may seem like those of ministers not conservative in doctrine. In any such case we do not claim a monopoly of preaching methods. But we do have a basis of authority different from that of many preachers not specially evangelical. Here again, we wish we could share our high privilege with every man who preaches. What is authority for us may well become the authority of any other Protestant divine. With us the authority rests in God and His Book, not in the minister or his Church. Ordinarily we say that the authority comes from the Bible, and of course that ever holds true, but only because the Bible is our supreme means of grace. Grace itself, with authority to proclaim it, proceeds only from the Triune God.

As the living Word, Christ speaks with the authority of His Father (Matt. 28:18-20). As the written Word, "the only inspired and infallible rule of faith and practice," the Bible also speaks with the authority of God (II Tim. 3:15-17). Whether we think of authority in terms of the living Word or the written Word, which always agree, we ought to remember that the authority to preach comes to a man now through the Holy Spirit (John 16:13). Herein lies the cardinal difference between our preaching and that of ministers not yet strongly evangelical: our authority is Biblical and objective.

10. *The Ministry of Christian Hope.* The climax of the Chris-

tian message has to do with hope for the hereafter. The golden
text of the Bible (John 3:16) starts with the love of God, en-
shrines in its heart the dying love of our Redeemer, and issues
in assurance of the life everlasting. When a minister preaches
the Good News of God he takes for granted the assurance of
sins forgiven, and then he deals with other spiritual truths dear
to the hearts of God's children. He comes to a Biblical climax
in assurance of Christian hope, not only for the redeemed of
God, one by one, but also for the triumph of the Kingdom, which
is "righteousness, and peace, and joy in the Holy Ghost" (Rom.
14:17b).

In a painting of the Madonna and Child, whether by Raphael
or almost any other artist of the Florentine School, there is at
least a glimpse of the open sky. When Raphael had to paint on
the top of a wooden cask, he showed a glimpse of the heavens
above. So in any true hour of evangelical worship, and in almost
every evangelical sermon, there is at least a little about the life
everlasting. As William Sanday used to say at Oxford, in the
New Testament the center of gravity lies beyond the grave. If
so, pulpit work that has New Testament balance and is not
"eccentric" gives a place of honor to preaching about the hope
for the triumph of the Kingdom, when the Christ of Calvary
will enter into all the crown rights of the Redeemer.

A glance over these ten elements of strength in the evangelical
pulpit will show that almost every one of them has come from
God. For them all we ought to give Him our hearty thanks, and
that most humbly. We ought also to learn through Paul that
even the best of ministers and churches have the Gospel treasure
in earthen vessels (II Cor. 4:7). This means in part that even
when we preach about the Resurrection of our Lord or the vision
of the Great White Throne our sermons are likely to show
human frailties and faults. To these we now turn.

II. WEAKNESSES IN EVANGELICAL
SERMONS

Sometimes as evangelicals we feel tempted to boast about our
heritage of preaching, and to feel proud of our pulpit attain-
ments. Lest we should become exalted above measure the Lord

has permitted us to learn what discerning critics say about our evangelical sermons. As a rule the strictures have to do with form rather than content; that is, with us and our efforts, not with our Gospel and our God. The most searching critique, and the most effective, comes from Harry Emerson Fosdick. In the leading article of *Harper's Magazine* in July, 1928, he discussed a problem, "What Is the Matter with Preaching?" Since many of his strictures (but not his doctrines!) still hold true, we evangelicals might well secure permission to reprint the article, and use it as a check list for our sermons. Many of the same ideas appear more mildly in Fosdick's autobiography, *The Living of These Days* (1956), which is also well written. Without specific mention, some of these charges emerge below.

1. *Ignoring the People Present.* The most serious charge has to do with our way of ignoring the hearers of a sermon. Under God, and for His glory, every such message has its being for the sake of the people in church, or else persons listening over the radio. When did any prophet or apostle, not to mention our Lord, ever preach without much regard to the interests and needs of the hearers? No one of those worthies, or of his evangelical successors, ever prepared and delivered a sermon for the satisfaction of the speaker, or the salvation of the sermon. So today, the preacher should look on himself in the pulpit as the local agent of God to interest and help the home people, and on the sermon as his appointed way of rendering this holy service.

How is it then with the evangelical pulpit today? Except perhaps in delivery, some orthodox sermons give no visible or tangible evidence of concern about the auditors as human beings in need of God. With commendable industry and zeal an able expositor makes ready to explain a Bible passage, or a Christian doctrine. In such a case Paul would have gone on to show the bearing on the lives of the hearers, or readers. What practical difference ought the truth to make here at home in the city, or else out on the busy street? For example, look at Romans 12-15, or at Ephesians 4-6. Every once in a while a present-day impersonal preacher may say "My friends," or "Dear brethren," but then he goes on to discuss the truth in terms of far away and long ago. Such pulpit work abounds in past tenses, plural pronouns, passive verbs, and impersonal nouns, which sometimes sound like "post-mortem preaching."

In all these matters there surely ought to be a golden mean. This applies both to the content of the sermon, and to its form. For instance, take the use of personal pronouns. According to a wise observer of current pulpit work, nobody but a dunce would keep saying "you" throughout a sermon, or even for any long stretch of time, but if in twenty-five minutes a man never says "you," probably he is not preaching. Where except in the pulpit does a man of learning and culture speak to people this long without once looking them in the eyes and saying something to them, kindly and directly? Why have a local preacher if his messages have no perceptible bearing on the interests and needs of the local hearers? On the other hand, the Lord pity the laymen if any discourse does not lead them out of themselves and up into the "air of increased visibility" where they can see themselves anew in light that streams from the open Book.

For preaching that ignores the hearers much of the blame must lie with us who teach and write. In class and with the pen we have exalted the preacher and the sermon. Our libraries contain volume after volume, often uplifting, about the preacher, his life and work, or "The Preparation of Sermons." But who can find more than one worth-while book about the hearers? Perhaps for this reason, many a young man does not learn how to preach until he has become a "good and faithful" pastor. When he gets to know men and women, boys and girls, preferably in their homes, he discovers that sermons in Cream Ridge or Middletown ought to differ from those in New York City or Hollywood. Let every minister determine that on the human level he will make every sermon people-centered, and that every Lord's Day he will look on the neediest hearer as the most important person in the house of worship, excepting only the ever-present Christ.

2. *Neglecting Bible Ethics.* Perhaps because he does not prepare and preach sermons with conscious reference to the interests and needs of the hearers today, an evangelical pastor may neglect to preach Bible ethics. He may boast that he "declares the whole counsel of God." If so, he ought to read a well-known essay about "a certain blindness in human beings." According to the

Westminster *Shorter Catechism,* "The Scriptures principally teach
what man is to believe concerning God, and what duty God requires of man." In other words, doctrine and duty, in this order
of importance. If so, what right has any Bible-believing minister
to follow an elective course in God's revealed truth? If a pastor
knows his people, at home and elsewhere, he discovers that many
of their perplexities have to do with duty as the "stern daughter
of the voice of God." Whatever the truth in a sermon, and however lofty its ideals, they have a right to learn how they can live
this way in a city much like Corinth, or in a smaller community
more like Sodom.

Perhaps unintentionally, ministers may shy away from ethical
preaching because of its difficulty. Among all the varieties of
pulpit work today, this is the hardest. How can a "live wire"
church leader find time to master a difficult Bible passage about
duty, learn how it should apply to local community needs, and
then figure out a way to prepare an effective sermon? If occasionally he does all of this, he discovers that some of the saints
wish him to "preach the simple Gospel," and not talk about
disagreeable duties. They have troubles enough elsewhere, without having more when they come to church to be "comforted
and inspired." They seem to wish the pastor to be like false
prophets who in the days of Jeremiah and Ezekiel shied away
from preaching duty, whether to one man, or to a multitude.

When a young minister goes to his first charge he may not
know how to "preach doctrine ethically, and ethics doctrinally."
Gradually, however, by living with the Book and with people,
he can learn how to choose a Bible passage, and how to preach
what the passage stresses. He will find that the Bible never "pulls
any punches." As with Paul in Romans, a sermon full of truth
will move in an ethical atmosphere, and a message about duty
will rest on a solid basis of doctrine. While he does not believe
in a social gospel, he feels a holy concern about living moral issues.
For example, he cares about everything that tends to make the
home community a place where it is difficult for teen-age boys
and girls to preserve "the white flower of a blameless life."

3. *Attempting Many Things.* In any one sermon many a zealous
young minister may try to do too many things. Instead of explain-

ing one text in its Bible setting, one character in Holy Writ, or one doctrine in terms of today, evidently he feels that if one message is good, three or four together must be that much better. Of course he scarcely has time to interpret one passage, one character, or one doctrine. Since that would require toil, he introduces another passage, another character, another doctrine, which he has not time to illuminate. In the hands of a master preacher, who has time to prepare a discourse ready for print, such a survey sermon occasionally may prove richly rewarding. As a rule, this sort of survey preaching tends to increase the muddle-mindedness of laymen who wish they knew what to believe, and how to live.

Some churchgoers enjoy and admire the skill and dexterity of a man who can keep several Biblical balls going up and down in the air. But what about the man fifty years of age who never began to read the Bible until he bought a copy last week? Now he has come to church hoping that the specialist in the Biblical field will show him how to "read, mark, learn, and inwardly digest" some important part of this holy Book. Also, what of boys and girls who have come to church hoping that they will learn what this Bible business is all about? If the minister settles down with one passage of the Bible, one character in a certain scene, or one aspect of a mighty truth, any of these novices can follow every word. But if the man in the pulpit starts playing hop-skip-and-jump, he may lose these hearers after the first or the second intra-Biblical hop.

In two churches that ministered largely to university students and professors the writer found that his occasional survey sermons, if well prepared, interested the people, but that he could accomplish far more by dealing each time with some vital aspect of a Bible passage or character, Christian doctrine or duty. He also discovered that if he could make a truth or a duty interesting and clear to a boy or girl ten or twelve years of age, the sermon was equally interesting and clear to every student or professor. Strange as it may seem, many a Ph.D. in science or philosophy does not know A B C about the Bible. Since the present-day preacher insists on "beginning with people where they are," let him know that some of the neediest persons in church should learn how to read a parable or a psalm, and how to approach a paragraph in Romans or Hebrews. If the minister contents himself with delivering only one Biblical sermon at a time, anyone can follow him, of course providing he knows how to preach Biblically.

As an example of an evangelical preacher who attempted only one thing in any sermon, take John Henry Jowett. In his "Yale Lectures" he told young men: "No sermon is ready for preaching, nor ready for writing out, until we can express its theme in a short, pregnant sentence as clear as a crystal. I find the getting of that sentence is the hardest, the most exacting, and the most fruitful labor in my study" (*The Preacher, His Life and Work,* 1912). Because of such simplicity Jowett's pulpit work impressed Dean W. L. Sperry of Harvard, and other brilliant critics, as being "thin." But it brought delight to hosts of evangelical laymen and ministers. J. Gresham Machen, for example, thanked God that even on Fifth Avenue he could hear simple preaching of the Gospel. He commended Jowett for having mastered the popular preacher's art of "making a little go a long way."

4. *Following Outmoded Customs.* With up-to-date hearers, especially if young, much of our evangelical preaching seems to be outmoded. Being timeless, Bible doctrines, duties, and ideals should never lose their appeal. When properly presented they seem as fresh as morning dew on mother's roses. But the form may seem old-fashioned. Especially since the coming of radio and television, people have changed their ways of thinking, feeling, and talking. Hence they may not be easy to please. They do not come to church in an ox-cart, or in a Model-T, and they do not wish the man in the pulpit to talk like their grandmother. This may be one reason why they often prefer a young man who has not yet fallen into a rut.

Outmoded customs have to do with every aspect of a man's pulpit work. Take, for instance, the matter of introduction. The approach to a sermon may assume any one of a dozen forms, but such an up-to-date preacher as James S. Stewart of Edinburgh normally begins with his subject as it now concerns the hearer, or hearers. In the published sermons of other days, one would have to search a while for this sort of introduction. In the ablest preaching of our time one might have to look about for an example of anything else. All of this has to do with the path of approach to Gospel truth. Much the same principle applies to other aspects of pulpit work. "Today is not yesterday."

Except in some pulpits, the whole conception of public speaking has changed since the days of Queen Victoria, Joseph Parker, and Henry Ward Beecher. As a rule present customs represent a partial return to the ways of our Lord and His disciples when they spoke to common people. In a current magazine a foremost United States Senator writes about the difference between the style of political addresses today and in the time of Webster, Clay, and Calhoun:

> Their oratory was involved and grandiloquent. In the mouth of a Winston Churchill or a Bryan this way of speaking has, even in modern times, thrilled millions. But today it is obsolete. . . . The emphasis [now] is upon exposition, not oratory. Here again, radio and television have had their effect. Clarity, directness, and logic are the qualities which the public wants in a speaker. Short words of Anglo-Saxon origin are preferred to Latinisms, and to be effective, sentences and paragraphs should be brief and to the point.*

5. *Having No Goal.* All these statements about pulpit weaknesses overlap. Such matters are closely related. In any sermon many of the defects may spring from the absence of a single controlling purpose. If only for variety, a good deal of a man's preaching during a year ought to be inspirational, rather than directly informative. When a man prepares to speak inspirationally he ought to have a purpose acceptable to God. As in a first-class novel or play, the purpose may not appear for a while, but the writer always has a purpose, and in time he makes it so evident that the hearer, or reader, will remember it as long as he lives. This purpose dominates the writer, or speaker, from the very first word. Robert Frost, for example, says that in making ready to write a poem he always has a controlling purpose. Before he puts pen to paper he feels free to go whither he will. But after he has written down the first line he has committed himself to

* Paul H. Douglas, "Is Campaign Oratory a Waste of Breath?", *New York Times Magazine*, October 19, 1958. By permission.

follow that line until he has completed the poem. As for the reader, he may have to go through it all before he figures out the controlling purpose. Sometimes, if he can, a minister ought to preach this way, inspirationally, and with increasing suspense. "Never do anything all the time."

Today, after several generations of inspirational preaching, some of which never got off the ground, people need more of what W. E. Sangster in London calls "teaching-preaching." (See his inspiring book, perhaps his ablest, *Power in Preaching*, Abingdon Press, 1958.) Whether the sermon deals with a psalm, a parable, a doctrine, or a duty, both preacher and hearer need the guidance and restraint of a controlling purpose. Many a young minister could practically double his usefulness in the pulpit if he formed the habit of putting at the top of every sermonic work sheet a sentence stating his practical aim, and then doing nothing else but follow this guiding star. Otherwise he might often almost as well shoot arrows up in the air.

In making ready for a sermon with "teaching-preaching," the practical aim guides in choosing a text both relevant and clear, in phrasing a topic both appealing and clear, in collecting materials both Biblical and current, in making a plan both sturdy and clear, in selecting a few examples both luminous and clear, and last of all, before the actual writing, in deciding on a way of introduction both interesting and clear, as well as brief and terse. Meanwhile among the most persevering church-comers there is a common complaint that the "parson" may always know what he is talking about, and why, but that half the time his hearers do not. If so, perhaps he has been mistaking mud for profundity.

> He that received seed into the good ground is he that heareth the word, and understandeth it; which also beareth fruit (Matt. 13:23).

6. *Employing Few Facts.* The best prose writing of our time shows a partial return to Biblical ways of presenting truth factually, often with reference to a person, or two persons in contrast. In the parable about the helpful traveling man (Luke 10:30-37), any reader can single out more "live words," fact words, than in an entire sermon of the impersonal sort. The

same holds true in any part of the Bible intended for devotional reading or public worship, rather than reference. In the First Psalm, for instance, a single verse contains these concrete terms: tree — planted — rivers — waters — bringeth forth — fruit — season — leaf — wither. By contrast, the next verse shows: chaff — wind — driveth away. To preach from such a text, a person needs to "see what he says." This whole line of thought relates not only to illustrations, but also to the texture of the entire sermon.

With such a glowing text the interpreter ought like Bunyan to enter the city of man-soul through "eye-gate." When he dares to preach about "The Searchlight on a Man's Soul" (Psa. 139:1 ff.) he finds that learned tomes discuss the omniscience, the omnipresence, the omnipotence, and the transcendence of God. All true, and wondrous, if understood, but not the truth in this difficult psalm. Such polysyllabic abstractions may come from scholastic tomes written by pundits who know more about Latin and Greek than about the King's English and the speech of common people, in whose hearts abstract impersonal Latinisms ring no bells of joy.

Like many another pontifical utterance, my sweeping pronouncements may go too far. In preaching about the latter part of such a wondrous chapter as Isaiah 40, a man would need to make clear and luminous the meaning of the word omnipotence. So in many a Gospel sermon there is need of such a dominant term as Incarnation, Atonement, or Reconciliation. If so, the word ought to appear at once, and without any apology. The first time Incarnation emerges it calls for illumination from within, such as comes from Charles Wesley's Christmas hymn, "Hark, the herald angels sing": "Veiled in flesh the Godhead see; hail th' incarnate Deity!" So let us venture on a simple working rule: "In any sermon let there be no more than one strong technical term, and be sure to make that one shine." After a while the church-comer will know as much about the terminology of historical faith as a football enthusiast knows about a triple pass or a quarterback sneak. For example, who can ever forget a sermon that brings out the pristine glory of the Christian word Reconciliation (II Cor. 5:17-21)?

7. *Using Poor English.* Perhaps because of failure to read

poetry, and to use the pen, some evangelical preachers do not in
the pulpit use correct and pleasing English. In the Philadelphia area of the Methodist Church Bishop Fred P. Corson
watches over more than a thousand local pastors. Recently he
reported to pastors that as a rule the lay officers like and respect
their minister as a man outside the pulpit, but that they do not
relish his way of abusing the King's English when he preaches.
They refer to ways of public speech that call attention to themselves by confusion, carelessness, and crudity. From radio and
television Protestant laymen may not learn much about the
Reformation faith, but after hearing and watching Fulton J.
Sheen they become aware of their pastor's shortcomings as a
public speaker for God.

The use of careless and incorrect pulpit speech is not con-
fined to illiterate local preachers, or to men in any one denom-
ination. In the past our own branch of the Church prided itself
on having an educated ministry. In recent years one of our largest
congregations sent committees to hear man after man. At last
they went outside our country to find a minister who could conduct an hour of worship without making grammatical blunders
and slips. On the other hand, in our largest seminary one of
the seniors told the professor and the class that he rather enjoyed hearing a preacher "pull a boner." Perhaps unkindly, the
professor replied that the young man surely must enjoy hearing
his own sermons. Being "a good sport," the student laughed. Out
in the pastorate afterward he may have married a high school
teacher of English, who would do for him what college and
seminary had failed to accomplish. A simple test of any man's
education and culture lies in his ability to speak and write English clearly, correctly, and forcibly.

8. *Lacking Quiet Beauty.* In the Bible almost every passage
suitable for preaching has a beauty all its own. Not every Biblical "form of sound words," inspired of God and profitable in
other ways, lends itself to use in a sermon. Once the Lord said
to Moses, "Take it by the tail" (Exod. 4:4), but He did not
intend that any homiletical magician should take this text for
a secular talk about the way to transform danger into docility.
As a rule a minister uses no more than a hundred preaching
texts in a year. Hence he need never select one that does not

shine with an inner light from God. Whenever he deals with a text full of quiet beauty, because fraught with feeling, he ought not only to make clear the meaning, but also bring out the beauty of God's revelation. Otherwise the sermon may be like a little boy's drawing of a man: "He does not look alive."

With a Biblical passage full of beauty, a pulpit exposition devoid of charm may seem more like a skeleton than like truth and grace that come from God. To show about a Bible passage everything except its spirit and "tone color" may mean to misrepresent the Lord of all beauty. It is a fearful thing for an ambassador by careless and ugly speech to misrepresent his country and his King. On the contrary, any minister who lives much with the beautiful parts of the Bible, and more than a little with John Bunyan, can learn to draw his words from a "well of English undefiled."

> God wove a web of loveliness,
> Of clouds and stars and birds,
> But made not anything at all
> So beautiful as words.

9. *Failing with Young Folk.* For reasons such as those above, the home pastor may fail to attract and influence young people by his preaching. In a typical place of worship young folk are conspicuous by their absence. Often the few who attend look bored. They do not specially object to the pulpit fare, except for its monotony and lack of seasoning, but they often protest about the way it is served. Here and there they find a minister whom they like as a preacher. They know that he understands young people today, believes in them, expects large things from them, attempts large things for them, and wants to work with them as "free, intelligent, and twenty-one." Like Paul, regardless of years, this kind of "pastoral director" soon helps to transform a local "young people problem" into an opportunity to enlist workers and leaders for the Church of tomorrow.

10. *Presenting Insufficient Variety of Biblical Fare.* Bishop Corson reports that laymen often object to the minister's preaching because it lacks variety. From the beginning to the end of a sermon, and from January through July, the pulpit work runs much the same. Instead of seeming like a joyous adventure

through a "land of hills and valleys," with an occasional vista
of the vast unknown, the sermonizing from week to week seems
more like a summer trek through level land so full of ripening
corn that the weary wayfarer can see little or nothing save tall
grain. Flat fields and towering corn have their uses, but when a
man comes to church he should lift up his eyes to the hills and
there behold the beauty of his God.

What of the remedy for a clergyman's sermonic sameness?
The cure for this common complaint may come through learning how to read and enjoy the Bible. Holy Scripture is far more
than a "form of sound words," with etymological significance
and theological implications. For instance, take the Gospel according to Luke. If a minister lives with it, and with commentaries, for three or four months, until he enters into the spirit
of the Gospel, as here recorded with quiet beauty, he can preach
from paragraphs in St. Luke as many as fifteen times, between the
middle of December and the climax on Easter Day. In these
successive sermons, not announced as a series, the element of
variety may come through steeping the soul each time in the
spirit of the chosen paragraph. For example, in the eighth
chapter note the difference in "tone color" between "The Members of Christ's Redeemed Family" (v. 21), and "The Healing of
His Seamless Dress" (v. 44).

Variety will also come at times if the minister adopts so-called
"newer ways of preaching," most of which appear in the reports
of sermons from Bible days. In no event does any such way of presenting a case interfere with the freest use of Biblical materials,
and preaching the old redeeming and transforming Gospel. In
Pittsburgh for twenty-six years, Sunday morning and evening,
as well as often during the week, Clarence E. Macartney preached
nothing but sermons from the Bible. In a downtown church,
especially at night, he delivered series after series, often as different and as distinctive in form as the printed publicity that
made him known everywhere in Greater Pittsburgh. In substance his pulpit work did not often differ much from that of
other orthodox men, but in form he felt free to adopt the problem approach, the psychological approach, the life-situation ap-

proach, the case method, the dialogue method, and other pulpit ways that have become known as modern and up-to-date. For many such reasons the common people heard him gladly.

In short, among high-minded evangelical ministers all of these pulpit weaknesses have to do with secondary matters. Alas, often "the things that matter most lie at the mercy of things that seem to matter least." Fortunately, every one of these weaknesses can be corrected, and that without leaving home, or taking time out for minor repairs in ministerial "technique." (What a cold word for our holy work!) If a minister would devote as much time and attention (not to mention meditation and prayer) to correcting his pulpit faults as an enthusiastic golfer spends improving his various strokes, there would soon be few complaints about the sameness, lameness, and tameness of the sermons.

To the minister these defects may seem far from serious. In the pulpit from week to week he serves an abundance of strong Biblical food, full of vitamins and not too full of calories. Why then should he trouble about niceties of form? Perhaps for the same reason that the Prophets and the Apostles, like their Lord, presented both truth and duty in forms full of beauty and power. So have the mightiest evangelical preachers throughout the Christian ages. In like manner our laymen feel that the successors of Bible preachers, and of evangelical heroes in church history, ought to show equal care in clothing their sermons with suitable garb (Isa. 50:4). Indeed, laymen expect much from a graduate of college and seminary who has dedicated to God all his gifts of thought and speech. What then is the hope for improvement in the evangelical pulpit of coming days? Let us see.

III. THE IMPROVEMENT OF EVANGELICAL PREACHING

After a long and careful study of evangelical preaching I feel encouraged and full of hope. Many of the faults I have pointed out lie on the surface, and are already being corrected. With some exceptions the young ministers who have been graduated since World War II show promise of better days for evangelical preaching. From this optimistic point of view let us think about certain factors that should enter into such a present-day reformation of the evangelical pulpit. To "reform" here means going back to Biblical ideals about the substance and the form of our preaching, and then going forward to discover the best ways of preaching "to the condition" of men and women today.

1. *The Primacy of Preaching.* The majority of evangelical ministers believe in the primacy of preaching. They look on it as an all-important part of public worship, and not as something that stands off by itself. They also feel that it should go hand in hand with pastoral care, which includes counseling, and with other related ministerial activities. But they believe, distinctively, that it still pleases God to save sinners and transform the saints through the ministry of preaching. More than at any time so far in our century evangelical pastors seem determined to recapture for preaching the sort of primacy that it enjoyed in Bible days, during the Protestant Reformation, and in every succeeding golden era of the Christian pulpit.

2. *The Strengthening of the Seminary.* The signs indicate that theological professors have caught a vision of what the Lord wishes them to do first of all. Of course they ought to guide young men in preparing for other sorts of full-time service of the Church, such as the chaplaincy. Like the graduate of a first-class medical school, who goes on to become a specialist, each of our ministers not called to the pastorate needs basic training in theology, both pure and applied. All the while the men and women who gave sacrificially to establish divinity schools did so mainly to insure well-trained ministerial leaders for local churches.

In pursuance of this practical aim every professor or instructor should have an important part in training men for the pastorate, or the mission field. This does not mean that all the professors ought to begin teaching practical theology, which calls for a teacher who has special gifts and training. In our better seminaries the professor of Old Testament now helps the student to prepare for using it in the parish ministry day by day, and most of all in the pulpit. Of what practical value is a knowledge of Hebrew, or of anything else in theology, if it does not help to prepare the seminary graduate to become "a good minister of Jesus Christ"? And so with every other professor. He has the glorious opportunity of helping to prepare young men for the

highest, the holiest, and the hardest work in the world today, that
of the pastor who prays and preaches.

3. *The Development of Personality.* Like everything else in the
work of a minister, the effectiveness of his preaching depends
largely on what he makes of himself. If wise he plans to make the
most of all his God-given powers, whether spiritual, intellectual,
or physical. All of this no family, school, or church can do for a
minister. Under God he should keep growing. Without God he
would not grow. Since preaching means the truth of God voiced
by a chosen personality to meet the needs of people now, the
ability to do it well depends on the size and caliber of the man
himself. If he keeps using aright his intellectual and bodily powers
year after year, he will have a stronger and a richer personality
with which to glorify God by helping people through his sermons.
Hence he may well say with Oliver Wendell Holmes, "Build
thee more stately mansions, O my soul!"

4. *The Zeal for Pastoral Care.* In contrast with ministers early
in the century, many pastors now feel increasing concern about
people, both one by one and in various groups, especially in the
home. This change for the better has come in part because of the
recent stress on counseling, and even more because of the return
to Biblical ideals about the ministry. Methods of pastoral care
may change, as they ought to do. Nobody has ever devised any
sort of standard pastoral procedure for a local shepherd. If he
loves sheep, and knows his flock, including the lambs, and any
older one in distress, his pastoral care will influence and color all
of his pulpit work. In due time he will receive the commendation
of the Good Shepherd (I Pet. 5:1-4).

5. *The Concern about Boys and Girls.* A wise farmer takes
special care for the growth of his seed corn. So does a Christlike
pastor feel daily concern about the Christian nurture of boys
and girls. A few generations ago, when we quit bringing to church
boys and girls old enough to attend the public schools, we soon began to rear young people who remained away from church. Now
the wide-awake pastor strives to reverse the trend by enlisting
boys and girls for regular and enthusiastic attendance at morning
worship. In a sense he looks on them as the most important human

beings in the House of God. "O satisfy us early with thy mercy; that we may rejoice and be glad all our days" (Psa. 90:14).

Methods of enlisting boys and girls for church attendance may vary. Some ministers still believe in the Junior Church, but that plan does not afford the minister an opportunity to lead boys and girls in worship, and preach to them as God's little men and women. Others prefer the Junior Sermon, especially if the lads and lasses sit with their parents and remain through the hour of worship. Otherwise they may never witness the celebration of the Sacrament, with its uplifting "Sermon in the Supper." In I Corinthians 11:26 the word translated "shew" or "proclaim" also means to "preach": "As often as you eat this bread, and drink this cup, you preach the Lord's death, until he comes."

Some of us believe in encouraging boys and girls of school age to attend and enjoy the regular hour of morning worship, which culminates in the sermon. Insofar as one can judge from the reading of ministerial and missionary biography, this is the method that has led most boys and girls to dedicate themselves to the pastorate and to service overseas. At Princeton Seminary one time a senior asked me how old I thought a boy ought to be when he starts coming to church regularly. I replied that I preferred to think of how young he ought to be. Then I asked the class of eighty men, "How many of you attended church regularly when you were six years young?" Almost every hand went up.

Has anyone ever had such visible evidence of God's blessing on methods "just as good" as the older way of bringing boys and girls to church to sit with father and mother in the family pew? If a traveling man is away from home all week, or a whole month, why not let him sit in church with his little daughter, and hold her hand while she learns to love the Lord and love her pastor almost as much as she loves her father? This older way still works. In a suburban church not many miles away forty-seven boys and girls not old enough for junior high school attended morning worship this past year on at least forty-eight Sundays. Why? Under God, because the pastor, beyond middle age, makes it one of his chief aims in life to enlist for public worship the men and women of tomorrow. Incidentally, a wise minister does not address them as "children," a term that he reserves for little tots. He wishes boys and girls to "put away childish things" (I Cor. 13:11b), and as God's little men and women to keep looking up to Him in church.

6. *The Sanctity of the Study.* The minister who wishes to keep growing as a preacher to men and women, boys and girls, needs a special place for study. He also needs a regular time, five days in the week, preferably early in the morning. At other times and places he should engage in counseling and other forms of pastoral leadership. In the study he devotes himself "continually to prayer, and to the ministry of the Word" (Acts 6:4). Lovingly he may dedicate to God this holy room in the "house of the interpreter." If at times other interests threaten to woo him away from hours dedicated to preparation for the pulpit, he may whisper to himself the words of a church leader who knew how to say No: "I am doing a great work and I cannot come down. Why should the work stop, while I come down to you?" (Neh. 6:3). Here some reader may protest: "That was feasible enough in Nehemiah's day, but it will not work now, at least not in my church." If so, why not? Nehemiah's ability to keep doing what the Lord wished him to do depended on his gift of leadership. He enlisted the aid of other workers. In churches large, small, and of middle size, here and there over the land, pastors are devoting themselves daily to long hours of study in the spirit of prayer. If they did not, they would soon cease to grow in ability to preach.

7. *The Preparation of Each Sermon.* Except when there is to be a celebration of the Lord's Supper, a Protestant sermon usually takes the place that the Roman Church gives to the Mass. Like everything else in the public worship of God, the sermon from week to week requires the most careful preparation, both in substance and in form. In the pulpit only a minister's best work can begin to be good enough to represent God before men. Contrary to a common impression, even such men as Spurgeon and Beecher, with all their gifts and powers, worked hard on their sermons, and, on the average, wrote out in full at least one a week. So one learns from the best biographies.

As a rule, with many exceptions, the men with most ability devote most time to the preparation of their sermons. They have such ability in large measure because they have previously worked on sermons. In almost every case this includes the "discipline of the pen." Except during a mid-summer vacation, when a man reads much and rests more, he may well set himself every week to write out a sermon in full, and then revise it with care. Otherwise he may wax wordy, and become known for his "much speaking," when he has not much to say. In addition to the one sermon that he writes out, but need not commit to memory, or read from the manuscript, what of other sermons and addresses through the week? These he may prepare in substance and speak from an outline, so simple that he can follow it with ease, preferably without notes. Whatever the method in detail, it calls for toil in the study. However impossible all of this may seem in some fields, the fact remains that a growing number of ministers are working this way, week after week. Hence they keep growing in favor with God and in power with men.

8. *The Growth in Preaching Ability.* As with any other God-given power, ability to preach grows with proper use, and declines through carelessness, or laziness. Not for the sake of becoming known as a great preacher, and the author of great sermons, but for the glory of God and the transformation of men, the evangelical pastor worthy of the name determines that he will keep growing in all-round pulpit effectiveness. By the grace of God he will preach better sermons at forty than at thirty: better in content, in form, and in delivery. During the most critical years in the ministry, between forty and fifty, he will keep on growing in grace and in knowledge, as in ability to use them both in preaching to common people. Even down to old age God's servant will prove that a man need never cross the deadline before he dies. With Paul when no longer young, the true evangelical pastor cultivates the forward look in faith and hope (Phil. 3:13, 14).

9. *The Freedom from Distractions.* Now we must face a practical issue that we may seem to have ignored. How can a minister today mingle among men and not feel distracted amid the world's rush and roar? Indeed, how can he keep from adding to the confusion among men, and the frustration? Herein lies the chief temptation of the zealous minister today. As a typical son of Martha he often feels "busy and troubled about many things," so as to neglect "the one thing needful." As one able minister

reported after he had served twenty years, in three congregations, each of them larger than the last, "In the seminary I won the first prize in homiletics. I started out into the ministry with lofty ideals about my preaching. But I have been so busy here and there that my ideals have escaped me." (See *The Organization Man,* by William H. Whyte, 1956.)

Let no one cast a stone at such a pastor if he seems to be distracted, like Atlas striving to carry a load weightier than God ever intended a mortal man to bear. In a workaday world full of confusion and fear, with the whir of machinery and complexity of organization, no minister can hope to escape from outer distractions, at least not before he retires or dies. But by the grace of God any pastor can learn how to "live on twenty-four hours a day," perhaps by lightening the load. By faith he finds and follows a God-given way to "live without worry, work without hurry, and look forward without fear." Is not the minister God's child? Is not this the Father's world? Why then should he not have here and now the peace of God that he often commends to others? This too is a beautiful theory. Thank God, it is also a fact of experience among ministers such as George W. Truett, who had a right to preach about the peace of God. When I spent a week with him at a Bible conference he had on his heart the welfare of 8,000 members, with numberless other concerns, none of them petty, and yet he did not seem to have a care in the world. "Cast thy burden on the Lord, and he shall sustain thee" (Psa. 55:22). A beautiful theory! Yes, and it works. Try it—by faith!

"No man has any more religion than he can command in an emergency." This old saying still holds true. But emergencies seldom arise, and when they do a man of faith can rise to meet them with power not his own. Ah, but it's the daily rub and grind of the world's machinery that drive a man to distraction. Not being given to drink, he may give way to Giant Despair. He needs a revised edition of the old saying: "No minister has any more Christlikeness than he can display in the midst of life's daily routine." As for preaching, if it means the truth of God through a minister's personality, how can he preach about heaven when he has in his heart no peace, no joy, no hope? Whatever the cost he must let the Lord Jesus cast out all the demons that dwell within. Otherwise, as Milton says,

> The mind is its own place, and in itself
> Can make a heaven of hell, a hell of heaven.

10. *The Call for Daily Dedication.* In view of all the ideals and the distractions in the ministry of one who believes in the primacy of his pulpit, a pastor may cry out with the Apostle, "Who is sufficient for these things?" In II Corinthians, which is Paul's spiritual autobiography, and especially in the part where he tells his philosophy of preaching (2:14—6:10), the Apostle gives the only answer to this ever-present question: "Our sufficiency is of God, who also hath made us able ministers of the New Testament" (II Cor. 3:5b, 6a).

For all these reasons the Lord calls on His ministering servant for daily dedication of himself, with all his talents, and all his limitations. If at times the obstacles in the way of his preaching ministry seem insurmountable, because mountain-high, still the Lord calls for daily dedication and for reliance on the promises:

Not by might, nor by power, but by my Spirit, saith the Lord of hosts. *Who art thou, O great mountain? Before Zerubbabel* [the servant of the Lord] *thou shalt become a plain.*

I. The Background of the Gospel

1. Billy Graham

William Franklin "Billy" Graham, Southern Baptist. Born near Charlotte, N. C., Nov. 7, 1918. Educated, Florida Bible College; Wheaton College (A.B.). A short pastorate and a brief radio ministry. President, Northwestern Schools, Minneapolis (1947-51). A general evangelist since 1946. A nation-wide radio and television program, "The Hour of Decision." Soul-winning crusades around the world, notably in London, New York, and San Francisco. Has probably preached to more persons than anyone else in history.

Billy's preaching is a saturated solution of well-known Bible truths, with stress on the doctrines of redemption. His messages are worthy of note for dependence on God, loyalty to the faith of his conservative fathers, and reluctance to fight anyone but the devil. They are simple, full of fervor, and strong in popular appeal. To others he leaves erudite discussion of vast world problems, and detailed teaching of Bible ethics to believers. He consistently shows humility and frankness, a radiant personality and a dynamic delivery.

As an ordained minister Billy Graham works with representatives of every Protestant church or group willing to cooperate on the basis of his clearly defined evangelical message. Like Moody, Spurgeon, Wesley, and other soul-winning divines, he has critics, chiefly among the clergy. Extreme conservatives censure him for working with churches and ministers more liberal, and for advising each new recruit to join the church of his choice. More liberal critics say that Billy makes the Gospel seem too simple, and that he does not stress its social implications.

If Billy tried to defend himself he might ask when Moody ever refused to work with others who wished to cooperate with him as a soul-winner, or when any effective evangelistic preacher has

43

ever consistently made an all-inclusive appeal. Graham feels that the Lord has called him and equipped him for a simple type of pulpit ministry, and that he should largely leave to others, especially local pastors, the teaching of the Bible about the ethical issues that every believer ought to face after he has accepted Christ as Redeemer and King. This matter has untold importance today, when every minister has to decide whether to keep his soul-winning messages simple or to make them complex.

The following sermon about "The Grace of God" bears the copyright of the Billy Graham Evangelistic Association at Minneapolis, and is used with its permission. The message appears first among all the thirty-seven because it sounds the keynote of the entire volume. Other sermons that also repay study appear in Graham's book, Peace With God *(1953). If anyone were to ask him, "Are these great sermons? Are you a great preacher?" he might well answer, "I prefer to think that I have a great Gospel and a great God. Have you?"*

THE GRACE OF GOD

"The grace of God that bringeth salvation hath appeared to all men, teaching us that denying ungodliness and worldly lusts, we should live soberly, righteously, and godly in this present world, looking for that blessed hope, and the glorious appearing of the great God and our Saviour Jesus Christ, who gave himself for us."   TITUS 2:11-13a

I CALL YOUR ATTENTION to a very important subject, "The Grace of God." My text is found in the tiny book of Titus with its forty-six verses packed with truth. In the second chapter, verses eleven to fifteen, we find these wonderful words about the grace of God. These truth-wrought verses comprise one of the classic utterances of the Scriptures. They take the simple, silver facts about the plan of salvation, embellish them with logic, deck them with eloquence, and place them in an understandable setting of digestible, acceptable truths.

Grace, according to the dictionary, is "the unmerited favor of God toward mankind." As the little boy said in Sunday school, when asked about the meaning of grace, "It's something for nothing!" Perhaps the simplest definition would be, "something granted as a favor, not as a right." Your human mind with its inherent reciprocal philosophy can hardly comprehend the full meaning of this grace of God, but when once through inspiration you catch its meaning you will leave the bounds of human logic and revel in the spiritual riches of divine truth and privilege.

This word grace appears in the Bible over 170 times, and that in the New Testament alone. I would like to take these five letters of the word grace, in the light of the verses I have quoted, and let these five letters spell out the majesty of the most wonderful of all words, the word grace.

I. THE FIRST WORD — GRACE

The first letter here is "G." It stands for God's grace that bringeth salvation to all men, teaching us that denying ungodliness and worldly lusts we should live soberly. Notice here the spiritual miracles wrought by the majesty of divine grace in the human heart and life.

Grace brings salvation. Where else can salvation be found? Go to Wall Street with its endless miles of ribbon and ticker tape, and its millions of dollars ready to be wagered, with the hope of making still other dollars. Study the intent expressions, as I have, on the faces of those men who have so much to do with the financial structure of America, and you will not find salvation there. Go to our halls of learning where the scholarly leaders of our educational institutions deal lavishly with knowledge and wisdom, with facts and figures. For the most part you will not find salvation there, for the primary responsibility of our schools is to train the mind, not to groom the soul.

Go into our shops and factories and the merchandising areas of our cities. You will not find salvation there, for they deal with the material needs of mankind. Grace is not to be sought, or bought, or wrought. It is the free, lavish gift of Almighty God to needy mankind. When I see Jesus Christ dying on the Cross, I see the free gift of God's grace in Christ, reconciling the world unto Himself. Hence we sing with John Newton of old:

> Amazing grace! how sweet the sound,
>   That saved a wretch like me!
> I once was lost, but now am found,
>   Was blind, but now I see.

The word grace calls for the fine art of self-denial: "teaching us to deny ungodliness and worldly lusts." Even our psychologists are learning that controlled living is the only victorious way of life and that no man is strong enough to control his life apart from the grace of God. One of the reasons for moral failure in America is that as individuals and as a nation we have tried to get along without God. We have tried to control ourselves without the Saviour. We have tried to rule ourselves without the Master. This attitude of godless living can lead only to ruin and decay.

May I add this in passing? The Christian religion consists not merely in negations. There is no particular virtue in leaving off all that is bad unless you replace these evil things with positive good. Certainly Christ taught this. Christianity is not just the absence of evil; it is the presence of good through the grace of God in Christ. When Jesus said, "If any man will come after me, let him deny himself" (Matt. 16:24), He did not necessarily mean that we were to deny ourselves things. He meant that we were to deny that inner self which refuses to follow the divine command, and that spirit within us which would rather live after the flesh than after the Spirit.

Grace teaches that we should live soberly. This does not mean that we should live without a smile. The Pharisees were solemn hypocrites, whom Jesus condemned for their insincere "piety." Grace imparts the life that was forfeited in Adam. In Adam all die, but in Christ Jesus shall all be made alive again. You haven't really lived until you have acquired the grace of God through faith in the Lord Jesus Christ. If you want in your heart something that will put a spring in your steps and a smile on your face, then receive Jesus Christ as your personal Saviour. Receive

the gift of God's grace and your life will be transformed from
despondency to peace and victory and joy.

All the way through the Bible the word "grace" is used far
more often than the words "wail" and "moan." Like all synthetic
stimulants, sin has its terrible after-effects. It leaves scars on the
soul, the mind, and the body. As the Bible says, "She that liveth
in pleasure is dead while she liveth" (I Tim. 5:6). Genuine victorious living begins when the grace of God appears to you in
its significance and beauty; when you actually commit and surrender your life to Jesus Christ.

II. THE SECOND WORD — RIGHTEOUSLY

The second word in our test is "righteously." The second
letter in the word grace is "R." Righteously! Without doing any
violence to the word, "righteously" can be interpreted as meaning
"rightly." There are not many ways of life. There are just two:
the right way and the wrong way. Life is an open-and-shut
proposition. As the Scripture tells us, "He that hath the Son
hath life, and he that hath not the Son of God hath not life"
(I John 5:12). The plan of God is plain and simple, so simple
that Isaiah said a wayfaring man, though a fool, need not err
therein. The trouble with our modern way of thinking is that
we have a conception of God as a haphazard God, with no set of
rules for life and salvation.

Ask the astronomer if God is a haphazard God. He will tell
you that every star moves in its celestial orbit with precision. To
ignore the rules of the universe would spell ruin to that star. To
deviate from its God-ordained course would mean deterioration
and tragedy. Ask the mathematical physicist if God is a haphazard
God. He will tell you that formulas and equations are fixed and
that to ignore the laws of science would be the utmost folly of a
fool.

If the laws of the material world are so fixed and exact, is it
reasonable to suppose that God could afford to be haphazard in
the spiritual realm, where the eternal destinies of souls are at
stake? I say no, a thousand times no! Just as God has equations
and rules in the material universe, so God has equations and
rules in the spiritual realm. The Bible says, "The wages of sin

is death" (Rom. 6:23). That is God's formula. When a man sins, he is going to pay for it, both in this life and in the life to come. That is just as certain as that two plus two equals four.

There is only one way of salvation. That is God's way. He has outlined the road to heaven. He has made the rules simple and plain. He has given us the equations and the formulas and the compasses. The way outlined in His immutable Book says to receive the Lord Jesus Christ as Saviour. Jesus says that he who climbeth up some other way is a thief and a robber. It is the way of the Cross that leads home. It is the grace of God, and only the grace of God, that bringeth salvation. Grace implies that you cannot work for salvation. You cannot make your own way to heaven. You can come only by God's way, and that is by receiving His unmerited favor in Christ Jesus.

III. THE THIRD WORD — APPEARING

Now we come to the middle letter in the word grace. So let us think about the word "appearing,"—"the glorious Appearing of the great God and our Saviour Jesus Christ." On a memorable night in Bethlehem 2000 years ago the angels hovered over the Judean hills and said in unison: "Glory to God in the highest; peace on earth, and good will toward men!" (Luke 2:14). The centuries have rolled by and still the world longs for and looks for the peace that the angels sang about on that first Christmas morning.

"Where is His peace?" you ask. I'll tell you where it is. It abides in the hearts of all who have trusted in His grace. And in the same proportion that the world has trusted the Christ, it also has peace. In his Inauguration Address at Washington, D.C., President Eisenhower called for peace. He said that one of the main objectives of his administration would be to work for peace. To the President and to the leaders of all governments I would say that there can be no peace on earth until Christ has come into the hearts of men and has brought His peace.

There is no discord in heaven, there is no strife, for Christ reigns supreme. There is no conflict in the heart where Christ abides, for His words, "Peace I leave with you" (John 14:27), have been proved in the test tubes of human experience over and over again in the lives of those who have trusted His grace. But His glorious Appearing means far more than an incident in the past; it is the Christian hope for the future. In the heart of every child of God there beats the glorious hope for Christ's Return. This hope is a stimulus toward righteous living and conduct, and makes Christ far more than a figure in history. This hope gives Him the living breath of reality. The expectancy of His coming again makes Christ a vibrant Being who even now prepares Himself as the Bridegroom to meet His bride, the Church.

IV. THE FOURTH WORD — CHRIST

In the word grace the fourth letter is "C," and "C" stands for Christ, "who gave himself for us." The motive of grace is the infinite, compassionate love of our merciful God, and the work of grace comes through the Death of Christ on the Cross. Unless we view the grace of God through the sufferings of the Lord Jesus Christ on the Cross, we cannot comprehend its true meaning and significance. When I see Christ hanging there, with the spikes in His hands and the crown of thorns on His brow; when I see His blood being shed for our sins,—I see the picture of God's grace toward men.

I know then that man cannot work his own way to heaven, and that flesh and blood cannot inherit the kingdom of heaven. Only as we bow at the foot of the Cross, with contrition, confession, and repentance, can we find forgiveness. There is the grace of God! We don't deserve it! Some time ago a man declared, "When I get to the judgment seat of God, all that I will ask for is justice." My beloved friend, if you get justice, then you will go to hell. You don't need justice. What you need is mercy. The mercy of God, the grace of God, as it is in Christ Jesus who died and rose again.

V. THE FIFTH WORD — EXHORT

Now we come to the last letter, which is "E." "These exhort," says the Scripture. I have given my life to this exhorting, and I am not alone in this dedication. Our team has gone up and down the country and around the world, preaching the Gospel of Jesus Christ in exhortation. There are thousands of missionaries, doctors, and nurses who have dedicated themselves to exhortation with these great truths that are the embodiment of the grace of God. Every Christian should be praying for these missionaries of the Cross who are preaching the grace of God.

Also, there are thousands of businessmen, housewives, college students, and shop workers, along with a great host of people from various other walks of life, who have been dedicated to the testimony of Jesus Christ. These people are rational, worthy citizens of your community. Their testimony would be accepted in any court of the land. With one voice they proclaim: "There is therefore now no judgment to them which are in Christ Jesus" (Rom. 8:1).

Yes, the grace of God is a reality. Thousands have tried, tested, and proved that it is more than a cold creed, a docile doctrine, or a tedious theory. The grace of God has been tested in the crucible of human experience, and has been found to be more than an equal for all the sins and the problems of humanity.

Hence I challenge you to let the Holy Spirit spell out upon the tablets of your heart this matchless word, grace. Let the Christ who has hallowed the pages of history with His presence sanctify your present and your future with His presence and His power. Receive Him now. You can know Him today. You can know the grace of God if you let Christ come into your heart right now.

2. Clarence S. Roddy

*Clarence Stonelynn Roddy, Conservative Baptist.
Born, Mount Vernon, N. Y., Jan. 30, 1898. Educated,
Gordon Divinity School (Th.B.); Colby College (A.B.);
New York University (M.A., Ph.D.) Served pastorates
(1922-44). Professor English Bible, Eastern Baptist
Seminary, (1944-51); Pastoral Theology and Homilet-
ics, Fuller Seminary since 1951. Former Vice-President,
American Baptist Convention. Conference speaker
throughout the United States and Canada.*

*The sermon that follows shows the practical wisdom of beginning
with a text that appeals to the imagination. This one suggests
something to see, to feel, to do, and to become. Starting with this
biographical cameo, the sermon presents a doctrine, indirectly.
The topic and the introduction show how the doctrine comes
out of the text in its background. Then the message concerns the
doctrine itself, in terms of the hearer today, or the reader.*

*The facts come mainly from the Bible, and also from life else-
where. The man in the pulpit wishes to interpret the life and
spiritual growth of the hearer, in light that comes from God
through this part of the written Word. The use of local color
from sources other than the Bible calls for notice. So do the headings, which serve as landmarks in such a pilgrimage of faith.*

*The number and order of the main headings will repay study.
Another minister would have only two main divisions, corresponding with the two parts of the text. This minister prefers to bring
out, successively, five aspects of present-day "fellowship with God."
In keeping with Spurgeon's call for "surprise power," the last
main heading unexpectedly relates to the genesis of such fellowship.*

*Why close the sermon this way? Because this is what the Lord
and His spokesman wish the hearer to do in his heart, right now.*

Let him resolve now to start on such a daily walk with God. If
he has already started, let him resolve to come closer and closer
still to God in Christ. So the sermon leads up, climactically, to the
text, and causes the hearer, or reader, to thank God for Enoch, and
to whisper, "He walked with God; why may not I?"

A MAN'S FELLOWSHIP
WITH GOD

"Enoch walked with God, and he was not, for God took
him."   GENESIS 5:24

FAMILY TREES ARE not devoid of interest, but the average
person would not spend much time in their study. Some things
with little interest, however, may reveal truths of large concern.
Such is the case in this fifth chapter from God's Book of Begin-
nings. There we have a record of Adam's descendants through
Seth to Noah. This is dry reading. It is only a family tree. The
casual reader skips this part of the written Word, and frequently
the serious student passes it by.

And yet upon this plain family tree there blossoms one of God's
fairest flowers, kissed by the everlasting sun, bathed in eternal
dew, and fragrant with the perfume of heaven: "Enoch walked
with God, and he was not, for God took him." This brief verse
seems like a diamond buried amid rocks; like a pearl cradled in a
shell; like a tree breaking the landscape of a prairie. Here in an
oasis is a touch of green that helps to redeem the waste of the
desert. What then can we learn from these few words of our text?

I. THE FACT OF FELLOWSHIP
WITH GOD

"Enoch walked with God." Walking with God means to have
fellowship. This beautiful picture of the deepest communion is

all the more noteworthy because of its setting. The chapter mentions fourteen men of old, thus recording a matter-of-fact genealogy, but this one man's fellowship with his God was so extraordinary that without a direct reference to his fellowship there could be no fitting mention of his name. Later in the Bible we have records of men walking with God, and He with them, but never a case like this one of Enoch. Abraham was called "the friend of God"; Moses, "the servant of God"; David, "a man after God's own heart"; Daniel, "O man greatly beloved" (of God). Enoch alone is said to have been the comrade of God, for "God took him."

Fellowship is one of the deepest and richest experiences of life. Without it a man's earthly existence would be like a barren wilderness. The human heart craves fellowship, and without it the soul of a man can not long be satisfied. Fellowship alone makes life seem worth living. Even on the human level there is a sweet fellowship of spirit with spirit, a fellowship that is clean, noble, and lofty; a fellowship whose gentle influence tends to sanctify and elevate the spirit. On the other hand, alas, much that passes for fellowship is not worthy of the name, for it tends only to degrade and debase the soul made in the likeness of God.

The experience of Enoch reminds us that the highest fellowship on earth is that of a man with his God. No matter how lofty a plane one may reach in the way of human fellowship, it can never approach the wonder of the divine-human friendship that is born amid the loveliness of heaven. Here is heaven come down to earth, in the form of a man's daily walk with his God. Here is the loftiest of all earth's spiritual mountain peaks; it is earth's nearest approach to heaven. This wonderful relation between a man and his God is the fountainhead of all wholesome human fellowships. Its influence flows out into other hearts and lives, and its Godlike graciousness makes all of a man's relations sublime.

II. THE ESSENCE OF FELLOWSHIP WITH GOD

What then is the meaning, the essence, of a man's fellowship with his God? "Enoch walked wth God." To have fellowship with God means to walk with Him. That in turn means to keep going forward with Him, and of course in His direction. In order to walk with Him, one must know Him, and know Him better from day to day. Without a certain heart knowledge of God, it is impossible to walk by His side, journey in His way, and enjoy the unspeakable bliss of communing with Him. "Can two walk together, except they be agreed?"

Fellowship between person and person grows out of mutual knowledge. Only through a study of knowledge can we enter into the deepest meaning of the word fellowship. So let us analyze the term knowledge in its various degrees, and see if we can discover the sort of understanding that enters into true fellowship with God. In order to have fellowship with his God what does a person need to know?

On the lowest level we speak of knowledge as purely intellectual. Here is a man who has read and studied his Bible for years. Within its pages he can trace accurately the vast and mighty movements of its history. He can picture vividly the life of Jesus when on earth. The reader finds no difficulty mentally in accepting the doctrines and the ideals of God's Holy Book. Does this man, like Enoch, enjoy a daily walk with God? The answer depends on what he does with his religious knowledge. Does his everyday life contradict the doctrines of the Bible, and contravene its ethical teachings? If so, he may have all sorts of intellectual comprehension, but he has not yet entered into the sort of heart knowledge that would make possible a life of deepening friendship with the God "whose presence is the happiness of every condition, and whose favor sweetens every relation."

The knowledge that leads to fellowship with God is to be found in another area than that of merely being aware of facts. The true kind of heart knowledge has to do with a personal relationship. Here again there are degrees of understanding. Enoch knew his God as a man today knows his dearest friend. Sometimes we employ the term knowledge to mean only recognition by sight. "Do you know John Bliss?" "Oh, yes, I know him by sight, but I do not have a speaking acquaintance." In like manner a man may have only a sort of "speaking acquaintance" with God. As Job cried out, "I had heard of thee by the hearing of the ear, but now my eye sees thee" (42:3). Then at last he was ready for a life of deepening fellowship with his God.

In the field of personality the deepest sort of knowledge consists in heart likeness. To know a person means to be like him in spirit. Above all, to know God means to be like Him. To know Him means by His grace to be in harmony with Him, to have sympathy for Him, and thus to enjoy increasing fellowship with Him. In the field of physics we speak of sympathetic vibrations of the same periods. If you sit down at a piano and press the loud pedal, singing into the harp the note C, you will get a response. Why? Because the two tones are alike. So in our lives we can know best those whom we at heart resemble most. Because at heart we are in the deepest accord, we can enjoy fellowship sweet and abiding.

So it is in a man's fellowship with his God. In contrast with the many who possess only an intellectual knowledge of Him, only a sort of "bowing acquaintance," let us view one of God's saints as he appears in the loving recollections of his son. In his *Autobiography,* John G. Paton, saintly missionary to the New Hebrides, tells how as a wee lad he would see his father, a humble Scottish weaver, after every meal retire to a tiny room for quiet prayer. When at length he came out his face would glow with the light of an indwelling Presence. Now let us listen to the son, who is writing near the close of a life full of faith like that of the father, and with a record of heroic adventure peculiar to the missionary son:

> We knew whence came that light, as of a new-born smile that always was dawning upon my father's face. It was the reflection from the Divine Presence, in the consciousness of which he lived. Never, in temple or cathedral, on mountain or in glen, can I hope to feel that the Lord God is more near, more visibly walking and talking with men, than under that humble cottage roof of thatch and oaken wattles. Though everything else in religion were by some unthinkable catastrophe to be swept out of memory, or blotted from my understanding, my soul would wander back to those early scenes, and shut itself up once again in that sanctuary closet, and hearing the echoes of those cries to God, would hurl back all doubt with the victorious appeal, "He walked with God, why may not I?"

If you would enjoy a like experience, warm your soul by bringing every part of your being into harmony with God. Interest yourself in Him, and in His work. With Him learn to love the right and hate the wrong. Above all, deny yourself, and give yourself for the sake of others, somewhat as God did when He gave His Son to redeem the world. Yea, if you would experience the depths of the fellowship divine, you must suffer with Christ. From Paul learn to pray that you may know God and the fellowship of His sufferings. Nothing else binds hearts together so surely as mutual suffering, in the spirit of Christ. In like manner, a man's fellowship with God thrives best in a vale of suffering, more or less like that on the Cross. Oh, what an ideal is this to which you aspire, "to walk with God"!

III. THE GROWTH OF FELLOWSHIP WITH GOD

"Enoch walked with God." Hence he grew more and more like God. This fact of progress always enters into the Biblical idea of walking. Whenever by faith a man becomes like Him, that man's fellowship with his Lord grows in depth, in richness, and in joy. The more knowledge of God he gains, the more he is sure to receive. The more he grows in Godlikeness, the more he increases the capacity for communion with his Maker and Friend. Since the Lord God wishes every one of us to be like Him in that other world, where we all shall see Him as He is, He desires each of us to know Him now in the most intimate fellowship. Through the Apostle He has instructed us: "Grow in grace, and in the knowledge of our Lord and Saviour Jesus Christ. To him be glory both now and for ever" (II Pet. 3:18).

A man's fellowship with God has to be progressive. As a babe in Christ a new convert begins by desiring the pure milk of the Word. As a growing believer, feasting on the rich meat of the Word, he grows more and more into the likeness of the Ideal Man, even Christ Jesus. Such growth of soul must proceed along lines that we call natural, though they all come from God. No one all at once can leap into the fullness of sainthood. When a babe enters the world he begins to have experiences, and what he learns he stores up in mind as a foundation for years of later mental growth. So does youth build upon the knowledge gained in childhood; manhood builds upon youth; and old age upon the experience of past years. Hence the poet Wordsworth sings about the way his heart leaps up whenever he beholds a rainbow in the sky:

> The child is father of the man;
> And I could wish my days to be
> Bound each to each by natural piety.

A man's fellowship with his Lord grows through the right sort of appreciation. The same principle holds true in all of life. A person trained to appreciate and enjoy profound music is rapt with aesthetic delight whenever he hears the rendering of a Bach fugue or Wagner's *Walküre,* whereas a person with an uninstructed ear would only feel bored. Where a mind cultured in the dramatic art is held spellbound by Shakespeare's *Richard the Third,* the untutored person finds it dry, dull, and drab. Where the artistic soul looks upon Turner's *Slave Ship* as a symphony in color, the eye of a novice sees in that masterpiece only a lot of daubs and blotches of wasted paint.

A Christian woman of mature years, who herself has passed through such an experience of love, can enter into the spirit of Elizabeth Barrett Browning in one of her *Sonnets from the Portuguese.* A girl of thirteen may memorize the words, and recite them perfectly, but only insofar as the words are concerned. She has yet to learn the meaning of the deepest fellowship, which consists in love:

> How do I love thee? Let me count the ways.
> I love thee to the depth and breadth and height
> My soul can reach, when feeling out of sight
> For the ends of being and ideal grace.

This principle of growth in excellence through appreciation of the highest holds true everywhere in the realm of the spiritual. If we would walk with God we must grow into His likeness. Is it not wonderful that we can walk with Him? Is it not still more wonderful that as we grow more and more like Him, He increases our capacity for Godlikeness, so that "we all, with open face, beholding as in a glass the glory of the Lord, are changed into the

same image from glory to glory, even as by the Spirit of the Lord"
(II Cor. 3:18)?

IV. THE GLORY OF FELLOWSHIP
WITH GOD

The supreme glory of a man's fellowship with God is that it
never ends, but continues through eternity. "Enoch walked with
God, and he was not, for God took him." Out from the confines
of earth the Lord God lifted Enoch up into the limitless bounds
of the heavenlies, there to walk with Him in the beauty of eternal
day. This inspired phrase, "God took him," is an early Old Testament assurance of everlasting fellowship with God, and not merely
a dim, misty "intimation of immortality." In like manner the
ancient Book describes the translation of the prophet Elijah, when
he bade farewell to the younger Elisha: "There appeared a chariot
of fire, and horses of fire, and parted them both asunder; and
Elijah went up by a whirlwind into heaven" (II Kings 2:11).

These two sacred writers are not alone in their witness to the
reality of a man's eternal fellowship with God. Either directly
or indirectly, other authors under the Old Covenant give evidence of assurance about everlasting fellowship with God, but
only for those who love Him. Many of these passages have to
do with only one person, more or less like Father Enoch. Amid
the mighty chorus hear Job singing with triumphant joy, "I know
that my redeemer liveth, and that he shall stand at the latter
day upon the earth: and though after my flesh worms destroy this
body, yet in my flesh shall I see God" (19:25, 26).

Again, give ear to David: "Thou wilt not leave my soul to
Sheol; neither wilt thou suffer thy Holy One to see corruption.
Thou wilt show me the path of life: in thy presence is fulness of
joy; at thy right hand there are pleasures for evermore" (Psa.
16:10,11). Once again David sings; "As for me, I will behold thy
face in righteousness: I shall be satisfied when I awake, with thy
likeness" (Psa. 17:15). Daniel adds with joy: "Many of them that
sleep in the dust of the earth shall awake, some to everlasting
life. . . . And they that be wise shall shine as the brightness of the
firmament" (Dan. 12:2,3a). Isaiah brings all to a supernal climax
in his paean of transcendent praise to the Lord of Hosts: "He will

swallow up death in victory; and the Lord God will wipe away tears from off all faces" (Isa. 25:8a,b).

In the New Testament of our Lord Jesus Christ this glorious river of truth about the hereafter flows on increasingly to its fulness. By His Death and Resurrection He has brought life and immortality to light. With the authority of God our Redeemer brings solace to every believer who mourns, solace in words well known to us all. Thus with certainty we may conclude that in the land beyond the river our fellowship with God shall continue and increase. What knowledge! What assurance! What peace! What bliss!

V. THE GENESIS OF FELLOWSHIP WITH GOD

You have in mind a question, have you not? Does it not run on this order? "If knowledge leads to likeness, and if one must be like God in order to grow, how can I begin? How can I start to become like Enoch, and thus to walk with God?" Dear friend, you are already like God in the sense that He has made every one of us in His own image. He has formed you for fellowship with Himself and He has given you all the faculties necessary for knowing Him well and loving Him much. Indeed, He has en dowed every human soul with capacity for the completest fellowship with the Creator. He has so constituted your soul that apart from God it cannot really live and realize its potential powers. What sound is to the ear, what light is to the eye, what air is to the lungs, what blood is to the heart,—all this, and vastly more, God is to the believing soul.

Though the image of God in many a soul has been marred, and even broken, it has not been lost, or destroyed. Though it has been battered and bruised, weakened and wounded, by the dominion of sin, the likeness to God persists. Though it lies buried under the debris and the corruption of iniquity, though it is smeared with the blackness of unspeakable vice, the soul may have a triumphant resurrection, a beautiful cleansing, and a triumphant restoration into the likeness of God.

> Down in the human heart, crushed by the tempter,
> Feelings lie buried that grace can restore;

> Touched by a loving heart, wakened by kindness,
> Chords that were broken will vibrate once more.

Like Enoch, each of us can know God, because He is love. His love is self-revealing, and self-imparting. In love He reveals Himself to us; in love He imparts Himself to us, supremely through Christ. He also reveals Himself through nature, as He did with Enoch, who must have walked with God in the vast outdoors, and thus enjoyed "open-air treatment of the soul." Enoch must also have come to know God through His Providence.

Today God does not stop with these lesser means of revelation, for He has revealed Himself to each of us in the written Word, and most of all in Christ, the living Word. Since the Lord Jesus came to reveal the Father, when once you behold the Son, you have seen God. "He that hath seen me hath seen the Father" (John 14:9b). If you can see God in the life of Jesus, how much more in His Death! Ah, here in the Christ of the Cross is God's supreme revelation of Himself! Here you see God in Christ pouring forth His love for the reconciliation of the world unto Himself. Here you behold God in Christ removing the barrier of sin, which would forever keep you from fellowship with God. Thus you can behold Him swinging open wide the gates of fellowship with Him forevermore. Thank God for the Christ of the Cross!

> There was a Knight of Bethlehem
> Whose wealth was tears and sorrows;
> His men-at-arms were little lambs,
> His trumpeters were sparrows;
> His castle was a wooden Cross,
> Whereon He hung so high;
> His helmet was a crown of thorns,
> Whose crest did touch the sky.

In Christ, "we have redemption through his blood, the forgiveness of sins, according to the riches of his grace" (Eph. 1:7), that we may walk with Him here and now, and also forever in the heavenlies. When by faith you receive Christ, my friend, you thereby receive God. By growing in Christ you become more like God. He is the Way to God, the Truth of God, the Life in God. He is the only Way, and there can be no other. All this by His grace you may have already experienced. If so, you know what it means, like Enoch, to walk with God here and now.

If you have so begun by faith in Christ, will you not like Enoch continue to walk with God? Will you who have started on your pilgrimage of faith not draw nearer and nearer to Christ? Yes, nearer to that thorn-crowned brow, nearer to those pierced hands and feet, nearer to that broken heart. Thus by faith you will walk closer and closer to the heart of God.

My friend, if you have not yet started on this walk of faith, let me appeal to you in person. Start now! You alone can make the beginning, for this matter of fellowship with God is entirely personal. No one on earth can provide it for you. No one else can do it for you. Like Enoch, enter into this fellowship of your own free will, and do it gladly.

Simply by trusting in Christ enter the beautiful portal of the new birth. To you He is calling from the transcendent glories of heaven, and also through the Holy Spirit in your heart. Through your walk of fellowship with God, the Lord Jesus is waiting to restore in you the image of God. So let your life now begin to be like that of Enoch. "Enoch walked with God, and he was not, for God took him."

3. Pierre Marcel

Charles Raymond Pierre Marcel, Reformed Church of France. Born, Paris, May 30, 1910. Educated, Paris and Amsterdam (degrees corresponding to A.B., B.D., and Th.D.). Pastor, Reformed Church, Saint-Germain-en-Laye, since 1942. Professor, Protestant Faculty of Theology, Paris, 1951; 1951-52. President, International Association for Reformed Faith and Action. Other such offices, notably, Director of Publications for the Calvinistic Society of France. Publications include: licentiate's thesis, comparing Calvin with Aquinas and Duns Scotus (1936); doctoral thesis about Herman Dooyeweerd (1956); A l'Ecole de Dieu (1946); A l'Ecoute de Dieu (1948); The Biblical Doctrine of Infant Baptism (transl., 1953); L'actualité de la Prédication (1951). Editor, Calvin's Institutes, Calvin's Sermons (selected), some of Calvin's Commentaries, and other learned works.

The sermon about "The Ordeal of a Man's Faith" shows the wisdom of here including messages from overseas. This one shows that "biographical preaching" need not seem easy and simple. Living in the midst of European trials, God's spokesman deals with Abraham as a noteworthy example of what it costs to live and serve as a child of God. Throughout the sermon the pastor engages in what the fathers used to term "continuous application." At every stage he brings the truth out of his text in its Bible setting.

The message consists mainly in exposition of relevant facts about this exemplar of heroic faith. Two modern examples—one from a poem and the other from a drama—show ability to use extra-Biblical materials effectively. However, instead of ranging widely in quest of materials to support his main thesis, this interpreter of God's truth for today focuses attention on facts about the Bible character in view. As a consequence, every hearer or reader should come away with a new understanding of these facts in Genesis, and of what they now teach concerning "The Ordeal of a Man's Faith." Let us thank God for what this learned brother has shown us about the riches and variety of evangelical preaching today. Let us thank Him far more for grace to pass triumphantly through "The Ordeal of a Man's Faith."

THE ORDEAL OF A MAN'S FAITH

"God tested Abraham."—GENESIS 22:1a

WHAT A TRULY amazing record you have just heard! What greatness, what simplicity, what intimate communion with God! Throughout his life Abraham has given astounding proofs of his faith. And now, all of a sudden, God asks him for a token greater than all those he has given. It is his beloved son Isaac, granted to Abraham in his old age; it is Isaac whom God demands as a burnt offering. Isaac, in whom lay all the covenant promise of God: the promise of Abraham's posterity, through whom all the nations of the earth would be blessed.

THE TESTING OF ABRAHAM'S FAITH

God wants to put Abraham to the test. God calls him by his name and demands this sacrifice, with a precision that must pierce his heart, and fill it with grief. Even as in former days, at various stages in the life of Abraham, God now renews to him the covenant promise: "In thy seed shall all the families of the earth be blessed." Abraham knows that this is the voice of God, and that His promise is sure.

It seems to us as though God has appeared to Abraham in two different aspects, and has spoken to him with two different voices. In other days did He not often promise His blessing? Then suddenly He seems to withdraw His promised blessing. Has He not often made to Abraham a covenant promise? Then suddenly He seems to waive that promise. The chief characteristic of a man's faith is to lean upon the word of God. But here does it not seem that His word is contradictory, and that God wishes to destroy Abraham's faith in those very promises that God made to Him years before?

Thus God tries Abraham's faith. It would seem that He wishes to turn Abraham against all the promises he has received concerning his son Isaac. Isaac, his only son, from whose seed, as Abraham knew, the Saviour of the world would come. Isaac, in whom lay not only the love of Abraham and his household, but all their hopes for grace and salvation before God. Isaac, in whom lay the hope for the salvation of the world. For all the promises that have been fulfilled in Jesus Christ, says the Apostle, had been definitely vouchsafed to Abraham.

And if Isaac dies, what will happen? Does it not seem that God has derided Abraham and his loyalty, forsaken His promises, and broken His covenant of mercy, tearing it up? Does it not seem that nothing is left for Abraham but to mourn the death of his son, and then await his own death and destruction? When we put ourselves in the place of this father, if we have any feelings and any imagination, with any spirit of Christian love, we can feel the grief in his heart. Think of the strife in his soul, between God's promise, which is God's word, and God's command, which is likewise God's word.

Nevertheless, Abraham does not argue. As the author of the Epistle to the Hebrews says, Abraham acted in faith. He firmly believed in the promise. He was certain that God would give back his son through some act of resurrection. So Abraham does not argue. He rises early in the morning, saddles his ass, and takes with him two of his young men. He obeys at once. To him God's promise is sure, and will bear all its fruits, even if the son who has been given him is taken away, and dies. Abraham believes that God has power to raise him from the dead.

What strong faith he has thus to cling to God's promise! What a struggle! What prayer, of which nothing is told us here, so simple and reserved is the record. Behold how Abraham, when he hears God saying these two things, between which he might naturally have hesitated, becomes certain that God's command does not abolish His promise; that God is not his enemy, or opponent; and that He does not seek a quarrel with Abraham. By faith he finds how all seeming contradiction, all apparent opposition between the promise and the command, may disappear; and how the promise and the command can be reconciled. Since God is loyal, He has prepared the solution to this enigma, this mystery. God Himself, in His providence, will see to it all.

Let us try even better to imagine Abraham's struggle. It was difficult and grievous for him to forget that he was a husband and father. It was grievous, perhaps impossible, to repress all his human affections, in parting from his own beloved son, thus bearing the reputation of having slain that son with the father's own hand. But for Abraham, the believer, it would have been still more awful to persuade himself that God had disavowed and contradicted His own word, and then finally to suppose that the hope of the promised blessing would be destroyed by Isaac's death.

Abraham believes God. When this man decides to believe that his seed may spring even from a dead body, when he faces the death of his dear son, Abraham comprehends the power of God, the miraculous power, of the One who cannot but be true to His promises. Then this man of faith emerges from his maze of temptations and perplexities. He holds fast to the promise. He sees only the promise, and he obeys. However, with his human intelligence, even while he obeys the mysterious command of God, he is unable to discover by what unknown ways the Lord will find the solution, and with what deliverance, what means of grace, God will keep His promise intact.

THE TESTING OF OUR FAITH

That, dear brethren, is Abraham's struggle. It may be applied to our own lives personally, for Abraham is the father of all believers in God. Nothing happened to him that may not happen to many believers, but not perhaps in a form so extreme. He was the father of the faithful, even as Jesus Christ was the firstborn of many brethren, which means in effect that by God's grace we are not and shall not be put to a supreme test like that of Abraham. However, this does not prevent our faith from being so precious that it must be put to the proof. By a mysterious providence of God, the faith of every Christian, in the measure that he believes, must during his life on earth be put to the test. Experience shows that every one of us, young and old, must meet the testing of his faith.

By this I mean, dear brethren, that it is not merely a question of subjugating our affections, and overcoming our base impulses. As with Abraham, God wishes us to give ourselves to Him completely. So it is that in a boundless variety of ways, often with much precision, each of us is put to the test. By a test I mean anything that places us in a difficult situation, a situation apparently beyond human endurance, whether it be illness or mourning, conjugal unhappiness or difficulties with children, quarrels, or it may be ruin. Each of us, sooner or later, at a given moment, has to endure an ordeal more or less like that of Abraham.

The extraordinary thing is that in this struggle which we cannot escape we find ourselves caught between the promises of God, which He has revealed in His Word, and the commands of God, which He may reveal in His Providence. Think about His promises of forgiveness, peace, tranquility, and joy; promises of His benevolent love toward us. Think also about the tragic realities of life, realities consisting in circumstances and events that appear to be God's actions and God's order, even if it is those who are nearest to us who are the occasions of our suffering. These commands of God seem to be in fundamental contradiction with the promises, the hopes, and the love of God, which He Himself has set before our hearts. What a trial of our faith!

The fight is hard! If we want to keep our faith, are we going to let God contradict Himself in our lives? Over against the promises of God are we going to set the events of life: this problem, this sorrow, this awkward husband, this unbearable wife, this incomprehensible child? Are we going to contrast the present event with the promise and the faithfulness of God? Are we going to oppose God with God? In consequence of the contrast, through lack of faith we may either abandon the promise of God and rebel against the circumstances in which He has placed us, or else we may not pay attention to the seriousness of our situation, and resign ourselves to it too lightly.

Brethren, many of us live amid circumstances that seem to be in complete opposition to God's promises. In these circumstances, like Abraham, we must persevere in believing the truth of God's promises, persevering with invincible tenacity. It is the promise of God, understood by faith, that must rule us in the events of life, with all our personal sufferings. It is the promise of God understood by faith that must prevent us from pitying ourselves in our sufferings. When we begin to pity ourselves, the situation becomes more or less desperate, for we have all but denied God, and we are unable to face the event or to find a solution.

By faith we know that God has prepared a way. He has prepared an issue, which, either suddenly or else after many years, will reconcile the hardships we have experienced and the promises made of God. Thus by faith we shall know that the promise has always been valid; that the love of God has always been real. This is the reconciliation that comes through faith.

THE OBEDIENCE OF TRUE FAITH

"Get thee up on a high mountain which I will tell thee of," God says to Abraham, "there give up thy son." These orders call for the lapse of three days between the command and the deed. What a crucial time of waiting! In his play, *Abraham sacrifiant,* Théodore de Bèze has tried to show us the attacks Satan made on this man's heart during those three days. What a tremendous struggle! And yet he obeyed, to the very letter!

What does all of this teach us? It shows that God plans each of our trials in every detail. This truth is most important. Our trials in every detail; all these pricks, these thorns, everything that hurts us, wounds us, upsets us. These things in their least extent, God knows them all. He wishes us to give up our wisdom and submit to His will. Above all, He demands our perseverance. How many of us would lightly, perhaps even happily, undertake to make a heavy sacrifice if we could do it all at once! "Let's get it over and be done with it!" But no, God leaves Abraham in suspense, and says to him, "Go thither, and I will show thee the mountain." This means three days of waiting in anguish.

"And Abraham rose up early in the morning, . . . and went to the place of which God had told him." What greatness appears in this faith of Abraham! His mind may be troubled by many thoughts, but still he remains stedfast. He sets to work, and he works methodically. He accepts the situation in which God puts him, and obeys the orders given. He gets up early, chops the wood, saddles the ass, and gathers the servants together. He gets the rope and the fire ready, and takes with him everything he will need to obey in faith the orders he has received. He is not prostrate with despair or with doubt. He suffers, he grieves, he is tormented, but still he is calm, and he sets to work methodically. Thus by faith he overcomes the temptations of Satan, and refuses to heed his insinuations.

How much we all should benefit, dear brethren, if in our trials we strove by faith to follow the example of Abraham! Too often when we are in trouble or distress we feel overwhelmed. We feel shut in. We know not what to do. Either we do too much, or else we do terribly little. If only we could set ourselves to do with precision exactly what God asks, in the situation where He has placed us! If only we could accept the situation as the will of God, the order of God, the command of God, like the captain of a ship who well knows what to do by looking at the waves, the speed of the wind, and the position of the ship.

On the third day Abraham comes within sight of the mountain. Then he sends his servants away. He does not ask for witnesses to stand by him. He is not going to let everyone know of his grief. He does not seek this person's sympathy, or that person's expression of esteem. In other words, he does not make a display of his ordeal. How often, brethren, our trials would be easier to bear if by faith we knew how to bear them together with God, perhaps with a single confidant, or confessor, without bringing in all our friends and relations. With Abraham we should learn when and how to keep people at a distance, and to refrain from making a display of our feelings.

On the way up the mountain Isaac speaks to his father, "Behold the fire and the wood, but where is the lamb for a burnt offering?" In all of Abraham's trials this one is the hardest to bear. With a quiet voice his son, perhaps fourteen or fifteen years of age, questions his father candidly. With the perseverance of faith, the father meets this test, also. Relying on the Providence of God, Abraham replies, "My son, God will provide himself a lamb for a burnt offering."

"And Abraham bound Isaac his son." A father old and gnarled binds a boy big and strong. Contrary to all our expectations, the son does not struggle, or even protest. He offers himself voluntarily. Here again, the record is wonderfully simple, and far more heartrending than if there were a long, tragic description. So it ought to be with us. In our ordeal, when we think we are in front of an insoluble problem, at least we can face it squarely, with faith and courage. Then by faith we may find, as Abraham found, that God takes the matter out of our hands.

THE REWARD OF SUCH FAITH

"God will provide himself a lamb for a burnt offering." So He did. When everything was ready, "Abraham stretched forth his hand to slay his son, and the angel of the Lord called unto him out of heaven, . . , 'Lay not thy hand upon the lad, for now I know that thou fearest God.'" Against all hope Abraham's sorrow is changed into joy. At such a time God takes control.

In our earthly trials, dear brethren, even when we are in agony, even if we should be at the door of death, let us consider how God brought Isaac back to life, how He again gave Abraham his son, as truly as if He had saved the lad from the grave. Let us consider how God has delivered us, and how He will deliver us again. Let us remember how with Abraham the angel of the Lord intervenes; how he holds back the father's hand; in short, how the Lord brings the ordeal to an end.

Let us note, also, how at each stage by faith Abraham accepts the command of God. Each time when the Lord calls, "Abraham," the man of faith immediately replies, "Here I am," ready to obey God's command. Especially note how with faith and obedience Abraham accepts the end of the ordeal. He does not protest against his deliverance, or wish to put it off until a later time. Even as in faith he has accepted his ordeal, so in faith he now

accepts his deliverance. In faith he has said "Yes" to grief. Now
he knows how to say "Yes" to God's command to rest and to
rejoice. This is the gift of God Himself, which without hesitation
He offers to everyone who by faith passes through such an ordeal.

Dear friends, by faith we too should learn how to say "Yes" to
God, and never to say "No." In the course of a hard struggle, during an ordeal for which we have had to muster all the resources
of our faith in the promises of God, when at length He gives us
a sure sign of our deliverance and our freedom, by faith like that
of Abraham we should know how to acquiesce immediately. We
must accept the Lord's will that our mourning be transformed
into gladness. For such acceptance we may need as much faith
as in going through the ordeal itself. Is it not amazing how many
believers deny themselves the joy of a true deliverance that comes
from God?

Through lack of faith many persons prolong their ordeal. By
attachment to the past and its trials, an attachment that becomes
idolatrous, they persist in not believing in their deliverance. As
Christians we ought never to bear any cross longer than God
desires. At the moment chosen of Him we should believe that
the ordeal is ended: that the home now rebuilt can praise God
in harmony and peace; that the child no longer in peril is now
again on the right road; that the suffering caused by illness has
given way to victory; that the former solitude has been vanquished
by the presence of Christ; that our temptation has been conquered; and that our enemy has become our friend.

In response to faith like that of Abraham, the Lord substitutes
for the ordeal of suffering the sacrifices of thanksgiving. If at
different stages of our Christian life we could but say and believe
with Abraham, "The Lord will provide," then as often as God
does deliver us, could we not with hearts free and at peace cry
out, "God has provided"? Whenever God asks us to suffer, let us
acquiesce and say,

> Beneath Thy chisel, Divine Sculptor of the soul,
> Let my happiness be chipped to pieces.

But when God delivers us from an ordeal, and bids us rejoice,
let each of us be able and free to say, "Here am I." And let us use

for joyous sacrifices of thanksgiving the blessings that He has conferred upon us at the end of the ordeal. Just as Abraham received and offered up in sacrifice the lamb sent of God to show that his son was safe, and that he remained, as we remain, overflowing with the mercies of God, so let us offer up our sacrifices of thanksgiving to the God of Abraham, who is to us by faith the God of our Lord and Saviour Jesus Christ.

4. Harold B. Kuhn

Harold Barnes Kuhn, Quaker, Ohio Yearly Meeting of Friends. Born, Belleville, Kan., Aug. 21, 1911. Educated, John Fletcher College (A.B.); Harvard (S.T.B., S.T.M., S.T.D.). Lecturer, Emmanuel Bible College, Birkenhead, England, (1936-37). Assistant, Dept. of History, Harvard (1942-44). Pastorates (1936-44). Professor, Asbury Seminary, Wilmore, Ky., since 1944. Educational consultant, U. S. Air Force, Europe (1951-52). Summer ministry in Europe with chaplains and refugees (1947-58). Editor, The Asbury Seminarian, *since 1946.*

The following sermon consists largely of exposition. It draws materials from various Biblical records concerning Moses, and then weaves them into a message about a faith worth sharing now. The man in the pulpit evidently takes for granted that the friend in the pew has brought his brains to church, and wishes to keep them busy. The result is a sermon that reasons things out on the basis of revelation. Such preaching appeals to thoughtful men, and many women, who enjoy the masculine note from a man who speaks with authority not his own.

The message has to do with practical aspects of faith. Without calling special attention to saving faith, as it appears in Romans, the spokesman for God shows the importance of serving faith as it shines out in the Epistle to the Hebrews, especially in the eleventh chapter, with its Hebrew Hall of Fame. Such a faith means God-given ability to see what is hidden from other eyes, to serve as He directs, even to suffer and die, all without sin. As for practical application, in terms of today, the sermon leaves it largely to the guidance of the Holy Spirit.

A FAITH WORTH
SHARING

"By faith Moses, when he was come to years, refused to be called the son of Pharoah's daughter."—HEBREWS 11:24

IN THEIR Bible setting these words show everyone here today the meaning and the glory of a faith worth sharing. The example of Moses in turning his back on all that the world prizes, and accepting a life work full of hardship and peril, ought to move every one of us to yearn after a like faith. The place of Moses in time and rank differed from anything that we know today, but his example in trusting the wisdom and power of God should teach certain lessons that everyone here ought to learn. Let us consider the facts in this case, so that each of us may receive from the Lord the dynamic of a faith worth sharing.

I. A FAITH THAT SHOWS MATURITY

The faith of Moses is that of maturity. Noteworthy in the text are the words, "Moses, when he was come to years." A brief statement about the known facts of his early life should help us here. At a period about as long before the birth of Christ as the discovery of America by Columbus came after, Moses was born to a couple who shared the enslavement of the Israelites in Egypt. His parents appear to have been above the average in comprehension of Israel's hope. At a time when Hebrew boy-babies were special targets for destruction by Egypt's rulers, Amram and Jochebed saw in this newborn child some indication of a providential purpose, and potential greatness. Hence, at vast personal risk, they concealed their wee son. According to the inspired record, "By faith Moses, when he was born, was hid three months of his parents, because they saw he was a proper child; and they were not afraid of the king's commandment" (Heb. 11:23).

We are all familiar with the way their plans, thus conceived in faith, matured in action. The infant Moses was adopted by the daughter of the reigning Pharaoh, turned over for a time to his own mother for subsidized care, and then reared as crown prince of Egypt. St. Stephen has indicated to us the quality and the extent of the young man's royal education: "Moses was learned in all the wisdom of the Egyptians, and was mighty in words and in deeds" (Acts 7:22).

Thus far the major lines of this man's career were laid out by others, evidently with a view to a career for him in the royal palace. But then something happened, of which we do not know. Here we should be glad to have details that have been withheld. In any case, some circumstance arose to demand that Moses himself make a personal commitment to the program laid out for him by others. How this came about we can only conjecture. Possibly there came a time when he was to be presented to the Egyptian people in an impressive public ceremony. In the light of what we know about the religiousness of Egypt in that day, we assume that such an occasion would have combined both religion and patriotism.

At this point Moses must have been put squarely on the spot. Then he proved the correctness of Lowell's words,

> Once to every man and nation comes the moment to decide,
> In the strife of truth with falsehood, for the good or evil side.

The issues must have been so transparently clear that there was no turning back from the choice that he registered. The age at which this experience came to Moses is not of consequence, but the fact that such a time arrived is crucial. Nor can we know all the other factors that entered into the choice he made. Without doubt his early thinking had been shaped by the faith that he had observed in others. The period during which he was reared at home, by the appointment of Pharoah's daughter, may well have continued for three or four years. During such a time he could have learned much about "the way of faith."

One element the early career of Moses has in common with our own. Each of us, also, is subject to strong formative influences from his placement and environment. It would be the sheerest folly to suppose that any one of us acts wholly from within, not being strongly shaped by influences from without. True freedom consists, not in the absence of shaping forces, but in the choice of the force that one permits to become dominant. Here Moses stands in a place of high example for us today. When confronted with the choice that would be determinative of his entire career, the element of faith became predominant as his shaping force. The element of faith gave tone to his moment of high decision. Such is the faith of one who has matured. This leads us to a consideration of the second element that he had in common with each of us who now believe.

II. A FAITH THAT CHOOSES THE RIGHT

At the crossroads of his early career, Moses made a decision profound and calculated. When a person has attained the maturity indicated by the term, "coming to years," he cannot act in a vacuum. At this stage in Moses' career, the element that challenges us is the fact that by this time a profound personal faith was shaping his thought and life. It detracts nothing to say that he had received this faith, imparted in large measure, no doubt, by his parents. During his boyhood, adolescence, and early manhood there doubtless were events that helped to clarify certain issues in his mind. For example, there must have been some searching comparison, on the one hand, between the promises given to Abraham, by faith kept alive among the Israelites, and on the other hand, the current lot of Moses' people as slaves in the province of Goshen.

We do not, of course, rule out the probability that Jehovah had dealt with the young man directly, providentially making clear to him that these enslaved people were nevertheless "the people of God," and that his identification with them would mean a special relationship to a providential history soon to be unfolded. Further, there must have been for him some clarification of the Messianic hope, so that his identification with the captives of Goshen would mean for him sharing in "the reproach of

Christ"; that is, having a portion in all that God would ultimately reveal through the coming of the Anointed One.

Also significant for us is the fact that there came to Moses a time when he had to make a decision, and when he could see clearly the two alternatives. We must bear in mind, of course, that over against the difficult and forbidding path that Moses ultimately chose, there was to him a clear alternative. From the human point of view, that alternative would seem to be logical, attractive, and easy. In its favor one could have brought forward the perfectly reasonable argument that this was what those in authority expected from Moses. Had not the royal family spent much upon his education? Did they not also with high expectancy look forward to his administration?

Moreover, would it not have seemed plausible for Moses to assume such a royal status, and then lead in enacting legislation that would bring to his captive people immediate and lasting relief? Might he not even have elevated them to a position of security and comfort? Indeed, it would have seemed strange if some such alternative had not suggested itself to the trained mind of Moses. This line of thought raises the entire question of "means and ends." He must have weighed the issues, by faith putting both means and ends in proper perspective. As for the outcome, that appears before us in a very few words: Moses "refused to be called the son of Pharaoh's daughter."

This was a measured choice. It was not a decision that he made on the spur of the moment, but one in which he weighed both the objective and the outcome. The final and decisive element in his decision was the faith by which "he esteemed the reproach of Christ greater riches than the treasures in Egypt; for he had respect unto the recompense [that is, the outcome] of the reward." This consideration brings us to a third factor in the account concerning Moses, another element that he held in common with believing men of all time.

III. A FAITH THAT LEADS TO ACTION

Having surveyed the two alternatives, and weighed the momentous issues at stake, Moses made his choice the basis for decisive action. By now it has become a commonplace that to experience a profound impression, and then give it no suitable and adequate expression in deeds, means to erode a man's character. On the contrary, the conduct of Moses underscores the clear-cut nature of his choice: "By faith he forsook Egypt." Worthy of note here is the restraint with which the inspired record describes his action. The same kind of restraint is evident in the account of Exodus 2. Such restraint stands in contrast with the tendency in purely human literature to overplay details of the sort. Thank God for the restraint of God's revelation!

The element that grips us here is that Moses' action was decisive. By an act visible to those about him, showing his resoluteness, he burned all the bridges behind him. Thus he made his own "point of no return." Insofar as he was concerned, the die was cast. And yet his action was capable of being misunderstood. In any case those who lacked the perspective of faith would consider his decision a manifestation of wasted opportunity and unrestrained fanaticism. Beyond all this, those who were accustomed to having their commands obeyed, as would have been the case with the royalty of Egypt, must have felt completely perplexed and frustrated.

Significantly, the inspired author of the Epistle to the Hebrews adds the words, "Not fearing the wrath of the king." Even a little degree of imagination will enable us to reconstruct the scene at the palace when the tidings of Moses' decision became current. With much show of justice, the king might accuse him of being an ingrate, an unworthy waif who had been rescued from the crocodiles when his infant cradle had floated among the rushes along the Nile. The king might revile him for having accepted the best education Egypt had to offer, and then frustrating the pattern of bright hopes that well-meaning minds and hearts had woven about his future.

Except for two facts, these considerations might have weighed heavily with Moses. First, none of these plans were of his own devising. Second, when he did make his decision, he stated it frankly and clearly. No doubt it hurt him to feel compelled to make a decision that so intimately involved those who had shown him the utmost personal kindness. Even more poignant must have been the problem of trying to explain his actions to those who were not equipped to comprehend his motives. After all, it was not faith that underlay the religion of Egypt, but the working of darkened minds that could see nothing incongruous in worshipping creeping things of every kind. Under such circumstances it must have proved frustrating for Moses even to attempt any sort of explanation.

Let us note with care that when Moses decided to forsake Egypt, he did not immediately begin to act with the utmost wisdom. Having once made the choice of all choices, he did some serious fumbling of the ball. He acted rashly and prematurely, so that instead of accomplishing the quick deliverance of his captive people, he himself felt compelled to flee from the country, and to take refuge with a kindly shepherd-priest in the peninsula of Sinai. But when we see that he had made up his mind, and had set his heart on doing right, we feel ready to forgive his errors in tactics. The grand strategy of his life was no longer in doubt.

The action of Moses in taking leave of Egypt's court led to a series of multicolored events: first as a shepherd in semi-waste land north of Mount Sinai; then as a son-in-law, a householder, and a father; and later as one whom Jehovah summoned to go as an uninvited ambassador to the court of Egypt. This line of thought leads us to consider a fourth and final feature of Moses' career. In this feature, also, we can see a parallel with our own common experiences.

IV. A FAITH THAT SUFFERS HARDSHIP

Moses endured! What a word full of challenge! When Moses forsook Egypt, the elements of high resolve and heroic decision may have tempted the cynically minded to exclaim: "But wait! How will this man react when his hopes backfire, and his ideals explode in his face?" Yet when we survey the career of Moses we are deeply impressed with the number and variety of the hardships he had to confront. Bear in mind that his mission compelled him to serve as military chief, civil engineer, Jehovah's quartermaster, legislator, civil judge, and religious prophet. Recall, further, that he was responsible for a childlike people as numerous as the inhabitants of our fifth or sixth largest city, a childlike people whose faith had been eroded through long years of grinding servitude. What a colossal task of discipline, and one that offered no visible compensation!

When we measure the difficulties that Moses had to face, we find his endurance all the more remarkable. Despite constant misunderstandings and slanders, loneliness among crowds, disloyalty of associates, and gross lack of appreciation on the part of so-called friends, Moses never once looked back. His people might yearn for the cucumbers and garlic of Egypt, but never once did their leader. The secret of his endurance is not merely a matter for our understanding: Moses was a man with iron-clad faith. "He endured as seeing Him who is invisible."

The vitality of this man's faith sprung in part from the fact that it was no spur-of-the-moment affair. True, there had come a moment of supreme commitment, a moment when he crucially confronted issues that he knew to be pregnant with eternal weight. But this moment of commitment had carried with it all there was of Moses, so that when his decision began to involve him in difficulties and perils, there was in him nothing that he had not committed to Jehovah, nothing that could ever draw him back from doing his duty. Moses had a faith undergirded by divine disclosure, a faith born of mature reflection, a faith tested in the crucible of suffering, a faith hammered out on the anvil of rugged experience. Nothing less than such a faith could enable a man to endure all that Moses suffered for his God.

Also revealing to us is the fact that his endurance was a derivative of his insight. "He endured as seeing Him who is invisible." Once over in England while conversing with an organist who was blind, the writer half in pity apologized for frequently referring to things visible, which of course the blind organist could not see. Then the organist made a discriminating remark. When asked how he had come to grasp a certain situation he replied: "Oh, I do not mean seeing in that way. Do you not catch what I mean? There are deeper ways of seeing things!" That man could see with the eyes of the soul.

In such a manner did Moses see the invisible God. His vision of God was no idle, theoretical seeing. That vision gave him new supplies of divine grace, and new qualities of human endurance.

Like Saint Paul, though with vastly less in the way of historical inheritance, Moses could live out in triumph the spirit of the Apostle's later words, "None of these things move me." Moses' faith led to a quality of endurance that revealed towering greatness of soul, and likewise added to his spiritual stature. His was a character of such dimensions that before it today any one of us ought to stand in awe. Even more than the magnitude of his achievements, the size of his personality ought to impress us permanently.

A FAITH THAT LEADS TO TRIUMPH

Finally, in all its major outlines the career of Moses was of one piece with the mighty central motivation of his heart. In the whole of that magnificent life there was a transcendent consistency, as well as grandeur. When at last complete, his career served as a majestic crown piece to the faith that he had begun to show as the self-renouncing crown prince of Egypt. In shining idealism his faith once began, and throughout long years until he brought the Lord's people to the threshold of the Promised Land, his faith continued to shine undimmed.

When at last this man went up to his last resting place on Mount Nebo, a place known only to God, the faith of Moses was most impressive in its quiet dignity. Centuries later on the Mount of Transfiguration the son of Amram and Jochebed talked face to face with the Christ whose cause he had long since espoused, and whose reproach he had then borne. On that mount of vision the faith of Moses shone with a splendor from above. Who can imagine with what emotions his heart filled up when he beheld his Lord, the Image of the invisible God, toward whom with steadfast faith he had looked forward throughout a long career.

May the Lord of all grace now grant each of you such a faith worth sharing. In its vigor may you live and serve with courage and hope. In its power may you complete your earthly course with fidelity and with joy.

5. Bryant M. Kirkland

Bryant Mays Kirkland, United Presbyterian. Born in a manse, Essex, Conn., May 2, 1914. Educated, Wheaton College, Wheaton, Illinois, (A.B.); Princeton Seminary (Th. B.); Eastern Baptist Seminary (Th. M.); D.D., Beaver College, Philadelphia. Visiting teacher of homiletics, Princeton Seminary (1951-56); declined invitations to become the head professor. Pastorates (1938-57), First Church, Tulsa, Okla., since 1957.

Among the hundreds of manuscripts before me, this one stands out for its strong ethical emphasis. In two large churches, as in two earlier pastorates, this minister has learned that countless problems among laymen have to do with personal purity. If his purpose and his text had to do with people en masse, the message would do the same. But even then it would be risky for the minister to keep using the plural pronoun "we," while talking about the act and the sin of adultery. Of course some pastors never soil their pulpit robes by referring to anything so sordid, but the Scriptures seem not to be so timid and squeamish.

According to Frederick D. Maurice, no minister can be of large use to his generation [or community] unless in the pulpit he deals with the spiritual problems of his time. Today no person can question the need for brave, strong, Biblical instruction about God's way of keeping a soul and a body pure in the midst of our impure society. This is perhaps the most difficult task that anyone undertakes in the pulpit, unless it be that of preaching on the larger aspects of Bible ethics, as in the prophecies of Amos and Micah.

This pastor shows a working knowledge of Bible ethics, with a sympathetic understanding of the temptations that beset a traveling man and his wife, while he is away from home for weeks. Without ever ceasing to give the place of honor to Christ, the *sermon evinces appreciation of modern psychiatry in Christian hands. The preacher even deals with pre-marital physical sin, a sort of discussion that most of us leave to the world, the flesh, and the devil. More concretely, to television, the novelist, and the stage.*

With a different sort of people, not yet accustomed to strong meat from the pulpit, a pastor elsewhere might deal with the subject of adultery more simply. Then a later sermon, or sermons, would reinforce the basic scriptural teaching. But in a series or a course from the Ten Commandments a minister has only one opportunity to deal with the Seventh, which Lutheran readers number differently.

By way of preparation for such pulpit work, a pastor may well study Christian Personal Ethics, *by Carl F. H. Henry, with the scholarly literature to which he refers. Better still, a local preacher of ethics ought to know well what the Bible teaches about this subject, as vital as it is difficult. The Bible study should include the Book of Hosea, the prophet of forgiving love, human and divine. Thank God for the "Cross of Hosea"!*

THE COMMANDMENT ABOUT PURITY

"Thou shalt not commit adultery."—EXODUS 20:14

IN OUR STUDY of the Ten Commandments we now come to the Seventh: "Thou shalt not commit adultery." In a more positive form the Scriptures teach, "Rejoice in the wife of your youth; be always infatuated with her" (Prov. 5:18-19).

Someone may ask, "If adultery is so obviously wrong, as forbidden in the commandment, why talk about the matter in the pulpit?" Because adultery is in all places both a present and a perennial problem. In this respect the times today resemble those of our grandparents. Their times were like the days of our Lord. According to the Gospels, He had much to say publicly about adultery.

TWO CASES OF ADULTERY

One day while our Lord was teaching, a group of men came rushing down the road dragging by the wrist a forlorn woman. Rudely they cast her down in the dust at His feet. Then they stood by to exclaim, "Master, we caught her in the very act! Moses says that she should be stoned. How sayest thou?" Jesus looked round the circle and then full into their eyes. Stooping down, with His finger He wrote in the dust. What He wrote we do not know, but it may have been a list of those men's sins.

Every man there must have understood what Jesus wrote. Man after man, searching his own heart, slunk back into the anonymous crowd, leaving the woman alone with the Lord. Then He said to her, tenderly, "Woman, where are thine accusers?" Here He used the same word "woman" with which He would later address His mother during the anguish of the crucifixion. Looking through the dust and the tears in her eyes, she said, "Master, there is no one." Jesus gently told her, "Neither do I condemn thee; go and sin no more."

One of the reasons He did not condemn her was that every person who commits adultery carries a heavy burden of guilt, and senses his own condemnation. No further healing would take place through heaping condemnation upon condemnation. The Lord showed His scorn rather for those who would deprive people of their good name. Adultery is a sin that stems from the wrong use of love, but pride and hauteur spring from hostility and anger. These latter sins do not carry in themselves a sense of guilt and oppressiveness.

In a later study of this human problem we come to 1850. In that year Nathaniel Hawthorne wrote *The Scarlet Letter,* which some have described as the greatest book ever written in the western hemisphere. In this poignant story, which centers round adultery, the stress falls, not on the sin itself, but on what adultery does to each of the four principals. Hester, enduring her open confession and vilification by the people while she stands before them in the pillory, is transformed into a humble, purified woman who spends the rest of her life in gentleness and deeds of mercy.

The minister, Mr. Dimmesdale, who secretly bears guilt eating within his heart, finally confesses his sin from the pillory in front of the people, and dies in the agony of his long-carried burden. Dr. Chillingworth, who at length discovers that his friend and pastor has been the violater of his marriage, takes out his vengeance in hostility and retribution. At the end he dies the victim of his own wrath. The most-wronged person, of course, is Pearl, the little child, who grows up to be a wanton, rebellious, undisciplined person, because she has been deprived of strong love from legitimate parents, and of the security they could have given her. . . .

As we sweep through history, from Bible times to the present, the main theme we wish to establish is that marital infidelity is always a symptom of a far deeper need or conflict within the human heart, a malady that Christ alone can heal. Sometimes He does so in part through psychiatry. The Bible teaches that out of the heart are the issues of life, and that out of the heart also come adultery, wantonness, and murder. The public in general deals with adultery as a thing by itself, as if it could be solved by legal punishment. The Bible views adultery as a symptom of a far deeper inner hurt, which needs to be healed. When the proper steps are taken, a marriage that has been fractured by violation of the seventh commandment can be restored. Two nobler, finer people, who now possess deeper self-understanding and receive prayerful support, can be restored to one another for all the years that lie ahead.

In support of this basic proposition let us suggest three avenues of discussion. First, a definition of what we mean by adultery and its involvement. Second, a broad description of the causes that lead to its being committed. Third, some indication of what hope and cure await those who are involved.

I. THE MEANING OF ADULTERY

Basically, adultery involves first of all a disrupted, deep, inner disloyalty, even more than it involves physical violation. Before the sinful act can take place, there has to be an inner spirit destructive of integrity in one's own personality. Hence we say that the act is only a symptom of a deeper disorder within.

In general there are three types of adultery. First, and obviously, it means the unfaithfulness of one or both parties to a marriage. Christ teaches that a man shall leave his father and mother, and shall cleave to his wife, and they twain shall be one flesh. This deepest of all human relationships is meant of God to be one of unity and permanence, which are violated by breaking the seventh commandment. Sometimes adultery is committed because of a sudden impulse. More often it is due to a deliberate triangular relationship. In either case, the act is an indication of a neurotic personality, or an unrealistic view of life.

Again, there are those who maintain this relationship in a way wholly legal, according to the codes of various states. From the Christian viewpoint they are violating the integrity of marriage. The Christian way of life is that of a minority, in the midst of a broad secular generation that always seeks to dim or "gray" the distinctive characteristics of Christian ideals. The Christian ideal is that of a marriage as permanent. The secular state makes rapid divorce readily available for anyone who wishes to change from one mate to another. More than one cinema star at Hollywood has had a series of successive marriages, preceded by a series of rapid divorces, easily obtained.

A comment on easy divorce comes from C. S. Lewis, the professor at Oxford, who has been converted to Christ. He states that it is better to have no marriage at all than to add to unchastity the compounded burden of perjury. This statement has both truth and sharpness, in keeping with the Biblical ideals we are seeking to uphold.

Once again, under the general subject of adultery we may include pre-marital relationships, which mean unchastity before marriage. Technically, this kind of sin is called fornication. We live in a generation that is continually incited to obsession about sex. More and more, young persons feel that they must violate their inner integrity, either because they think that the other partner expects it, or that their comrades do. Such pre-marital experiences tend to produce an immunity to that love which is the chief characteristic of a man and a woman as they look forward to a successful marriage. Pre-marital relationship dulls the beauty of a union that God intends to be lifelong and healthy, pure and beautiful.

Whether we think about the pressures put upon unmarried young persons, the tensions that exist between those already married, or the experiences of those too often married, we ought to consider the causes that lead persons to violate the seventh commandment by committing adultery.

II. THE CAUSES OF ADULTERY

Our basic theme is that the act of adultery, or marital infidelity, is always a symptom of a far deeper inner personal disorder, which can be healed only through conversion and restoration by Jesus Christ. The healing may come in part through the insights and re-education of pastoral or psychiatric care.

The causes of marital infidelity may be classified under three heads. First, an immature personality, or a neurotic way of life. When we say that those who commit adultery are immature, we mean that they have a deep-seated need, which consciously or unconsciously they are trying to meet through excursions into sin. For example, a man who goes from woman to woman may unconsciously be looking for a mother. A woman who hates her father, for reasons justified or unjustified, may unconsciously seek to wreak revenge upon man after man, whom she humiliates in one intrigue after another. Some are not able to face the facts of responsible support and loyalty. They constantly seek to be reassured by a series of infidelities that only add to their feelings of insecurity. Trained counselors agree that dissatisfaction in a marriage is only an expression of a deeper unmet personal need, which leads a person to commit adultery.

A second cause has more to do with the body. Christian people need to realize that even the noblest saint has a body, with normal appetites and drives. Christians also need to remember that even the grossest person, with the crudest physical appetites, still has a soul and a conscience. We all need to consider the care and preservation of our purity and integrity, lest the normal impulses and appetites of the body yield to the allurements of life, so that possibilities become actualities. We live in the sort of world where every person needs to defend his integrity by maintaining the health of both soul and body.

The third and most common cause of adultery is plain selfishness, or character failure. People in general feel that sexual violations destroy character. The considered opinion of those who write upon the subject is that the reverse holds true. First comes character failure, or disintegration of loyalty, and then comes the sexual violation. As a rule infidelity is committed by a selfish person who wishes to use another person as a thing. Such a relationship, though it may endure for a dozen years, does not culminate in a fruitful, unselfish, devoted union, which a normal man or woman wishes to enjoy through all the days on earth.

If these are the basic causes, then the only way the Gospel of Christ and the healing of our Saviour can penetrate the situation is by thorough-going forgiveness and restoration at the deepest level of the human heart. Healing and restoration come, not merely through dealing with adultery alone, but rather through dealing with the prime causes: an unrealistic personality; insufficient guardianship of the two natures in one's personality, both soul and body; and the dominance of uncontrolled and undisciplined selfishness. It is not by legalistic action, or by retributive revenge directed against the act itself, that we can rescue people from such obsessions. It is by the transforming love of Christ.

III. THE CURE FOR ADULTERY

For those who wish to be delivered from the burden of their infidelities, and from their feelings of guilt, the cure is as follows. For those who wish to be set free from circumstances that may lead to adultery, the remedy is the same. These three stages all have to do with Christ.

In the cure of adultery and the preservation of one's loyal integrity the first stage may be personal and psychological. This means to take a good look at one's self, to understand one's nature, and then determine to overhaul it with the help of Jesus Christ and competent professional care. This means to build a stable, loyal, generous, pure-minded personality on the abiding love of Jesus Christ.

One of the early symptoms of emotional need is a habit of

"being hurt." This is where the average person may well begin to work on his own inner self. To revel in hurt feelings is to develop a self-centered obsession that is destructive of personality, and may lead to the kind of dependent attitude that we have been talking about as the route to adultery. On the other hand, cultivating a generous, outgoing, other-seeking personality is a healthy way to achieve a stabilized, loving Christian marriage relationship.

A second thing that a person can do is to avoid circumstances and occasions that may lead to marital infidelity. We are living in a society so sex-stimulated that we have almost achieved a national obsession about our physical relationships. Many men are forced to travel away from home from four to six weeks, and are often lonesome. Even a long-distance telephone call to hear the warm voice of wife and children at home is not a satisfactory substitute for being in their midst, and enjoying the radiance of their love, with the laughter of their voices. At such a time it is easy for a lonely man to get into what may seem like a perfectly normal situation, which may turn out to be full of peril. By the same token, the wife who remains at home may through her long weeks of loneliness gets into a situation fraught with danger.

With our free and easy social conditions of life today, we must face the fact that this freedom promotes situations in which it is easy for infidelity to take place. For example, anything beyond the moderate use of alcohol (I speak as a total abstainer) puts either a man or a woman, especially a woman, into a position that may easily lead to infidelity. The use of alcohol involves a chemical-mechanical process that lowers the discipline center and the loyalty value of a person, thus permitting the physical passions to become dominant. In any such situation infidelity may follow.

Many people think that men and women commit sex violations because they drink excessively. The present-day teaching of psychology is that men and women probably drink excessively in order to commit sexual violations, which they orginally wished to perform. There is such a strong conscience for purity and integrity that the man or woman who desires to violate these standards must first suppress this moral center by excessive use of alcohol. So, instead of alcohol's causing infidelity, alcohol may be a tool used excessively by a brute who already has in his heart a desire to commit adultery. But what about his victim?

IV. THE PREVENTION OF ADULTERY

This third stage has to do directly with Christ. Any step that deepens the discipline of character control in a Christian person, enabling him to say "Yes" and "No" clearly and sincerely, is an aid in preserving the purity and integrity of his life and marriage. The man who makes Christ the Master of his life is in a far better position to defend the honor of his home and the purity of his heart. The man who makes himself his own master,—or money, or fame, or fortune,—actually becomes the slave of his own deepest interests, and is not able to control himself and his passions. The same holds true of a woman. Those who yield to self-pity, self-interest, and self-reference, by constantly having their feelings hurt, are living a life of narcosis where they receive "ego shots in the arm," and need increasing doses. This sort of self-indulgence may easily lead to physical sin.

But when Christ is the Master of a life, the body becomes a temple of the Holy Spirit, which the custodian keeps pure and noble. The Lordship of Christ leads to discipline of the body. The finest way for a man or a woman to keep pure is taught by St. Paul. He says that if a man gives himself to his wife, and if she gives herself to her husband, with the sincere love of a Christian marriage, then they will both be able to keep themselves pure by the strength of the love that each of them calls forth from the other. As André Maurois says in his book, *The Art of Lasting Love,* "I have chosen. Now my aim is not to search to please myself, but to please the one whom I have chosen to love."

When a man or a woman looks forward to marriage, or else looks back on it, reflectively, the chief desire through long turbulent years is gradually to achieve wholesome character and fruitfulness of love, and never to be drawn aside to some liaison not conducive to personal growth and not productive of household happiness. When a man and a woman sincerely love each

other in the Lord, either of them can say to the other these
words from a poet, Roy Croft,

> I love you
> Not only for what you are
> But for what I am
> When I am with you.
>
> I love you,
> Not only for what
> You have made of yourself,
> But for what you are making of me.

With such a love in the heart of a man and of a woman, the
two Christians can recognize their mutual needs, both of soul
and body. They can deal objectively with the disappointments,
the temptations, and the failures of ordinary life. And they can
meet emergencies. Out of the years they can achieve a radiant
love on the basis of their loyalty to God and to each other. The
poignant attachment of husband and wife appears in beautiful
lines by an unknown poet, who entitles them, "Walk Slowly":

> If you should go before me, dear, walk slowly
> Down the ways of death, well worn and wide,
> For I should want to overtake you quickly,
> And seek the journey's ending by your side.
>
> I should be so forlorn not to descry you
> Down some radiant road and take the same;
> Walk slowly, dear, and often look behind you,
> And pause to hear if someone speaks your name.

In conclusion, to fulfill our obligations we need to deal severely
with ourselves. In our dealings with those who have fallen into
temptation we need to deal as compassionately as Jesus would do.

For ourselves, we need to be severe in order to achieve the
fruitfulness of purity, and the depths of true love to enhance
the loyalty and dignity that come from giving oneself whole-
heartedly to one's Christian partner in marriage. Only the love
of Jesus Christ to us can make us loving and beloved. Only the
healing power of Christ, who suffered for us on the Cross, can
enable us to go through the fires of temptation, and to reach
the depths of inner, personal integrity. By prayer and by faith-

fulness to Him we shall receive strength to be loyal to ourselves
and to our partners.

As for those who bear the heaviest weight of guilt by reason
of their past infidelities, and who now seek to be delivered from
the burden of their sins, our prayers should constantly arise to
God. Here we need not condemn, nor need our non-condemnation
be misconstrued into condoning. We need to rescue the lost, to
seek the bewildered, to encourage them, and to lead back to
Christ those who are frightened, so that they may have their
inner souls healed, and be delivered from the burden of their
infidelities.

Even though the seventh commandment has been broken,
many a marriage can be restored. Every person caught beneath
this burden, who truly turns to Jesus Christ, repenting and pleading for His love and forgiveness, will be restored to a new personality. Thus he will receive integrity, loyalty, and purity, to go
forth into a deeper life of true loving and self-giving, from Him
who is ever loving and ever giving Himself to the one who turns
to Him in faith believing.

6. Paul S. Rees

Paul Stromberg Rees, Mission Covenant Church.
Born, Providence, R. I., Sept. 4, 1900. Educated, Uni-
versity of Southern California. (A.B.) D.D., Univ. So.
Cal., Asbury College; LL.D., Houghton College. Pas-
torates (1920-38); First Mission Covenant Church,
Minneapolis (1938-58). A leader in Billy Graham's
City Crusades; also in conferences with pastors in Asia,
et al. Now serving with World Vision as evangelist and
Bible teacher. Books: If God Be for Us (1940); Things
Unshakable (1947); The Radiant Cross (1949); The
Face of Our Lord (1951); Stir Up the Gift (1952);
Prayer and Life's Highest (1956); Christian, Commit
Yourself (1957); The Adequate Man: Studies in Philip-
pians (1958).

*The message about silence before God shows how the purpose
and "tone color" of a sermon ought to accord with the character
and spirit of the text in its Bible setting. Here the text has to do
with a person who believes in God, and the spirit of the psalm
is devotional, with a touch of quiet beauty. Hence the message is
devotional, and for one of God's children. While the minister
appeals to the head, he speaks more to the heart. Such pulpit
work the fathers used to term "pastoral," since it aims to comfort
and cheer a person who already loves the Lord.*

*The speaker catches attention at once by pointing out a con-
trast between the restfulness of the passage and the rush of a
modern city. Later he keeps one interested by using non-Biblical
materials, none hackneyed, and all showing how to enjoy "quiet
seasons of the soul," even amid the roar of city life today. Such a
spokesman for the Lord of all grace needs himself to have a love
of beauty in the world about him, in the poetry of the Bible,
and in the lives of men, one by one, as they reflect "the beauty
of the Lord."*

THE SERVICE OF SILENCE

"Commune with your own heart upon your bed, and be still."   PSALM 4:4

OTHER TRANSLATIONS prefer the word "silence." Horace L. Fenton has it, "In silence reflect." The American Revised Version says, "Be silent."

For our noise-numb age could anything be more timely? Our cities are cities of the three s's: swoosh, screech, and shrillness. The swoosh of huge buses, the screech of brakes and sliding tires, and the shrillness of the policeman's whistle. They are cities of the three r's: rumble, rattle, and roar. The rumble of subway trains below, the rattle of delivery trucks at the curb, and the roar of airplanes above.

Speaking of her own New York City, Dorothy Kilgallen says: "You can't walk ten blocks without passing a street repair man leaning on his jack hammer, which can do worse things to your eardrums than it does to the Gotham pavement." And then one thinks of Stephen Harold Spender's lines:

> Swear never to allow
> Gradually to smother,
> With noise and fog,
> The flowering of the spirit.*

If the summons to stillness, the healing ministry of silence, was urged upon spiritually-caring people in the comparatively quiet times of long ago, how urgently important is it in these days of turbulence and tension! An age that measures the noise of applause with a meter and reckons the thunder of explosions in decibels needs to reach out for a medicine that isn't found in sleeping tablets. It is found in something much simpler. It is found in a stillness that somehow becomes alive with God. "Be still, and know that I am God."

I myself have felt such stillness, and so have many of you. In some degree I have felt it often. On occasions I have felt it over-poweringly. One night, deep in the south of India, following dinner in the Episcopal residence of an Indian bishop, a companion and I walked out of the house and into the garden. Serene stars were shining. The hillside was quiet. The trees were motionless. The town was still. Presently, as we sat on a bench, we were joined by our host, the godly bishop, resplendent in his scarlet robe, venerable with his long black hair and his well groomed beard. In a voice softer than chamber music he told us the story of his conversion.

The bishop also told us, ever so quietly, how God had baptized him with the Holy Spirit, and thus introduced him to the discipleship of freedom and fulness. When he had ceased talking, the silence of that moment, as we sat there in the noiseless flooding of that Travancore moon, was something I shall remember as long as I live. It was a silence so pregnant with God as to make you feel that even one audible word would be sacrilege. It was a moment when, without forcing yourself, you could enter with Whittier into the significance of the poetic exclamation:

> O Sabbath rest by Galilee!
> O calm of hills above,
> Where Jesus knelt to share with Thee
> The silence of eternity,
> Interpreted by love.

"Commune with your own heart upon your bed, and be still." "Be silent." "In silence reflect." What is the service of these quiet and yet creative interludes in the life of one who is a child of God?

I. SILENCE AS AN AID TO MEMORY

Certainly, for one thing, we are warranted in saying that silence serves as an aid to memory. It is when we are still that the past comes trooping back, perhaps to haunt us, perhaps to humble us, perhaps to make us happy. In our psalm, the fourth, note two past tenses. In verse one David remembers: "Thou hast enlarged me when I was in distress." In verse seven he recalls: "Thou hast put gladness in my heart, more than in the time that their corn and their wine increased." When David is quiet, his memory goes to work. He looks back upon those troubles which, however unbearable they seemed at the time, have left him nevertheless a bigger man, with a richer soul and a finer faith.

Some time ago I read a prayer that is posted on the door of a guest room at Bridgewater College in Virginia. As I share with you this prayer, I want you to notice the prominence it gives to the value of remembering and the peril of forgetting:

> Let me do my work each day, and if the darkened hours of despair overcome me, may I not forget the strength that comforted me in the desolation of other times. May I still remember the bright hours that found me walking over the silent hills of my early childhood, or dreaming on the margin of the quiet river, where a light glowed within me, and I promised my early God to have courage amid the tempests of the changing years. May I not forget that poverty and riches are of the spirit. Lift my eyes from the earth, and let me not forget the uses of the stars. . . . Let me not follow the clamor of the world, but walk calmly in my path. Give me a few friends who will love me for what I am, and keep ever burning before my vagrant steps the light of hope. And though age and infirmity overtake me, and I come not within sight of the castle of my dreams, teach me still to be thankful for life.

Can you conceive of anyone writing a prayer like that who did not know the sanctuary of silence as a place for the soul's retreat and renewal? Can you imagine anyone who can read it and enter understandingly into its beauty without first stilling, as far as possible, the noises that chug and chatter around him? Yes, silence is the setting in which memory has its best chance, and does its noblest work. "Be silent." "In silence reflect."

II. SILENCE AS A RESPONSE TO MYSTERY

Think too how silence often serves as a response to mystery. See how David begins the verse from which our text is taken: "Stand in awe, and sin not." When the universe and all of life draw aside their thick curtains and permit us to catch a glimpse of their innermost marvels, the vision is not likely to send us into gales of laughter and roars of applause. It is more likely to leave us speechless.

Fourth of July firecrackers go off with a pop and a jump, and the neighborhood young life squeals and shouts. But not long ago when an atomic explosion was shown on television, a strange hush fell while that ghastly mushroom took shape before eyes curiously quiet. Silence, or near-silence, was our response to the awesome mystery that man's ingenuity had lately unveiled.

To be sure, science takes the mystery out of some things by giving us understanding in place of ignorance. To a savage a Swiss watch seems completely mysterious. A civilized man appreciates the watch, and knowing how it works, he is not awed by it. However, when science has said its last word, there are mysteries that still remain mysteries.

Take birth, for example. When our first child was born I was permitted to be in the delivery room. I can still see that tiny human form in the hands of the doctor. I can still feel the inexpressible sense of mystery, the wonder beyond words, that took possession of me. The dryness in my throat and the wetness of my eyes were part of the silence that I gave as my response to the marvel of life's beginning.

Or think of great art. At Forest Lawn Cemetery in Los Angeles the colossal painting of the Crucifixion is viewed by hundreds of spectators every day. You cannot rush in and take a "quickie" at it, as you can in some art galleries. The large viewing room, with comfortable seats, is first filled. As the crowd waits for the curtain to be parted, whispering and low talking may be heard throughout the room. Then the great curtains are drawn aside, the vast picture confronts all eyes, and a hush as of eternity falls everywhere. How can brush and pigment come so close to the lineaments and the luster of real life? The low gasps soon subside into stillness. The silence is the tribute that admiration and awe are ready to pay to the undying mystery of great art.

Or else consider the holiness of God. Do we stand in awe of holiness, as most assuredly we should? "As he which hath called you is holy," cries Peter in a solemn address to his fellow Christians, "so be ye holy in all manner of conversation," or "conduct," as an improved version has it (I Peter 1:15). Whether it is a whole nation of men, or just plain "John Smith" on Fifth Street, there is a hushed reverence that should be evoked by the unsullied holiness that our poor eyes behold in God. It is a part of worship. It is a part of penitence. It is a part of all sensitive discipleship.

"Be still!" says our text. In the presence of life's mysteries, we know how useful silence can be. When no other response is possible, this is it. "Be silent." "In silence reflect."

III. SILENCE AS A FORM OF MINISTRY

Still another service that silence may render is this: strange as it may seem, silence itself is a form of ministry. It is a form of ministry to ourselves. In verse two David is mightily stirred because of the stubborn rebelliousness and the stupid hypocrisies of wicked men. Whether he is speaking for God, or for himself, he cries out: "O men, how long shall my honor suffer shame? How long will you love vain words and seek after lies?" Such concern and such a protest are not out of place today. Without them something is missing from our moral fiber.

But even in the warfare against wickedness there are dangers. Our own souls can become strident and harsh, hectic and strained. Hence the need of stillness, and of those luminous insights that come with quietness before God. Here in verse three is one of these insights: "But know"—just quietly recognize, and as you recognize, rejoice—that "the Lord hath set apart him that is godly for himself."

Harry A. Overstreet, the author of such a widely read book as *The Mature Mind,* has some viewpoints that I do not share. But in *The Great Enterprise* he has a fine passage: "Times of silence are times when we have a chance to be loosed into affection. Too much noise, too many voices, too many suggestions and counter-suggestions, too many calls to do this and that,—all tend to put edginess into life. To be still is to give ourselves the chance to recover kinship and friendliness" (p. 197).

"Know that the Lord hath set apart him that is godly for himself." What is this if it is not recovering a sense of the highest kinship, our kinship with God as His twice-born children; and the highest friendship, our friendship with God in Christ?

But silence, I would remind you, is also a form of service to others. A little girl's favorite doll was broken by someone who, not realizing how dear that doll was to the heartbroken girl, said instantly, "I'll buy you another one." Those words, however well intended, seemed to convey no appreciation of how irreplaceably precious was that doll. When the mother also tried to give some word of comfort, the little daughter, with a dignity of sorrow that seemed beyond her years, looked up into her mother's eyes and said, "Don't talk about it, please, Mummy." Because the hurt was too deep for words, words could not reach it.

More times than I like to recall, I have gone to a funeral parlor, or someone's home, to face a father or a mother, a husband or a wife, to whom grief had just come, acute and desolating. My first ministry there—if please God it has been a ministry at all—has been with no smoothly turned sentences, no glib and conventional condolence, no attempt at explanation of what had happened. No, not any of these, but a clasp of my hand and whatever of Christ's tender care I could convey with my eyes. When the heart is throbbing with its most acute anguish, it isn't speeches that are needed so much as Christ's healing silence.

IV. SILENCE AS A SYMBOL OF MAJESTY

Let us acknowledge, finally, that silence can serve as a symbol of majesty. In verse six David seems to hear some mocker of the good life, saying, "Who will show us any good?" This is the language of the cynic who affects a proud scorn of purity and truth and goodness in general. Now mark David's way of treating this cynical outburst. He refuses to argue with it. He simply ignores it. With sublime indifference he turns and says, "Lord, lift thou up the light of thy countenance upon us." Not upon the cynics, but upon us!

Jesus was like that. Pilate said to Him, "Whence art thou?" Jesus, having already declared Himself, gave no answer. Again, there was Herod. Wanting only to make a plaything of Jesus, Herod "questioned Him with many words," says Luke. But Jesus "answered him nothing." Our Lord met him with majestic silence.

A little later, when He was near the end, up on the Cross where He was suspended, the taunting mob hurled at Him their cruel challenge, blind as it was callous: "If thou be the King of the Jews, save thyself!" What was His reply? A silence so noble and so noteworthy that the centuries have had to reckon with it.

In company with the Saviour we too can hardly escape occasions when the best weapon of moral dignity is silence. There are times when the hurtful, gossipy word against the fair name of another is best rebuked by silence. There are times when some proposal of dishonesty or dishonor is best flung back in the face of the proposer in silence, with a wordless look and with lips from which no syllable escapes.

Silence! Let no one imagine that it is useless. Whether as an aid to memory, a response to mystery, a form of ministry, or a sign of moral majesty, the soul has need of silence. Give it, then, I beg you, a larger and a more significant place in the life of your soul.

And whatever you do, don't treat Jesus Christ with such carelessness and flippancy that He can return you nothing but His awful and dooming silence. The fear of such a thing once laid hold of the Psalmist, resulting in a cry that more than one of you should make your own: "Be not silent to me, lest if thou be silent to me, I become like them that go down into the pit" (Psa. 28:1).

His silence unto you can be terribly fatal. Your silence unto Him can be tremendously fruitful.

II. With Christ Before Calvary

7. Samuel M. Shoemaker

Samuel Moor Shoemaker, Protestant Episcopal Church.
Born, Baltimore, Dec. 27, 1893. Educated, Princeton
University (A.B.); General Seminary, and Union Sem-
inary, New York. D.D., Virginia Seminary, Alexandria,
Va.; S.T.D., Berkeley Seminary, California. Y.M.C.A.
Secretary (1917-24). Rector, Calvary Church, New York
(1925-52); Calvary Church, Pittsburgh, since 1952. Sun-
day night radio program, "Faith that Works." Nation-
wide radio broadcast, "Episcopal Hour" (1957-58).
Author, 25 books, including How You Can Help
Other People (1946); Revive Thy Church—Beginning
with Me (1948); By the Power of God (1954). Also,
The Experiment of Faith (1957).

In Battell Chapel of Yale University on a Sunday morning this
minister recently dared to preach the evangelistic message that
follows. In it he did not apologize, hesitate, or try to steal up on
the hearer unawares. Neither did he talk down by pausing to
identify Paul Tillich and G. K. Chesterton, Blaise Pascal and
William James, the latter of whom once wrote, "My attitude to
religion is that of deference rather than adoption." In pleading
for adoption the advocate of the Gospel speaks about decision in
two contexts familiar to every university man: his job and his
girl. Especially does the latter decision emerge at strategic intervals, but never in such a fashion as to cause distaste or mirth.

Without ever seeming shallow the style keeps simple and clear.
The sermon aims to let Christ stand out at Yale as the most
appealing character in history. When the manuscript first came
to me it caused me to feel, as I still feel, after repeated readings:
"This man has a message from Christ for me. I wonder why more
men do not preach this way in university chapels." I thank God
when a written sermon brings me face to face with my Redeemer
and King, moving me now to confess Him before men.

THE CHRISTIAN DECISION

"As he passed by, he saw Levi the son of Alphaeus sitting at the place of toll, and he saith, 'Follow me.' And he arose and followed him."   ST. MARK 2:14

WE SHALL THINK together about the Christian decision. We shall begin with this refreshingly clear encounter between Jesus and Matthew, or Levi. In the world Jesus had a tremendous task to accomplish. Here was a man He felt sure could help. So our Lord called him, and the man responded with his life. How very different from the sometimes hesitant efforts we put forth to arrive at a religious conviction! It is much like a man's jumping at a job that his mouth has been watering for, a job with the National City Bank, or with Alcoa. It is still more like the spirit in which he sets out to visit the girl of his heart when she has crooked an interested finger in his direction.

Emotional? You'd better have some emotion in the enthusiasm with which you undertake a new job, and certainly in relation to your heart's intended! But there is much more than emotion. The whole of your personality—reason, emotion, imagination, and will—the whole of your being is involved in a decision like this.

Before the conversation, this man surely had known something of Jesus and His purposes. He must have heard the Master speak, and have seen Him at work. Jesus must have observed Matthew and decided that he was the sort of man He wanted to call. Like many another passage in the New Testament, this study is surely foreshortened. But there cannot have been a very long exposure, only enough to give the man a basis for such a commitment of himself. The incident illustrates the basic necessity for Christian decision. As Paul Tillich says, "The Christian Gospel is a matter of decision. It is to be accepted, or rejected. All that we who communicate this Gospel can do is to make possible a genuine decision."

I. A RESPONSE TO CHRIST

In this record we see that the Christian decision is a response. We ourselves do not create the Christian encounter. We do not go out looking for God, and stumble on Christ. If the Christian Gospel is true, in Christ God has made the first step in our direction. Through Christ God seeks us. You may not believe that a man is "lost," in the sense of his being damned, but you must accept this belief in the sense that he does not know the meaning of his life, or what to make of his own existence. As Gilbert K. Chesterton said, man has always lost his way, but now he has lost his address!

It is well for us to accumulate all the findings we can about life and existence, but there still remains the question whether or not it means anything, and if so, what. Christ claims to be the Way, the Truth, and the Life. He claims to have a unique relation to God. He healed men's bodies and He healed their minds. He even pronounced on individuals the forgiveness of sins. So we have a far better opportunity than Matthew to form our opinion of who this is that asks from us the response of faith and obedience. But the same encounter that took place between Him and Matthew is taking place at this moment, in this house of worship, between Him and ourselves, with exactly the same issues involved.

II. A GAMBLE OF FAITH

The Christian decision is a gamble of faith. We consider the claims of this Person: His effect upon history and upon human lives; His views and values over against those of other seers and sages. Then we decide. It is a gamble of faith. So is choosing a job, or taking a wife. So is all living that is not purely academic. You will never know whether or not the object of your faith is worthy of it until you risk the gamble. Such a gamble requires all our powers, including our emotions. As William James said, in the *Will to Believe,* "Our passional nature not only lawfully may but must decide an option between propositions, whenever it is an option that cannot by its nature be decided on intellectual grounds; for to say under such circumstances, 'Do not decide, but leave the question open,' is itself a passional decision, just like deciding yes or no, and is attended with the same risk of losing the truth."

And Blaise Pascal said, "There is a necessity to wager; the thing is placed beyond your will. . . . By not laying that God is, you in effect say that He is not." This kind of thinking, I believe, is characterized not so much by pure reason as by the reasonableness of common sense. Is there not a great deal of the gamble of faith in the hypotheses that science must assume to be true till further experiment proves them true or false? In religion, also, we shall need the gamble of experimentation. Some of the illumination that you want on this side of a decision, before you make it, will come to you only on the other side of the decision, after you have made it.

III. A COMBINATION OF QUALITIES

The Christian decision involves a combination of personal loyalty to Christ and of dedication to His task in the world. There is much danger that people who think themselves Christians will remain content with a theologically reasonable and satisfying view of Christ. I judge that He cares very little about this. "If ye love me, keep my commandments." "Not every one that saith to me, 'Lord, Lord,' shall enter into the kingdom of heaven, but he that doeth the will of my Father which is in heaven." Really we shall never truly know who He is until we let Him call us into the kind of life that is impossible without living faith, which means faith in action.

In Pittsburgh a while ago a remarkable missionary named Donald McClure was speaking about his wonderful work with the Anuak tribe in Africa. He was also asking for helpers. A young engineer in the city asked him how you knew when you were called to be a missionary. McClure replied: "We have orders from the Commander-in-Chief. He told us to go into all the world. Are you 4 F?" Today the young engineer is with McClure in Africa, laying out airstrips and helping to erect new buildings. Call this impulsive, if you will. I judge that it is a good deal less so than many of our calculated and prudential decisions, with self-regard as their real basis. The young engineer's experience certainly sounds like the encounter between Jesus and Matthew.

IV. A FACTOR IN CONVERSION

Christian decision, I believe, is the most important factor in Christian conversion. In conversion there are two parts. There is God's part, which consists in His approach to us through Christ, and in His dealings with each of us as an individual with particular needs and possibilities. Here the initiative is on God's side. Then there is our part, which consists in our initial dedication of ourselves to Him, with our acceptance of Christ and His forgiveness, in an act of will that is as complete and wholehearted as we can make it.

Sometimes we think of conversion as so overwhelming an experience that we can do nothing about it. We think that it is either for the very bad, or else for the very good, and that we are not in either class. So we do not feel eligible. Now the gift of redemption which Christ offers us is there already. It has been extended to us. But it takes two to create a gift, both a giver and a receiver. Our decision does not convert us, but it puts us in the way of being converted. I have never seen anyone fail of being converted because God withheld conversion from him, but I have seen many fail of it because they withheld themselves. When we come in need, in honesty, and in openness, offering ourselves in a definite decision, God acts. He accepts us, forgives us, and begins dealing with us. He can do all this without trespassing upon our freedom. "Our wills are ours to make them Thine."

V. THE SURRENDER TO CHRIST

Christian decision therefore means the personal surrender of ourselves to Christ. We should begin our discipleship with the same undivided wholeheartedness that we have toward marriage. No one of us does a perfect job of giving an undivided and selfless love to a wife, or a husband; but we begin by promising to "keep ourselves wholly unto her [or to him] as long as we both shall live." We spend the rest of our lives trying to fulfill the vows we took the day we were married. Surely the initial completeness and wholeheartedness of the transaction is of the utmost importance.

I know a marriage that is going on the rocks today because the initial wholeheartedness was wanting. Many a nominal Christian, also, is dull and lacklustre because he has never even tried to surrender himself to Christ completely. We begin by surrendering to Christ as much of ourselves as we can, to as much of Christ as we understand. But our pride resists surrender to anybody, even to God. William James called self-surrender "the vital turning point of the religious life." Our performance will never come up to our promise, but we need the initial promise as the lasting guide for our subsequent living.

A certain psychiatrist has for years been very close to the movement called Alcoholics Anonymous. He believes that the reason the A.A. succeeds in so many cases where medicine and psychiatry fail is to be found in the alcoholic's surrender to a "higher power." Alcoholics generally are self-centered and defiant people who develop expansive egos. This psychiatrist thinks that the usual therapy of building up the patient's ego and self-confidence is misplaced.

But if an alcoholic first admits that he is powerless against strong drink, and then surrenders himself to whatever he considers to be the Higher Power, his ego gives way. Says this psychiatrist, "Surrender means cessation of fight, . . . logically to be followed by internal peace and quiet. Loss of self is basic. And when the individual surrenders his ego, God automatically steps in." But what about the rest of us whose egos are just as expansive as theirs, and who constantly get "tight," not on whiskey and gin, but on self-inflationary ideas, on dreams of success, on feelings of resentment, and even on intellectual pride?

VI. THE MISSING FACTOR

Christian decision, I feel sure, is the missing factor in the spiritual pilgrimage of many a decent but powerless nominal

Christian. Such people have beliefs and convictions, but they do not have power. They may worship in Christian churches. They may work for good and Christian causes. These things may bring them within the reach of deep Christian conversion, or may provide a substitute that keeps them from knowing in their lives the power of Jesus Christ. You can rub your arm rapidly with a smooth stick, and produce an abrasion that will admit of a vaccination, or else you can rub it slowly with the same stick, and merely produce a callus. That's what often happens in churches.

Recently I have been in touch with a man who bears one of the great names in American business, a graduate of one of our foremost schools and universities. Some years ago he was confirmed in one of our educated, well-established churches. What I believe to have been the objective grace offered to him in that ceremony did not reach in to his personal problems and enable him to solve them—such problems as drink, nerves, and a feeling of futility. Later on he came in touch with some of Billy Graham's people, and made a life-changing decision.

There are many of us who through our membership in one of the standard-brand churches do not find a decisive Christian experience. I was one of them, and in the churches I sense a lack that needs to be met. For the last five years this businessman has been growing in his faith, learning to pray, studying his Bible, deepening his relation to Christ. He used to be a personable playboy, living a selfish, useless life. Today he is searching after the right place to invest his life for Christ. He says that to him nothing else is so important. He is a privileged man whom Christ has confronted. He is responding with his whole life, and if I may say so, he is getting a terrific bang out of it.

VII. THE HOW OF DECISION

How does one make the Christian decision? The "how" is wrapped up with the "who" and the "what." Christ confronts you and me, and asks of us the commitment of ourselves to Him in faith as His disciples. Christ—and you! These are the persons in the play. I know, and you do, that the closer we come to knowing Him, the more insistent becomes the decision that this confrontation involves. It is because of our simple human need for redemption from ourselves and from our meaninglessness without faith. Because of something deep within us, somehow we know that He is the Truth. We may fear this decision because of its consequences, but we cannot forget His claims upon us.

It will help if we now begin honestly to face what there is in us that He does not want. Someone has said that we take hold of God with the handle of our sins, and in the saying there is a real truth. God can transform all of our instincts, but in the raw many of them are His rivals. Everyone is more or less beset by a desire for money, for sex, and for power. We all want security, we want affection, we want prestige. All of them may rival Christ till we have given them to Him, that they may serve Him, as all of them can when they are surrendered. But be specific. Make a list of the things in you that you know Christ does not want to see in you. Such a list will give you something to go to work on. Like a doctor, Christ comes to us at the point of our need.

In all of this you may want some human help, some other Christian whom you know; it may be a minister, or someone else to whom you feel drawn, and to whom you think you can talk. This person may help to answer some question, and to nail down the decision as a kind of witness. Or maybe you want to make the decision by yourself.

In whatever circumstances seem to you right, make the decision. Tell Jesus that you want to say "Yes" to Him, to accept the redemption that He offers you, to receive His forgiveness, to become His disciple, and to let Him be your Lord. He is not a logical proposition, or a theological problem, or the head of an ecclesiastical system. He is a living Person, alive in this world, alive in this church, alive in your heart, and waiting to be more alive through your conscious decision and acceptance. Make the decision now, and do not endlessly delay.

Every man who dares to appear in this pulpit stands here in Christ's name and by His commission. We are recreant to our calling if we try to preach to you only little religious essays that do not offend your intellectual and aesthetic sensibilities.

We speak in His name. His cause in the world still needs disciples and recruits. To this He calls you. You will not be a perfect disciple, for no one of us is. But give Him your heart, your loyalty, and your life. This is where it all begins. Let Him take on from here.

8. Alan Redpath

Alan Redpath, Baptist. Born, Newcastle-on-Tyne, England, Jan. 9, 1907. Educated, Durham University School; Wyclif Hall, Oxford. Business executive (1930-36). Itinerant evangelist, Christian Youth Movement (1936-40). Pastor, Duke Street Baptist Church, Surrey (1940-53); Moody Memorial Church, Chicago, since 1953. Books: Answer for Today *(1951);* Victorious Christian Living *(1956);* Victorious Praying *(1957);* Victorious Christian Service *(1958).*

In its form the following evangelistic sermon differs from "the run of the mine." The text is most familiar, but the treatment is unique. In a message about Christ's question this minister often asks questions. Count them; also the number of interjections, which might be more, with a different kind of punctuation. Often he addresses the hearer, kindly, but searchingly. Again and again he uses direct discourse, or vivid dialogue (even hypothetical words from Christ). There is also much repetition, but never of aught not worth repeating. There is little extra-Biblical material.

The minister is speaking at the home church on a Sunday evening. Evidently he assumes that the hearers know the Book and the Gospel. Still he serves as a surgeon of the soul, gazing into it with the searchlight of divine truth, and standing ready to use the scalpel, "quick and powerful, piercing." Everywhere is a sense of onward motion, urgency, and a sort of suspense, one scarcely knows why, unless it be that the speaker's soul is moving Christward, and that his words flow from a heart surcharged with feeling. Thank God for the burning heart! See St. Luke 24:32.

CHRIST'S QUESTION WITHOUT AN ANSWER

"What shall it profit a man if he shall gain the whole world and lose his own soul?"   ST. MARK 8:36

THIS QUESTION from our Lord must be hypothetical. It is impossible for anybody ever to gain the whole world. You might get a bit of it, you might even gain a lot of it, but you could never own all of it. But suppose you could! On one scale the Lord Jesus puts the world in its entirety, and on the other scale He puts the soul in its eternity. Side by side He puts the two, and says: "Just suppose that you gain the whole world, every bit of it. What will it profit you if in the getting you lose your own soul?"

Our Lord's question is provoking. It isn't just shot at us out of its context and at random. The question is the climax of a tremendous message that the Lord Jesus spoke to the hearts, not only of the disciples in Galilee, but of all those within earshot today. I want the background and the principle of this text to be clearly understood by all of us, because through this searching question the Lord Jesus Christ is facing all of us with a principle of life. The contrast is between living for things that are temporal and living for God and eternity.

May I remind you of the circumstances in which our Lord asked this question? He had been preaching for about three years, and He knew perfectly well that the Cross stood a few months ahead. He had spoken to large multitudes. He had also spoken to persons one by one. He had given them abundant opportunity to arrive at a clear verdict concerning Himself. The time had come when they should not simply know something of His teaching.

The hour had arrived for everyone in that crowd to come to grips with God.

I feel as I speak to you that the time has come for many of you to do this very thing. You have heard about Jesus, you have listened to His teaching, and you know something about the Gospel. Surely the time has come for you personally to come to grips with God in Christ.

At such a moment the Lord Jesus faced the few disciples and said, "Who do men say that I am?" The answer was, "One of the prophets." Then He brought the question a bit closer and said, "Who say ye that I am?" You remember the answer that came from Simon Peter, "Thou art the Christ, the Son of the living God." Thou art the Christ!

I. A PROFESSION EVERYONE SHOULD MAKE

Here is a profession that every one of us has to acknowledge. I doubt whether a single person here would deny that statement by Peter. We don't think of Christ as simply one who lived in history. Everybody beneath this roof would say without reservation exactly what Simon Peter said, "Thou art the Christ, the Son of God." Of course we all believe that! The whole evidence of the Bible is here to prove it. We know enough about the Book to say that without any hesitancy. Therefore it wouldn't be a bit difficult for any of us to come to the same conclusion as Peter. He had walked with Christ, talked with Him, and watched His miracles. There was plenty of evidence for this man to say without any hesitancy, "Thou art the Christ."

Very well, let me assume this much. I trust that I am safe in doing so. I hope that everyone in this congregation will go that far and say, "I believe that Jesus Christ is the Son of God. I believe that He came into the world to save us from our sins. I believe that much of the Bible." What then? Simply to believe that truth makes no difference to me at all. I can believe it and still be lost. I can believe the right things about Christ and still be completely unsaved. I can accept these things theoretically, and still set myself to gain the whole world, and then at last lose my own soul.

II. A PRINCIPLE EVERYONE
SHOULD ACCEPT

You see, my friend, in this message that Jesus brought to His disciples, following the profession that had to be acknowledged, there was a principle of life that had to be accepted. What was this principle? After our Lord had spoken to Peter about his confession of faith, immediately Jesus said, "The Son of man must suffer, and be rejected, and must be killed, and the third day must rise again." You remember what happened next. In a moment the Lord Jesus turned His back upon Peter, and said, "Get thee behind me, Satan. Thou savourest not the things that be of God, but those that be of men." That's pretty strong language! "Get thee behind me, Satan!" to a man who just a minute ago had said, "Thou art the Christ, the Son of the Living God"!

In a simple statement—"Lord, be it far from Thee; not that way of suffering, not that way of pain, not that way of death" —Simon was expressing the very voice of the enemy of souls. Today what is wrong with our world? Why is it in such darkness, in such a mess? Simply because it is in revolt against its Creator. Simply because every human being is basically in revolt against God, refusing to acknowledge His authority and His right to rule over our lives. Into this situation God has sent His Son, to end this rule of rebellion, to wind up this era of anti-Godism, to bring men and women to their senses, and to faith and trust in God.

The fruit of our rebellion, the effect of our wanting our own way, is seen in suffering and misery and agony, in pain and warfare, in bloodshed and unhappiness. Into this situation comes the Christ of God to do the will of the Father, to fulfill His holy plan, to obey Him completely, to satisfy all of His holy law, and to lay down His life for us who have rebelled against God. Christ never for one moment allowed any deviation from God's will for His life. On Calvary He offered a perfect sacrifice for your sin.

For a world living contrary to the will of God, there was no other answer than Christ on the Cross. Here is Peter expressing the very language of the devil when he says, "Not that way, Lord. I want to follow Thee. I believe that Thou art the Christ. I believe all that about Thee. I believe right things about who Thou art, but I don't want anything in life that's going to upset this principle of self-pleasing."

Immediately Jesus confronts him, and says, "That's the very voice of the devil. That's the one thing which has landed men in a lost eternity. That's the principle which brings to earth suffering and misery, pain and agony." There is only one answer to such a saying as that of Peter. The answer is this, "If you would save your life, lose it. If you lose your life, for my sake and the Gospel's, you will save it." "What shall it profit a man if he shall gain the whole world, and lose his own soul?"

III. A PROBLEM EVERYONE SHOULD FACE

How do you think a man is lost? By direct defiance of God? Oh, yes, you can be lost by defiance of God, but not many people are lost like that. You can be lost by denial of God in your life. I don't think that many people are lost like that. Listen, especially young folk, you can be lost by sheer drift. That's all! Just sheer drifting through life. A refusal to accept the principle of the Cross, and a determination to live your own life and carve out your own career. That's how people are lost.

It's the voice of Satan that says, "Not the way of the Cross, Lord, not the way of suffering, not the way of sacrifice, not the way of blood. I want an easy path, an easy road. I want it all to be simple. I just won't put my back into anything. I am merely going to drift through life, and not care." How is a soul lost? Not simply by denial, not simply by defiance, but just by drifting. That's how many a soul is lost.

How is a soul saved? "He that saveth his life shall lose it. He that loseth his life for my sake and the Gospel's shall save it." This does not mean that the soul of a person is saved merely because he volunteers for the mission field. It doesn't mean anything except staying right where God puts you, and living there on this principle: that you have given up your own independence, and that your sole concern is to live for the glory of God. This is conversion.

Now I trust that you and I know the meaning of what it is to be saved. Not a cheap decision for Christ! Not simply a belief in certain facts about God! To be saved means that in your own will and in your own heart you are saying to Christ, "Lord, I understand that Thou didst come to save me, that Thou didst lay down Thy life for my sake, in order that I might be saved from sin and redeemed unto God. Because this tremendous love is calling for a response, I can not simply go on drifting, seeking to please myself, with no real purpose in life. I see that to be saved means the end of having my own way, and following my own wishes."

Oh, how many people just say, "I don't feel led to do this," and "I don't feel led to do that." "It's going to cost me too much! It's too hard!" It is so convenient to be "led" like that! I very much question whether this is the leading of God. Have you ever faced the principle that conversion—a real experience of the new birth—is simply laying down at the feet of Jesus your right to be your real self? Have you ever faced that? Have you really been through that experience in your heart?

Yes, you believe the correct things about Christ. You read your daily psalm and you say your prayers. All that you believe about the Gospel with your head is correct: that Jesus is the Christ. And yet in your heart, in the matter of experience and application, you are still saying "no" to the Lord, to the Cross, and to the principle of "Not your way, but His." You are still saying that you want to run your own future, and choose your own friends. You want to make your own marriage, and select your own partner in life. You want all of this for yourself.

This is what we are doing today, many of us: believing aright, but living wrongly. Deep down in our souls there is a spirit of rebellion against the whole principle of Calvary. Beloved, if this is true of you, I am sorry. I must say this to you: you are not yet a Christian. This is how a soul is lost. But how is a man's soul to be saved? By laying at the feet of the Lord Jesus his right to his own way, to his own ambition, and to his independence. Here is the principle that he must accept: the principle of the Cross. "What shall it profit a man if he shall gain the whole world, and lose his own soul?"

IV. A PERIL EVERYONE SHOULD AVOID

In the text that I have chosen I want you to notice that there
is a peril here to be avoided. What does Jesus say at the conclusion of the passage? "Whosoever therefore shall be ashamed of
me and of my words in this adulterous and sinful generation, of
him also shall the Son of man be ashamed, when he cometh in the
glory of His Father, with the holy angels." Here you see the
tremendous power of Christ's question in its own setting. Here
our Lord says, in effect, "If you want to save yourself, if you
want to live for yourself, I am warning you that some day you
are going to forfeit your life. Some day you are going to lose out."

Perhaps in your own experience there are all the marks of
losing out. A man's soul is not lost simply at the moment when
he dies. It is being lost all through his life. There's no peace of
conscience. There's no rest. There's no spirit of contentment.
There's no sense of poise. There is a certain sort of shriveling.
When a man seeks to live for himself, his soul gets smaller and
smaller. When a man is wrapped up in his own selfish pleasure,
he is losing his own soul. This is not merely something that he
loses when he breathes his last. He is losing out day after day.

Jesus says, "You want this principle. You want to live for yourself. Well, then, if you get the whole world, what are you going
to gain if you lose your own soul? Because when a man lives
on this principle, a person who is ashamed of me and my words,
ashamed of the Cross, ashamed to be identified with the church,
ashamed to lay down his life at the foot of the Master, of him
one day I shall be ashamed." "If you reject me now," says Christ,
"I shall be ashamed of you then."

Oh, the awful peril to be avoided! The peril of setting my
teeth and refusing to accept in my life the principle of the Cross!
Ashamed of Jesus, ashamed to bear His Cross, ashamed to be
known as a Christian, ashamed to live for Him, ashamed to be
identified with Christ, ashamed to do the thing that is right,
ashamed to go straight, ashamed to be true! In school, in store,
in business office, ashamed to be known as a child of God! The
Lord Jesus says that if any man lives this way, one day He is

going to be ashamed of that man. Oh, the peril of living on such a basis!

My dear friend, this is the simple challenge that lies behind the Lord's question. Do you see the principle? Do you sense the power of His question in its own setting? To His question there is no answer. What is it going to profit you if you satisfy all your selfish ambitions, and if you gain the whole world, but lose your own soul?

V. A QUESTION EVERYONE SHOULD ASK

Let me conclude by asking you a straight question. Are you a Christian? Are you? Don't answer this question lightly. Don't say, "I've been a member of this church for twenty years; of course I am a Christian." Don't answer easily by saying, "I believe everything that the Bible says about Jesus; of course I am a Christian." Don't say, "I've been brought up in a Christian home; I have been taught the right things, and now I am in college; I'm studying to be a missionary; I'm going in for Christian training and Christian work; therefore I'm a Christian."

None of these things can make you a Christian. The simple basic issue that I present to every one of you is this: Has there been a moment when the power of the Cross has gone right down to the citadel of your heart, a moment when you've laid your life down at the Master's feet, so that you are His forever? This is what it means to be saved. This is what it means to lose your life for His sake and the Gospel's.

Are you a Christian? All through the years the matchless spell of the Christ on Calvary has gripped the hearts of business people, of kings, of rulers, of common people in every country, race, and clime, with every tradition and background. Sunday by Sunday young men and girls have come to this church, and ofttimes with tears have laid their lives down at the Master's feet, stopping life on the self-principle, and beginning to live on the Christ-principle. This is conversion, this and nothing less.

Is this true of you? Do you now face the Cross in your own life, and accept the principle of "no" to self, and "Yes" to Jesus Christ forever? "What shall it profit a man if he shall gain the whole world, and lose his own soul?"

9. Leslie R. Marston

Leslie Ray Marston, Bishop, The Free Methodist Church. Born in a parsonage, Maple Ridge, Mich., Sept. 24, 1894. Educated, Greenville College, Ill., (A.B.); University of Illinois (A.M.); University of Iowa (Ph.D. in psychology). Professor of psychology (1920-26), Greenville College; President (1927-36). Member, White House Conference on Child Health and Protection (1930). Bishop since 1935. President, National Association of Evangelicals (1944-46). Books: The Emotions of Young Children, Monograph (1925); From Chaos to Character (1934; rev. ed., 1944); Youth Speaks (1939).

The following radio sermon differs from a regular message in church. Unless the radio speaker catches attention at first, and unless he holds it, he will go unheard. With no Scripture lesson, the hearer may have foggy ideas about the parable. In fact, he may never have read it or heard it. So the speaker tells the salient facts, and stresses what the Lord Jesus makes prominent, the folly of the man who tries to feed his soul on things.

With various sorts of local color the minister portrays such a personal heart hunger today. Gradually the horizon broadens so as to show the folly of our so-called "sensate civilization," which puts things ahead of God. The sermon leads up to the Gospel truth that Christ alone can satisfy the heart hunger of humanity, and of any one hearer. This radio message has more Gospel truth and soul food than most "religious talks" of the sort. It likewise shows a young minister the wisdom of clothing a pulpit message with a garb of fitting words, more or less like those in St. Luke. According to Renan, that is "the most beautiful book ever written."

THE HUNGER OF THE SOUL

"I will say to my soul, 'Soul, thou hast much goods laid up for many years; take thine ease, eat, drink, and be merry.' "

ST. LUKE 12:19

Emerson ONCE WROTE that the health of a man means an equality of inlet and outlet, a balance of gathering and giving, and that any hoarding brings disease and tumors. Jesus taught this truth in His parable of the rich farmer, his goods, and his barns. One day this farmer walked over his fields and beheld their promise of a plentiful harvest. He was sorely perplexed because his barns already were bursting with the bounty of past harvests. He thought only of inlet, not of outlet; only of gathering, not of giving. He would distribute his goods neither through the regular channels of trade nor yet through the special channels of charity. Rather, he would get and have and hold all the good gifts of God, seeking only to consume them with the quenchless fire of his own appetites and desires.

So he pondered the matter, asking himself, "What shall I do, because I have no room, where to bestow my goods?" Then there came to him what seemed a happy thought, so that he answered his own question, "This will I do: I will pull down my barns, and build greater; and there will I bestow all my fruits and my goods And I will say to my soul, 'Soul, thou hast much goods laid up for many years; take thine ease, eat, drink, and be merry.' "

THE CONCERN ABOUT SELF

Ten times in this brief parable the farmer uses the perpendicular pronoun "I," or its possessive "my." Impoverished indeed is the life thus hedged about with self! This man is already dead, spiritually dead, for he has mistaken the nature of his soul-hunger, and has starved himself on goods, those gifts of God that he has not shared with others. Hence God says to him, "Thou fool, this night thy soul shall be required of thee. Then whose shall those things be which thou hast prepared?"

Yes, the miser, the glutton, the greedy one must some day let go all of his goods, which will be distributed by others after death has garnered his poor, shriveled soul. Many are the modern versions of this life story about the rich farmer, the records of multitudes, each of whom would gain the whole world at the price of his own soul. Out of the gold fields in the Klondike, Robert Service once wrote about such a wretch's disillusionment:

> I wanted the gold, and I sought it;
>   I scrabbled and mucked like a slave.
> Was it famine or scurvy, I fought it;
>   I hurled my youth into a grave.
>
> I wanted the gold, and I got it;
>   Came out with a fortune last fall.
> Yet somehow life's not what I thought it,
>   And somehow the gold isn't all.*

Neither goods nor gold can ever satisfy the hunger of a man's heart. Dwight L. Moody once said that a person's soul is so much bigger than the world that to pour the whole world into a man's soul would be to leave it still empty. Verily, so vast is the soul of a man that the world would rattle about in its resounding emptiness. Life's insistent hunger can not be satisfied by feeding the soul with the husks of material plenty, by narcotizing it with sensual pleasure, or by drowning it with delirious passion. In all such endeavors a man lives on earth's lowest levels, forgetting that he is overbuilt for this world. According to the chaplain at my university, "Man is built for the universe, for eternity, and for God. Out and on and up to that heritage the normal living heart is ever pressing." No marvel then that Jesus warns, "What shall

---

* Reprinted by permission of Dodd, Mead & Company from *The Collected Poems of Robert Service.*

it profit a man, if he shall gain the whole world, and lose his own soul?"

After all, what are we? Children of God, or only superior animals? The crown of creation, or merely "a boisterous bit of the organic scum of one small planet"? Rob a man of God and level him to the brute, convince a man that this life ends all and that he has kinship only earthward, then "chaos is come again," even a hell here on earth. A man cannot for long surrender his faith in God and still retain a belief in the meaning of his own existence.

THE NEGLECT OF GOD

So it comes about that the loss of faith in God brings from a despairing modern this cry, "I catch no meaning from all that I have seen, and pass quite as I came, confused and dismayed." Failure to believe in God permits a cynical modern to flaunt his impious creed: "The universe is a gigantic wheel in rapid revolution; man is a sick fly dizzily riding on the wheel's whirling rim; religion is the fly's delusion that the wheel was constructed for the express purpose of giving him this ride." The rejection of God prompts a flippant modern to call man "an ape that chatters to himself of kinship with archangels, while filthily he digs for groundnuts." This way of thinking, or not thinking, brings a disillusioned modern to lament "the old age of thirty-five."

This last reminds one of Lord Byron's entry in his journal on his thirty-fifth birthday: "I go to bed with a heaviness of heart at having lived so long and to so little purpose." Byron here touches the secret of today's cynicism, disillusionment, and despair. These all-too-common modern moods come from living in the present moment, with no eternal purpose; from accepting material and sensuous facts, but denying spiritual and eternal truths. Without an eternal purpose, life shrivels up in all its four dimensions of length, breadth, depth, and height; shrinks to a mere point in time, a fleeting moment. Striving to press from each passing moment its last drop of pleasure brings old age prematurely, "the old age of thirty-five," or it may be, twenty-five. How pathetic are such life-weary, already-aged youths of our day, "without hope, and without God in the world"!

THE PERIL OF OUR NATION

Even as disillusionment comes to every person who seeks satisfaction in things, so it is with every nation. History clearly writes the record that the noontide of the nation's triumph over the material order is too often the fading twilight of the spiritual. Only a few generations have passed since our pioneer forefathers set their God-given energies to the task of subduing this continent, and today America is ours. But how greatly changed by the courage, the industry, and the faith of those pioneers!

Once-virgin prairies now yield rich harvests. Primeval forests have given way to the onward sweep of civilization. In their place now stand teeming cities, quiet hamlets, scattered farmsteads. Rivers that through millennia flowed in primitive quiet now carry the fruits of forest and field, mine and manufacturing, thus driving the wheels of commerce and industry. Like arteries in the body of our nation, railroads and highways interlace our many commonwealths, and the loftiest clouds provide thoroughfares for giant airplanes, while beyond in outer space we seek our new frontier. Threads of copper have long carried our words to the ends of the earth, and now with radio even the thunder galleries of the clouds have become our speaking tubes. Television brings into our homes the most distant objects and events, so that the unseen world may become our clearest vision. At last, even the atom has surrendered its secrets of power, by which we may control vast areas of nature.

Oh, if only we could learn how to control ourselves! Long ago the wise man wrote in the Book of Proverbs, "He that ruleth his own spirit is better than he that taketh a city." Modern nations have taken cities and kingdoms. They have conquered their environment, but they have not mastered the world within, and so anarchy prevails. For this reason the very power by which nations seek security brings insecurity, with "men's hearts failing them because of fear."

Back in the nineteenth century Herbert Spencer remarked that to educate reason without changing desire is to place high-powered guns in the hands of savages. His meaning becomes clearer in our day of A-bombs and H-bombs, when these instru-

ments of destruction may easily become the playthings of men
with shrewd, trained minds and skilled hands, but with savage
and wicked hearts. Science and technology have brought great
power to nations that have no ethics for the righteous control of
these titanic forces, which they can summon either for human
welfare or human destruction. At the moment, some nations seek
to direct this power principally to destruction, vying with one
another to gain dominance in the mad handling of nature's forces.
Control without self-command guided by righteous desires may
spell tragedy for our race. In terms of this world's time schedule,
it may indeed be much later than we think!

A cartoon in *Collier's,* appearing not long before that magazine
ceased publication, foreshadowed with grim humor the collapse of our civilization, and man's return to caves. In front of
a cave dwelling on a devastated and smoking terrain the cartoon
showed two savage creatures in the midst of a welter of prehistoric
bones. One of the two, evidently representing the scientist of the
distant future, holds a bone in his hand and announces to his
neighbor, "As nearly as I can figure out, we are descendants from
a creature called 'man,' who lived in the atomic age." "Vanity
of vanities!"

THE HOPE OF THE GOSPEL

Nations as well as individuals that forget God finally come to
despair. But is there no hope for men and for nations? The
Apostle Paul gives the answer in his letter to the Ephesian
Church, where he recalls the depths of moral degradation from
which these Ephesian Christians have been lifted by the power
of God's love. To them he writes, and also to us:

> To you, who were spiritually dead all the time that you
> drifted along on the stream of this world's ideas of living,
> and obeyed its unseen ruler (who is still operating in those
> who do not respond to the truth of God), to you Christ has
> given life! We all lived like that in the past, and followed
> the impulses and imaginations of our evil nature, like every-
> one else. But even though we were dead in our sins God
> was so rich in mercy that He gave us the very life of Christ,
> . . . and has lifted us right out of the old life to take our
> place with Him in Christ in the heavens. . . .

You had nothing to look forward to, and no God to whom you could turn. But now, through the blood of Christ, you who were once outside the pale are with us inside the circle of God's love and purpose. For Christ is our living Peace (Eph. 2:1-6, 12d-14, Phillips Translation).

There is hope, then, because God cares! It was not to save worlds whirling into collision and catastrophe that God sent forth His Son into this world, nor was it to hinge a new solar system into space. Not to dig deep the Royal Canyon, nor to pile high the Rockies and the Andes, did God send His Son to this earth. But God sought out this distant planet so that by the gift of His Son He might span heaven and earth, and thus bring us back to Himself.

Even in our rebellion and despair God seeks to draw us unto Himself, that He may satisfy our deepest heart hunger and our most intense soul thirst. In lines that have lived through three centuries George Herbert shows how our restlessness should lead us to God. He tells how in creating man God gave him all of life's blessings save one. He gave man strength, beauty, wisdom, pleasure, and honor. Finally, in the bottom of the glass, rest alone remained, and that God withheld:

> For if I should, said He,
> Bestow this gift upon my creature,
> He would adore my gifts instead of me,
> And rest in nature, not the God of nature;
> So both would restless be.
>
> Yet let him keep the rest,
> But keep them with repining restlessness;
> Let him be rich and weary, that at least
> If goodness lead him not, yet weariness
> May toss him to my breast.

God made us for Himself; then He gave Himself for us. Jesus Christ is God's good Gift to man, answering his heart cry in the words of a blessed I AM passage: "I am the bread of life: he that cometh to me shall never hunger; and he that believeth on me shall never thirst" (John 6:35).

The drawing power of God's love is greater than the destructive force of the atom, and nothing now can save the world but the power of God changing the hearts of men. Education, social betterment, statism, and all the other human schemes to bring Utopia, work too slowly to avert the impending destruction, even if in any case these man-made devices were adequate to save the world. In human society no leaven works so quickly and so powerfully as the regenerating power of God's grace. This power of God worked in the Evangelical Revival, which saved eighteenth-century England from such a revolution as came to France. A like transformation can come in America, or Russia, when men seek in Christ the satisfaction of their deepest desires. For now, as in the days of Paul and the Roman Empire, the Gospel is the power of God unto salvation, both for men and nations.

THE HOPE FOR THE PENITENT

This is the hope for our nation, and for every nation, that men will seek in Christ the fulfillment of their deepest longings. Such fulfillment is first of all a personal matter. The saving work begins with the individual. As transformed individuals increase in number, the social order is changed, a nation is reborn, a world is made new. What an ideal! And so we close with a few words concerning a man's personal faith when he responds to the promise of Christ to satisfy his deepest and direst need.

Through faith, responding to the promise of Christ, the promise of the Gospel, a man becomes indeed a child of God, by grace restored to the divine favor that he has forfeited through sin. This change in a man is far more than a mystical idealism stirring him to noble sentiments; it is a vital fellowship with the Divine Person. It is far more than a change of mind bringing assent to Christian truth; it is a life made dynamic by the In-dwelling Christ. This change is far more than moral heroism striving for salvation through strenuous efforts; it is childlike trust resting securely in the Father's love. The response of our faith to the promises of God goes deeper than our religious sentiments, our reasoning about truth, our fullest purposes to be good and to do good. This faith is the response of our inmost, utmost self to the call of God, uttered in unmistakable accents about Jesus Christ as our only Saviour.

Because this faith is the response of our total being, it is simple, even as a child's trust in an earthly father is simple and unquestioning. The prodigal son made a simple reponse of faith to the love of his father. Perishing with hunger in a far country, he came to himself and remembered that in his father's house even the servants had bread and to spare. So he arose and came to his father, confessing his sin, his waywardness, his unworthiness to be a son, and begging rather for employment as a hired servant. Then his father forgave him, clothed him, and fed him, not as a servant under a legal contract, but as a son under the favor of his father's love. God's response to our need is like that; it is far greater than our faith. He can do for us exceeding abundantly above all that we ask or think!

To the hungry wanderer, perishing now in some far country of sin, pride, and self-will, Jesus Christ offers bread, the bread of life. Let such a one say with a sincere purpose, "I will arise and go to my Father." While the penitent one is still afar off, the Father's love revealed in Jesus Christ will meet him. Faith is that simple: coming to Christ, we are fed. Believing in Christ, our thirst is quenched.

Yes, God satisfies our hunger. He did not make us with a boundless craving without providing for its satisfaction. So with Saint Augustine we too may say, "Thou has made us for Thyself, and our hearts are restless until they find their rest in Thee."

10. V. Raymond Edman

Victor Raymond Edman, Christian and Missionary Alliance. Born, Chicago, May 9, 1900. Educated, Boston University (A.B.); Clark University (A.M., Ph.D.); University of Illinois; Columbia University. D.D., Taylor University; LL.D., Houghton College. Instructor, Missionary College, Nyack, N. Y. (1921-22). Director, El Instituto Biblico, Guayaquil, Ecuador (1923-28). Professor, Wheaton College, Ill. (1936-42); President, since 1941. Author of 12 books, including: Finney Lives On (1951); In Quietness and Confidence (1952); Great Is Thy Faithfulness (1954); Sweeter than Honey (1955); Not Ashamed (1955); Just Why? (1956); Fear Not (1957).

According to the author, the message that follows has a definite aim: "I have found this type of approach very effective in reaching those who think that they themselves have no need of the Saviour." So the advocate of Christ makes clear and vivid the way the Master replied to His critics. The gist of the sermon is easy to recall and to apply, because the minister deals in turn with three familiar parables that Christ used in answering His critics.

The treatment throughout is concrete, in the sense that the parables are factual, with facts from the lives of persons, often one by one, or with two in contrast. Such a pulpit expositor "sees faces." He shows that a popular interpreter of the Bible need not depart from his passage in quest of other revealed truths about the subject in hand. Elsewhere the Master answers similar charges in still other ways, but they would call for other sermons. See The Galilean Gospel, *by A. B. Bruce (1884).*

Not only does the present message about Christ and His critics show how to deal with such a difficult subject today. The sermon also affords a practical answer to present-day critics of expository preaching. According to a foremost critic of such pulpit work, it is "predestined to dullness and futility." Such a critique shows as little understanding of real expository preaching as of sane beliefs about predestination. Why blame God for our ministerial "dullness and futility"? All the while the Lord stands ready to honor and bless the right sort of expository preaching (Isa. 55:10, 11).

THE MASTER MEETS HIS CRITICS

"This man receiveth sinners, and eateth with them."

LUKE 15:2

EVERY GENERATION has its Pharisees and scribes. They are well taught in the Scriptures, and are proud of this knowledge. They are confident of their own orthodoxy, and so they can be caustic in comments about others who do not measure up to the same standards. These critics are instructed in the letter of the Law, even to its minutest implications, but they are totally unaware of its spirit.

Such Pharisees are always critical of those who seek the welfare of sinners. In their own opinion these critics are infallibly correct. Can they not quote the Bible, chapter and verse, as the basis of their barbed criticisms? In the passage before us the Pharisees and scribes were sure that their indignation against Jesus of Nazareth was wholly righteous. Why should He mingle with such outcasts from society as those tax-gatherers, cheap politicians, renegades, sinners? No self-respecting person would associate with them in any way, much less eat with them!

To this way of thinking there was just one thing that the Lord Jesus could do. In response to murmured criticisms He could leave that motley group of sinners, and come over to the side of the "upright," the highly regarded. He did nothing of the kind. On the contrary He arose and began to defend the publicans and sinners! To be sure, He did not palliate or excuse their sin. That He recognized, but in compassion for them He had come to turn them away from their sins.

The Friend of Sinners recognized that their invitation for Him to dine with them was an indication of their desire to turn away from their unsavory past into ways that were right. Like their contemporaries who had repented at the preaching of John the Baptist, these publicans and sinners were desirous of coming to God. Would Jesus come and help them? He would, and He did!

In defending these sinners against the unwarranted criticisms of the Pharisees, the Lord Jesus gave three parables that are timeless in power and pungency: the lost sheep, the lost coin, and the lost sons. The three parables all appear in one chapter.

I. LOST THROUGH STUPIDITY

Some men, declared the Saviour, are lost because they are stupid. Sheep, you know, wander away from the flock and the fold. They are lost because they are foolish and careless. Once separated from the flock and the shepherd, a sheep drifts farther and farther away, without any sense for returning. In this regard other animals are not so stupid as sheep. A dog or a cat may wander all over the neighborhood, and even farther afield, but by and by either of them will come home. Cows can graze out in the pasture all day, but when the shadows begin to lengthen toward evening they stand in the lane, waiting to come into the barn. But it is not so with sheep!

Therefore in the parable the shepherd set out to find the one that had gone astray. "All we like sheep have gone astray," insisted Isaiah, and rightly so. The Good Shepherd came to seek and to save us who were lost. In the parable when the shepherd found his sheep he brought it home on his shoulder, rejoicing. The sheep that was lost had been found.

"Lost like sheep!" So the Pharisees began to murmur among themselves: "Does He mean to insinuate that these 'foxes' and 'wolves' are in reality lost sheep?" Yes, He did so teach, and He does today. He teaches that many are lost because they are stupid, careless, indifferent. The sheep do not hate the shepherd or the fold; they merely drift away. This explains why many now are lost out in the wilderness of the world. They are lost simply because they are unconcerned.

II. LOST BECAUSE OF SOMEBODY ELSE

Others are lost because of somebody else. Not all men are lost alike. Some, says the Lord Jesus, are lost like sheep, and some like money. Money, we know quite well, does not lose itself. A coin is not stupid. It does not drift away from its owner. Contrariwise, it is the owner who loses the money! The woman who lost her coin was under obligation to find it herself. After a diligent search she did find it. Then she called on her neighbors to rejoice with her.

"Does Jesus insinuate that these publicans and sinners are lost because of somebody else"? "Undoubtedly!" murmured the Pharisees and scribes among themselves. Of course they were correct. This is exactly what He was telling them. Were these sinners confirmed in their wrongdoing because they had discerned the spiritual inconsistency of the Pharisee? Had they understood that while the Pharisee proudly stood praying on the street corner, secretly he was plotting to foreclose the mortgage on some poor widow's house?

Of course the publicans had seen all this. They knew that the Pharisees talked much about God, but that in reality the gold of mammon was their god. They could quote Scripture glibly and accurately, but all the time they were consummately selfish. To the unthinking populace the Pharisees seemed to be spiritual men, because they sat in the chief places of the synagogue, but still they knew nothing about the spirit of love.

In substance the Saviour was saying to the Pharisees: "Because of you, these men, like money, have been lost. Your inconsistency, your indifference, your smug conceit, your spiritual pride,—all these have caused publicans and sinners to stumble from paths of righteousness into ways of sin."

While it is true that before God everyone is responsible for his own soul, it is equally true that many others are more sinned against than sinning. In men like the Pharisees these other persons have seen cheating, lying and stealing, malice and evil speaking, hatred and spite—all in the name of religion. With indignation the onlookers have turned away from everything that savors of religion. They have stumbled over those who by their mouths have professed that they were believers, but whose actions have spoken louder than words. Yes, even today, people may be lost because of somebody else.

III. LOST BECAUSE OF STUBBORNNESS

Some are lost because they are stubborn. The prodigal son did not go into the far country because he was stupid, drifting aimlessly, like a lost sheep. He was determined to go away from home. He had decided upon his destination, and he could not be dissuaded from his decision. He preferred to be lost! In the account there is no inkling that the home had been unhappy, or that the parents had been inconsistent in their love for God and for their sons. On the contrary, when the prodigal later came to his senses he expressed the highest regard and reverence for his father. Father and mother had not been stumbling blocks in his pathway.

The prodigal son had been aptly portrayed in the Mosaic code: "a stubborn and rebellious son, which will not obey the voice of his father, or the voice of his mother, and that, when they have chastened him, will not hearken unto them" (Deut. 21:18). This part of the Law required that such a son be judged by the elders of the city, and if guilty, that he be stoned. Nevertheless, the gracious and godly father gave this lad his portion of the estate.

There is a strong intimation, also, that a part of the prodigal's decision to leave home was caused by the attitude of the elder brother. The latter was intelligent, industrious, diligent, frugal, and faithful. Because of the "model behavior" of this older brother, no doubt well-meaning neighbors made critical comments about the younger man. The older brother was not unfamiliar with his own supposed superiority, and commendation from his neighbors would only increase the pride of his heart, and the contempt for his far less dependable brother.

To the younger brother the far country, so fair in prospect, proved to be a bitter disappointment. Sin is always a robber. At first its pillage may not be apparent, but in time it can rob one of health and happiness, of home, and finally of heaven. "All have sinned and come short of the glory of God," declare the Scriptures. All do not sin alike, or to the same extent. But all are included under sin, and all need the Saviour.

In time the prodigal discovered that he was hopelessly lost. Unless he made a decision to return, he would die in that far country. Here is a strange anomaly. When the sheep went astray, the shepherd himself sought for it everywhere. When he had found it he said to his friends, "Rejoice with me, for I have found my sheep which was lost." When the coin was mislaid the woman herself had to seek for it. So she did, and when she found it she said to her neighbors, "Rejoice with me, for I have found the coin which was lost."

But no one went into the far country to seek out the lost son. Why not? The answer is elementary: he had known better than to be lost. He had known what to do, and where to go. Later, in the far country, the decision for true repentance lay entirely with him.

Never has anyone made a decision more important and far-reaching: "I will arise and go to my father." And so the prodigal son did! His heart attitude toward father and home had now become one of utter humility. His true repentance showed itself in remorse. There was no self-justification, no fault-finding with anyone else, not even with the elder brother who had been so brutal in caustic criticism of the prodigal. He recognized himself as unworthy to be called a son. If only he could be at home again with his father, the prodigal was willing to become one of the servants.

Who can measure the gladness and the gratitude of the father as he ran to receive his son with kisses and tears? Under other circumstances the substance of that father's joy was mine years ago when the first of our lads returned after long service overseas in the South Pacific. Just before Christmas, 1945, he returned home. That night, as I locked the doors before retiring, I recall lifting up my heart to say: "I thank Thee, Father, that he

is under our roof again. From beachheads of blood and fox-
holes of fear he has been preserved. As I shut the door, he is
safely home again!" All of this, and more, was the joy of that
other father when the prodigal came home. He had been lost
because of his stubbornness.

IV. LOST BECAUSE OF SULKINESS

Some are lost because they are sulky and stiff-necked. When the
elder brother learned that the younger one had come home, and
that a feast was being prepared, "he was angry, and would not
go in." At last his real heart attitude became evident. To his
old father, who had come out and begged him to come in, this
elder brother boasted of his service, his loyalty, and his depend-
ability. For many years he had been faithful. He claimed never
at any time to have transgressed any commandment from his
father.

This elder brother was caustic and cruel to his father, as well as
bitter and unforgiving toward his younger brother. The older
one was sulky, obstinate, opinionated, ungrateful. He was the
perfect portrayal of the Pharisee and the scribe.

In answering the criticism of the Pharisees and the scribes the
Lord Jesus has given us three illustrations. His parables began
with the Pharisees standing outside the feast to murmur, "This
man receiveth sinners, and eateth with them." From the lost sheep,
the lost coin, and the lost son, He brought the story round full
circle to a scene of joy and gladness, emphasized by the fatted
calf. It was the elder brother who stood outside with cutting
criticism for the father's compassion and with utter contempt
for the repentant prodigal.

Only the Pharisee was lost! Lost because of his sulkiness! The
stupid, careless one, lost like a sheep that had strayed, was sought
and found by the good shepherd. The one lost because other
men had been stumbling blocks was found, like the money that
had been misplaced. The stubborn prodigal, though perhaps he
had been a glutton and a drunkard, repented of his waywardness
and wickedness. He came home and there found forgiveness, with
a welcome like that of heaven. Only the self-sufficient, sulky,
sullen, stiff-necked critic remained lost.

Herein lies a warning to anyone who seems to be outwardly upright, but who inwardly despises those that go astray. As with those Pharisees of old, the very rectitude of such persons today, enhanced by the commendation of others, may create within them the spirit of the Pharisee. It is "not by works of righteousness that we have done," but rather by God's mercy, that we are saved. "By grace are ye saved through faith." We are not saved by works, "lest any man should boast."

11. Alan Walker

Alan Walker, Methodist. Born in a parsonage, Sydney, Australia, June 4, 1911. Educated, Sydney University (A.B., M.A.); Leigh Theological College, Sydney (B.D.). Director of Youth Work (1936-38). Pastor (1939-44). Superintendent of Mission (1944-54). Director, Mission to the Nation (1954-55). Order of the British Empire, from Queen Elizabeth (1955). Mission to America (1956-58). Superintendent of Central Methodist Mission, oldest and largest Methodist church in Australia, since 1958. Fourteen books. Recent: Christianity on the Offensive *(1949);* Love, Courtship, and Marriage *(1953);* Australia Finding God *(1953);* Start Where You Are *(1954);* My Faith Is Enough *(1955);* Plan for a Christian Australia *(1955);* The Whole Gospel for the Whole World *(1957).*

This man from "down under" has a world view, quite unique. Preaching in New York City, he turns to the edifice of the United Nations. There he singles out the tiny chapel set apart for meditation. In it he points to three symbols of "religion," apart from Christ: "curtained walls, a vase full of flowers, and silence." These three symbols emerge at times throughout the sermon, and help to give a sense of unity to surveys of four vast areas in which the Gospel of Christ differs from "religion." Not everyone may agree with some of the heart-searching words about war and peace, but everyone can learn much from Alan Walker's way of presenting a strong case for Jesus Christ over against religion as it appears in "curtained walls, a vase full of flowers, and silence."

In showing Christ as God's way of meeting the world's needs, the local color consists of concrete cases about persons near and far. These facts show the basic difference between a Christian and a Moslem; the way a home-born missioner of India presents Christ to Hindus; a "little bit of America" over in Australia; the heroism of a German pastor in defying Hitler; a California ranch with four adopted waifs, from four different races; and a middle-aged criminal, now converted, who is making ready to become an ordained minister. Not every sermon needs so many examples from life, but it would be difficult to know which of these one could drop out. Facts, facts, facts! All of them clear, and all about Christ as God's Answer to the world's supreme questions today!

RELIGION OR CHRIST?

"Behold the Lamb of God who is to take away the sin of
the world."   ST. JOHN 1:29

A FEW WEEKS AGO I stood at the United Nations in New York City. Not far from the entrance door I found a small chapel for meditation. The place is unpretentious, actually only a tiny room. As you enter it you notice only the curtains on the walls and a potted plant on a table. At once you are aware of the quietness, the stillness of the chapel. Now this chapel is all of religion that has been introduced into the United Nations building. With the Moslem bloc, of course, solidly opposed to anything Christian, with the Russian section officially atheistic, and opposed to any emphasis on the world of the Spirit, this is the most that can be achieved religiously in the United Nations: a tiny chapel with curtained walls, a vase full of flowers, and silence.

I am not thinking of the matter politically. As I stood alone in that silent chapel I found myself asking questions about religion: Is this chapel and what it contains enough to help a man find God? Is this a sufficient highway into the presence of our God? Is it enough to have silence, roses, and curtained walls? I found myself also facing other questions. Where does Jesus Christ come into this picture? There is no symbol of Him here.

There is no Cross on the altar. Do we really need Him, or is religion sufficient in itself? Are silence and an emblem from nature, with art in the way of curtained walls—are these enough to help us toward God? Or do we need this Christ whom the Bible calls the Son of God? Well, what do you think?

This is a real issue. Around the world today, especially in America, there is a new concern about religion. There is a new awareness of God. Is it enough, though, just to be religious, merely to have vague ideas about a Supreme Being, and perhaps occasionally feel like praying? Where does Jesus Christ come into the picture? Why is He necessary? This is the question that I pose to you. Why do we as Christians say that if we are to find our way to the living God, a chapel with quietness and emblems of nature and art is not enough, but that there needs to be the story of the Christ, with emblems of the Cross and the empty tomb? Well, let me try to answer the question I have posed. Why is religion not enough? Why is Jesus Christ necessary?

I. THE WAY TO THE CHRISTIAN GOD

First of all I suggest that Jesus Christ is absolutely essential because only through Him can we come to the Christian God. What a man believes about God is all-important. What kind of God? This is really the basic question. Only through Jesus Christ do you come into the presence of the Christian God.

This truth was posed for me most vividly two or three years ago when I was taken from Australia to the Middle East for what happened to be the first convocation between Moslems and Christians. There for six days we sat round tables, thirty-five representing each faith. We tried to find points of likeness, as well as points of difference, between the two great world religions. It was not long before it became quite apparent that the one point where we differed most was regarding our conceptions of God. Early in the conference a debate developed about the Republic of Lebanon, where roughly fifty per cent is Christian and fifty per cent is Moslem. Would it be possible to find for the schools a common prayer, so that each school day could open with Moslems and Christians saying the same prayer?

I remember asking, innocently, "Would it be possible for a

Moslem child to repeat the Lord's Prayer?" At once an old sheik
from Saudi Arabia leaped to his feet and exclaimed, "Impossible!
We couldn't get past the first phrase, 'Our Father who art in
heaven.' God is not our Father. Our God has no sons! He only
is God!" Later on another scholar of Islam declared, "You can
talk about the slaves of God, if you like, but not the sons of
God." Afterwards we discussed the difference between our ethical
standards. There was a Moslem justification of polygamy, and a
defense of the slavery that still operates in Saudi Arabia. But
when you penetrated to the heart of it all, everything went back
to the different ideals that we held about God.

In America and in Australia we have become used to a society
which, even though men may reject Him, still is penetrated by
the Christian understanding of God. We do not know what
it would mean to live apart from Christ's revelation of Him.
What would we know of God if we merely stood under a towering mountain, in a woodland, or by a lakeside? What would we
know of God if we tried to interpret Him in history? What
would we learn about Him if we listened only to our own whir-
ring minds, and to the voice of conscience within us? Soon we
would meet all sorts of contradictions. Without Jesus Christ we
would have no clear understanding of Him whom we have come
to know and love as the Christian God.

In Australia a little while ago we had the Ceylonese leader,
D. T. Niles. After a radio forum he was asked a question: "You
live in Hindu Ceylon. In a society where everybody believes in
many gods, how do you present the necessity of Jesus?" I'll never
forget the answer of D. T. Niles. He smiled, and replied, "Oh!
I just repeat to them the words of Jesus, 'No man cometh unto
the Father but by me.'" Then he went on to say, "I tell them
that they can come to some other sort of god through a Hindu
idol, but that apart from Jesus of Nazareth no one can come
to the One whom we know and love as our Heavenly Father."
"No one cometh to the Father but by me." Oh, my friends, the
chapel with silence, curtained walls, and roses on the table is
not enough, because it does not tell who God is. We need the
historic life and teachings, the Death and the Resurrection of
Jesus Christ, to bring us into an understanding of the Christian
God.

II. THE WAY INTO THE CHRISTIAN CHURCH

Secondly, I suggest that Jesus Christ is so essential to our life because He gives us the community of Christians called the Church. No other religion has a church. Some of us who are near to the Church are disappointed in it. We find it so much of a human institution, full of jealousies, nationalism, and other limitations from our contemporary scene. And yet there is no alternative to the Christian Church. In the midst of this human thing there is that which comes from God, and so the Church persists. It is a part of the fact of Christ, an essential part of the contribution that He makes to mankind.

In the early chapters of the Book of Acts, have you noticed that long before Christians were called by that proud title they were known as "People of the Way"? When you come to think of it, that is a very good title. "People of the Way"! You see that in the midst of the ancient world there began to emerge a new community of people. In a world like ours, which has reserved its loudest plaudits for the harsher military virtues, they held aloft the softer virtues of magnanimity, forgiveness, and love. They sold their possessions and gave help to such as needed. And so, as others watched this new community move through the world, they said, "Ha! People of the Way!" But it was precisely because those "People of the Way" moved through the earth that the downward progress of Greece and Rome was arrested. Presently, their decadence was halted, because new life sprang out from the cells of those "People of the Way." Precisely because there was a new community of Christian people, throughout that ancient world there emerged something of a new and Christian culture.

Over in Australia, you know, or in any other land where your country is represented, you have a little bit of American territory. Right at the heart of Canberra, our national capital, there stands the United States Embassy. There is a little piece of land that is really America. If you step on that little bit of earth, the laws of the Queen of Great Britain and the Commonwealth of Australia do not operate. You are now under the President of the United States. There it is! A little bit of America! According to normal diplomatic usage, that is America. And we Christians, if we are obedient to the Lord Jesus, are set down of God in the Church, set down in this colony of heaven, set down where the laws of heaven operate, and where the ways of God's people may be seen.

My friends, unless there are "People of the Way" to challenge this world of ours, how do you think it is going to be deflected from its poverty-stricken living and its evil activities? For example, unless there are people who in their daily lives express the purity of Jesus, how do you think His purity is going to endure in our sex-saturated society? Or think about the flood-tide of liquor that is moving out over all our communities. How is it going to be stopped in its fallacious propaganda, and kept from gripping society in its tyranny, unless there emerge Christian people who say, "As for me, I can't touch it. I will not succumb to its appeals. I follow another way"? So you can carry this question to the mighty issues of race and war. How shall this world be challenged unless there keep emerging people who think differently from contemporary sub-Christian America, or contemporary sub-Christian Australia? How shall there be an elevation of our society unless there arise persons who are truly "People of the Way"?

In our time we have had a striking illustration of the power of a group of Christians who challenge a mighty contemporary movement. I am thinking of Nazi Germany. Apart from the witness of the Confessional Church, did anything decent come out of modern Germany under Hitler? Men like Pastor Niemöller, Dietrich Bonhoffer, and Paul Schneider stood out against the Nazi State, and declared, "The Lord is my Führer." Those were men who set flowing the forces that would help to redeem Germany.

Do you know, for example, the name of Paul Schneider? He was a humble German pastor, but he knew the difference between right and wrong. When Hitler first issued his anti-Jewish decrees, this man stood up to preach in his country church, where he quietly voiced his protest. News of that sermon quickly reached the Gestapo, and in a few days Pastor Schneider was arrested. After a time, unaccountably, he was released. But everyone knew, especially the pastor himself, that he had received his warning. A few weeks later came another decree that offended his Christian principles, and again in the pulpit this brave man voiced his convictions.

After the service, his wife reports, they two walked across the little bridge that led to their home. In the middle of the bridge they stopped. Then she looked into his eyes and said, "Paul, must you speak like that? You know what it is going to mean to our children and to me. Couldn't you be a little more cautious?" After a moment of silence, she reports, her husband replied, "My wife, shall I care for our children's bodies and fail their souls? Shall I feed them, clothe them, educate them, and yet not show them what is the truth? No, my wife," he continued, "maybe if you and they are to be kept faithful, I shall have to die."

Well, Pastor Schneider did die. Within a few days he was arrested again, and no one has heard of him since. But through men like Paul Schneider, God has been able to set loose forces that can help to redeem Germany and the world.

It is not just vague, sentimental religion that we need, not merely casual prayer, but members of the Christian community, "People of the Way," led by Jesus Christ as Master. These are the need of our world.

III. THE WAY TO THE CHRISTIAN CONSCIENCE

Again, I suggest that Jesus Christ is so essential because all of us need the conscience of Christ. Has it ever struck you what a miracle is the conscience of Jesus? In primitive, out-of-the-way Palestine He lived almost two thousand years ago. Yet no one can say that He has ever been a brake on human progress. No matter what moral issue arises, you will never find Him away yonder in the past dragging humanity backward. At certain points Mohammed and Buddha have done so, but never Jesus Christ. He is not now away back there; He is far ahead of us all. His conscience is far beyond any point that we have yet reached. The conscience of Jesus is one of the miracles in history.

We have reached a day when the conscience of man needs rapidly to expand. In one of his books J. Middleton Murry says, "The time has come when man's mind must jump forward." That word "jump" is well chosen. A gulf has developed, and we must summon all of our strength. In order to catch up we shall have to jump forward. Here we are suddenly plunged into an atomic age. The peril now is that into the atomic age we are taking stale old ideas that belonged to the pre-atomic era. Unless man can find something that will cause him to jump forward, he is lost.

Let me take as an illustration perhaps the most difficult issue of all, the whole question about war. We have reached a point where we can not make war any more, and still live. Can we? Peace is no longer an option; it is a stark, an absolute necessity. America, Britain, and Russia are saying openly, "If war comes, we must plunge into atomic war; all our plans are geared to atomic war." What does all of this do to a Christian? Can you or I as a Christian imagine that we could fly five miles high and touch a button to wipe out a million people so that none would escape, not a one, of all those men and women, old people and children? Could we do it? That is why war has become the most difficult question in Christian ethics. With tortures of conscience many of us keep wrestling with this issue. What is the will of God about war today?

We now stand at one of the most critical turning points in history. For example, take slavery. For about eighteen hundred Christian years men lived with slavery. During those years even the Christian said, "Slavery is all right as long as you have a good slave owner." Then, after eighteen hundred years God put into the hearts of Wilberforce and Lincoln, and into the hearts of men everywhere, hatred of slavery. No longer did man say, "Slavery is all right as long as you have a good slave owner." He began to say, "The institution of slavery is wrong, and it must go."

For almost two thousand years of the Christian era we have lived with war. The Church has said, "War is all right when carried on by justifiable means." In other words, "War is all right as long as you can have a good war." But now we are not so sure. A new stage has been reached, because war has now become total war. No, I suggest, we can not any longer speak about a good war or a bad war. Today we can talk about war only as hellish and obscene. Just as Wilberforce and Lincoln were led at last by the Spirit of God to say, "The institution of slavery is wrong," I suggest that perhaps we too are being led to the point where we shall see that the institution of war is wrong!

Today most of us are proud of the speeding bomber and the battleship riding at anchor. I suggest that in a hundred years a Christian will be as much ashamed of a battleship, or of an airplane that carries hydrogen bombs, as we today are ashamed of the whip in a slave-owner's hand. The institution of slavery was wrong. Today is one of the supreme moments in history, when God in Christ is calling on us by His conscience to rethink this terrible issue of war. He is calling us to move forward, with Him. The conscience of Christ—and not merely a religion that endorses our national purposes and pride—this is the need of our world today.

IV. THE WAY TO CHRISTIAN SALVATION

There is one other declaration that must be made. More than a chapel with silence, roses on a table, and curtained walls, Jesus Christ is absolutely essential because every one of us needs Him as Saviour. His best name is Saviour. It has not been long since we were treating sin lightly. We said that it was only a growing pain of the human family. "Throw a man a bit more education. Let him become a bit more civilized, and he will grow out of his sin; he will leave evil behind him." But now we are not so sure, are we? We have looked into the gas chambers of Germany, where one of the "most civilized" countries on earth pushed six million innocent people to their death.

In imagination perhaps we have walked through the streets of Hiroshima, a few hours after the so-called Christian West dropped an atomic bomb on the so-called pagan East. We have read about the Weinberger case in New York, where a man takes a little baby, throws him beside a highway, and lets him cry himself to death. Modern New York! We have seen men ready to sell narcotics to teen-agers. Could anything be more diabolical? We have looked into our own hearts, when jealousy, sex, or greed were astir, and we have been frightened by what we have seen of ourselves. So it is that many of us no longer prate about sin as only a growing pain. We are far more prone to speak about it as worse than cancer, the deadliest of all diseases.

What is the answer to this fundamental problem of evil? Deep down in the basement of our lives there is a twin issue. Most of us are grappling both with the problem of evil and with the problem of ignorance. Often we have imagined that education could grapple with both ignorance and evil. But education can grapple only with ignorance; it does not necessarily touch evil. That is why a very clever man can be a very clever devil. That is why George A. Buttrick says, "The only thing worse than a devil is an educated devil." Oh, yes, education may merely sharpen the wicked wits of man. It is time that we now see clearly the limitations of education. Education can never begin to solve the problem of evil. In the Lord Jesus Christ, through His Death and Resurrection, only God can overcome our evil. The need of men today is to have education come to grips with ignorance, and the Saviourhood of Jesus come to grips with sin. Every one of us needs Christ Jesus as Saviour.

A little while ago I was out in Los Angeles. One Friday there, I think, was the most thrilling day I have spent in America. In the morning I went out to Roy Rogers' ranch. I suppose it was my own four children who made me so interested in Roy Rogers, but anyway I went. I did not find him at home, but I met his wife, Dale Rogers, and talked with her. Before that I had heard something of her story; here was the confirmation. Running around the house I saw four adopted children: a little Korean child, a little American orphan, a wee Scottish orphan, and a small Indian child of America.

As a Christian Dale Rogers feels that she must do something to meet the world's need. When I talked with her as a mature Christian, I realized that five or seven years ago she was just another one of the shallow people who abound in Hollywood. But something had happened. Christ had come into her heart, and into her home.

I stayed at the ranch so long that I was late for my next appointment. When I got back to my hotel I found a man sitting in the foyer, waiting for me. He was to drive me to the next church.

As we walked out to the car he said, "You know, I'm in training for the Christian ministry. How long have you been a preacher?" I told him. "Oh," he replied, "I'm older than you are, and I'm just beginning." Then the tears began to run down his cheeks. Later he told me his story. In Kansas City he had been a criminal, right down in the depths, one of the wickedest men in that city. Then one night over in Kansas, feeling distraught, he stepped into a church. There the minister found him, and began to talk with him. Something happened. Jesus Christ, the Saviour, came into his life.

Though he was older, he felt that he ought to do something for Christ. One day he read the story of Peter, how he was probably over forty years of age when Jesus finally picked him up after the Resurrection, and said to him, "Feed my sheep." So, the ex-criminal told me, "I suddenly took heart." Today, past forty years of age, he is in a theological school, getting ready to give to the service of Jesus Christ what is left of his life.

That night I went to bed thinking about the wonder of it all. Dale Evans at the top of the entertainment industry in America, and another person from the depths of the underworld in a large city! Both of them finding the same Christ, the same Saviour, the same answer to the needs of their lives!

Why is Jesus Christ necessary? He is necessary because the Saviour is necessary. We need not merely a chapel, with silence, curtained walls, and roses on a table. We need a lonely hill with the Cross on its rim, an empty tomb in a garden, and the Risen Christ, Saviour and Lord. This is the need of all our hearts. Have you received Him? I offer you Christ.

Let us all pray: O God, who hast made the way so plain in Jesus Christ Thy Son, we worship Thee. We would now open our hearts for His coming. We pray that by committing our ways to Him we may discover His Saviourhood. Grant this our prayer, and keep us true to Him in every department of life. This we ask for Christ's sake, and for ours. Amen.

12. Clovis G. Chappell

Clovis Gillham Chappell, Methodist. Born, Fleetwood,
Tenn., Jan. 8, 1882. Educated, Bell Buckle School;
Duke University; Harvard. D.D., Duke U. LL.D., Bir-
mingham-Southern College. Pastor, leading downtown
city churches in the South; most recently, First Church,
Charlotte, N. C. (1945-49). Retired since 1949. Author
of thirty books, one homiletical, others sermonic. Recent volumes: When the Church Was Young—Acts
(1950); Anointed to Preach (1951); The Seven Words
(1952); In Parables (1953); Meet These Men (1956);
Sermons from Job (1957); Sermons on Simon Peter
(1959).

Like Clarence E. Macartney, this other downtown preacher has
sent out many widely read books of sermons, based on the Bible,
and often biographical. With human interest materials he appeals
to common people. He excels in illustration, often from his boyhood farm. The form of the sermon is simple, and the spirit is
sympathetic. Sometimes Chappell indulges in humor, but never
in horseplay. In books as in person, he preaches with irrepressible
optimism.

Such pulpit work aims to put heart and hope into the hearer.
It should also encourage the young ministerial reader: "If this is
the way to preach, I can do it. My sermons may never appear in
print, but by the grace of God I can deal with facts about a Bible
passage or character so as to make them clear and helpful to the
sort of persons who once heard the Master gladly. Also, I can keep
on reading, writing and preaching, so as not to cross the deadline
before I die."

THE MAN WHOM CHRIST REMAKES

"You are Simon—you shall be called Cephas."—JOHN 1:42
(Weymouth)

THUS JESUS GREETED blustering Simon when they two came face to face, perhaps for the first time. No sooner had Andrew performed the introduction than our Lord told this young Galilean fisherman that he was destined to become a man of character like a rock. Even to Simon that must have sounded a bit incredible. Had his acquaintances heard it they would have chuckled behind their hands. Had his enemies heard it they would have laughed with cynical scorn. "Whoever else among the followers of Jesus may be destined to become a man of rock," all would have agreed, "that can never prove true of young Simon!"

Yet Simon did arrive, to an amazing degree, even in the life that now is. So outstanding did he become that the Roman Catholics claim him as their first Pope, though, I believe, without a shred of evidence. Be that as it may, according to the Gospel records he surely was the acknowledged leader among the Twelve. Afterwards in the Book of Acts he stood out with Paul in the leadership of the Early Church. Even now, if a popularity contest were conducted, he would be selected as the most beloved among the apostles. Not only so, but I have an idea that among all the radiant characters who walk across the pages of both the Old Testament and the New, Simon is probably the most beloved.

Of course this was not the case because of his superior ability. I do not feel sure that he was the most nearly brilliant. But we never love any person merely because he chances to be clever. No more do we love Simon because he was flawless. We love him in spite of his faults. Not only so, we may love him because of his faults, which are much like our own.

More than once I have laughed and wept under the ministry of a unique genius named Bud Robinson. He was totally lacking in formal education, and he broke every law of grammar. But while he was breaking the laws of grammar, like Moody, this other man also broke our hearts. Instead of detracting from his forcefulness, his faults added to his appeal. So it was even with Simon.

I. SOME OF THIS MAN'S VIRTUES

Let us look at some of Simon's virtues.

1. He was genuinely human. That is wholly to the good. Whenever a minister becomes more of a minister than a man, three strikes have been called on him. But Simon was always himself. He never struck a pose. He never pretended. He never tried to conceal his ignorance. He always said what he himself thought, instead of trying to say what he thought others desired him to think. Even in Jerusalem, which was the Boston of that day, instead of trying to speak with a Harvard accent, he continued to use his own Galilean brogue. We appreciate that. It is the naturalness of our own Bing Crosby, as well as his ability, I think, that has made him perhaps the most popular person on the screen today.

2. Simon had gifts of leadership. He had the something that we of today call personality. We may not agree in our definitions of personality, but whatever it is, we all count it of untold worth. It is that something the lack of which makes a man largely ineffective. On the other hand, if a man has enough of it, he may get along with little else. Because of this something, when Simon said, "I go a-fishing," his young friends all said, "We will go with you." If Simon had lacked personality, they would have yawned and gone on their own way.

3. Another quality that we like about Simon is wholeheartedness. Sometimes he was on the right side of the fence, and sometimes he was on the wrong side, but he never straddled a fence. There were times when he was enthusiastic to the boiling point. There were other times when he seemed to be below zero. But he was never lukewarm. When he denied his Lord he might swear like a trooper, but he would never—

Damn with faint praise,
Assent with civil leer,
And without sneering
Teach the rest to sneer.

"I hate men who are half and half," declares a certain psalmist (119:113, Moffatt). We are close enough of kin to the ancient band to share his aversion. So does our Lord: "You are neither cold nor hot—would you were either cold or hot! So, because you are lukewarm, I am about to spit you out of my mouth" (Rev. 3:16, Moffatt). Hence we applaud Simon for being wholehearted. Even when he lied about knowing his Lord, I think that he loved Him.

II. A FEW OF THIS MAN'S FAULTS

Along with much that was good in Simon, there was much that was not good. Look at a few of his faults.

1. Simon was a man of too great self-confidence. He seems to have been so sure of himself that some students think he may have felt a sense of inferiority. Personally I do not agree. His conceit is of the "purest ray serene." In fact, it is so pronounced that it often has a sort of boyish charm; it tends to change our frowns into smiles. If Peter had a sense of humor, he must at times have laughed at himself. But there is no indication that this self-confident fellow ever saw himself as a joke, even when he looked at himself in an oldtime mirror. Therefore, because he constantly takes himself seriously he impresses us as being about as humble as a majorette leading a high school band.

Though doubtless he was willing for fellow apostles to take the second and third places, he must always be first. For instance, when by a word of warning Jesus sought to pierce the armor of Simon's self-assurance, that warning had about as much effect as modern B B shot would have on a battleship. "It may be possible," Simon seems to assert, "for the two Sons of Thunder to fail. It may even be possible that my brother Andrew will collapse. But, whatever the circumstances, failure on my part is simply unthinkable!"

Not only did this conceit color Simon's attitude toward his fellows; it also affected his dealings with his Master. Simon was deeply devoted to Jesus, and believed Him to be possessed of a wisdom beyond the human. But even at that, did He not need a bit of wise guidance from Simon? For instance, a certain woman had been ill for twelve years. One day she came up in the crowd and touched a tassel on His robe, so as to find healing. Having gained her purpose she sought to slip away with only half a blessing. But the Master, eager to bring her to fullness of life, would not allow her to leave. Therefore He asked, "Who touched me?" At this amazing question Simon was almost embarrassed. To save His Lord from making Himself seem ridiculous Peter rushed into the breach. "Don't be absurd!" he seemed to say. "You asked who touched you. Scores have touched you!" How fortunate that Simon was at hand!

A little later when Jesus proposed to wash the feet of this disciple, Simon made a flat refusal. That his Lord should even offer to perform such a slavish task was unthinkable. Therefore with a sense of bewilderment, and of proud self-assurance, he declared, "You shall never wash my feet!" "I am not going to allow you to humiliate yourself in any such fashion!" Simon was entirely too sure of himself.

2. He was also exceedingly impulsive. He relied on his feelings rather than his mind. He was guided by his emotions rather than his reason. First he spoke; then he considered. First he took his position; then he looked about for a reason to prop it up. Often I have marveled at the care with which a good golfer strokes his ball. My tendency is just the opposite. Usually I become careful after I have made my stroke. Hence I am not a champion.

3. Living thus within the realm of his emotions, Simon was unpredictable and unreliable. Neither he nor anyone else could know what he would do under a given set of circumstances. Sometimes he spoke with wisdom. At other times he did the very opposite. At one moment he felt so heroic as to move others to stand up and cheer. But the very next time he was so cowardly as to bring a blush of shame. At one moment he might kick a tossing boat from beneath his feet so as to walk upon the waves of a stormy sea. At the very next instant he might be up to his chin in turbulent waters, and frantically crying out for help. He was, therefore, as changeable as a weathervane. He was entirely too emotional and impulsive to be reliable.

In thus criticizing Simon I do not mean that feelings are to be repressed altogether. Recently I listened to a certain ministerial doctor of philosophy as he warned us against the danger of too much emotionalism in religion. It was hard for me to restrain either a smile or a tear. I was quite convinced that the pews in his church exercised little more self-control than the people accustomed to sit upon them. We may shun a man with too much gush, but even he is more winsome than a monkey. As for me, I should choose impulsive Simon any day, in preference to some unfeeling Herbert Spencer, flipping a coin to decide whether to marry the woman who loves him, or else to break her heart. Even so, Simon was conceited, impulsive, and unreliable.

III. A VIEW OF HIS REMAKING

It was out of this bewildering mixture of strength and weakness, of stardust and mud, that Jesus proposed to make a man of rock-like character. How did He go about it?

1. He gave Simon a glimpse of his possibilities. Our Lord, seeing Simon for what he was, also saw what he might become. Out ahead of the Simon who then was, Jesus pointed to the new man whose weakness would become power, whose pride would become humility, and whose ugliness would become beauty. "There," He told Simon, "is the realization of the dream that I have dreamed for you. That is the kind of man you will become if you fulfill my purpose for you."

This word to Simon may seem unique, but really it is universal. Even now our Lord looks on us not simply as a congregation but also as individuals. He never loses sight of the one among the many. To each person here He is saying, "You are; you shall be." What you are is of vast importance, but what you are becoming is of far more importance. Some are braver and stronger than others. Some have climbed up the hill far higher than others. But still this is true of us all: not one of us has yet become his best. There walks ahead of you, as there walks ahead of me, a far more Christlike person than either of us has yet become. This is not our despair, but our inspiration and our hope.

Somewhere I read of a youth who one day stood before a canvas on which Titian had splashed one of his marvelous dreams. That youth had not yet found himself. But as with glowing cheeks and sparkling eyes he looked on the thrilling picture, he murmured softly to himself, "I too, Titian, I too am an artist." From that moment of inspiration the young dreamer went out to realize his possibilities. So it was with Simon. So it may be with each of us.

2. Our Lord is not only giving Simon a pledge of his possibilities, but is pledging His help in the realization of these possibilities. If this were not the case, then His word might be no more than a mockery. None knew better than our Lord how impossible it was for Simon to reach the promised goal in his own strength. Jesus' words, therefore, were not only a prophecy but also a promise of divine strength. "You are Simon—you shall be Cephas" [a man of rock].

One day our Lord made a personal call on a human derelict who had lain flat on his back for thirty-eight years. To this bit of wreckage He puts what at first seems like a queer question. "Do you want to be healed?" By this question our Lord is facing the man with the fact that he is not healed. Jesus has to do so in order to gain the man's confidence. But along with this He is assuring the paralytic that healing is possible. If this were not the case, then the question would not be divine, but devilish. "In spite of the fact that you have been worse than worthless for half a lifetime, you may still stand upon your feet as a creature of worth. This is the case because I am at hand and able to help you." Even so our Lord pledges Himself to help Simon, and to help each of us.

3. Finally, if Simon is to become Cephas, it must be by his own choice. He must be willing to obey. The best name of Jesus is Saviour. He and He alone can save. But even He does not save without co-operation. Without human co-operation He does not save physically. I know a man who convinced himself that he could live without eating. He was going to be "clothed in the Godhead bodily." All that prevented him from being clothed in his own shroud was that when he fell into a coma, friends rushed him to the hospital and gave him forced feeding. But there can be no forced feeding with the bread of life.

Did you ever undergo surgery? If so, you know what it is to exercise your faith. "You are ill," said your physician. To that you had to agree. "I think that I can cure you," he continued hopefully, "but in order for me to do that you must put yourself absolutely into my hands." This you did. In spite of the fact that you knew your physician was not infallible, you dared to go into a sleep almost as deep as death. You did it knowing that one single mistake on his part might cost you your life. Such a faith directed toward our Lord is the one sure road to spiritual health.

This road of faith Simon took, and at once Jesus began to bring him to his best. His decision to follow was the work of a moment. But for the final winning of the goal he needed the whole of time and eternity. Often his rate of progress must have seemed pitifully slow and disappointing. The graph of Simon's life no more climbed upward in a straight and unbroken line than does your graph or mine. Today the proper noun Peter also becomes a verb, to "peter out." As for the reason, even Webster is not sure. I have an idea that Simon's new name Peter is now forced to do double duty because its wearer made so many failures. He petered out so many times.

In spite of all these falls, a little later we read in the Book of Acts that people brought their sick into the streets that even the shadow of Peter might fall on them and thus enable them once more to stand on their feet. That is, his very presence came to have in it both shelter and healing. The picture suggests that fine passage in Isaiah, "a man shall be as the shadow of a great rock in a weary land." Already Peter had become so rocklike that under his shadow weak and weary souls could find shelter and healing.

How did this come about? There was in it no magic. Having once dared to begin following Jesus, in spite of the fact that Simon fell again and again, he kept bravely on. He never allowed any fall to become final. The decisive difference between those gaining ultimate victory and those suffering ultimate defeat is not in the fact that the latter sometimes failed and that the former never did. The difference rather is this, that the one dared to start anew, while the other groveled in self-pity and remorse. If Judas had returned to his Lord, instead of resorting to a hangman's noose, he might have become as saintly as Simon Peter. Simon won out because he knew from experience that we fall to rise; we are baffled to fight better. If we thus refuse to quit, nothing can defeat us. "In due season we shall reap if we faint not." "You are Simon—you shall be called Cephas."

13. G. Ernest Thomas

George Ernest Thomas, Methodist. Born, Bolton, Eng., Feb. 16, 1907. Came to the States, 1910; naturalized, 1915. Educated, Boston University (B.S., S.T.B., Th.D.) Pastorates (1929-50). Director, Spiritual Life, Board of Evangelism, since 1951. Published works include: An Adventure in Stewardship *(1944);* To Whom Much Is Given *(1946);* What Jesus Was Like *(1946);* How to Live Your Faith *(1948);* Faith Can Master Fear *(1950);* Holy Habits of Spiritual Life *(1951);* America—Whither Bound? *(1952);* Spiritual Life in the New Testament *(1955);* Steps to the Christian Life *(1956).*

Sometimes we wonder why soul-winning sermons seldom appear in print. One reason may be that the evangelist feels untold concern about purpose and content, but little about structure and style. Here the spokesman for Christ deals with the human side of salvation, and that in the way of adventure. Like other editors, this one shows what Bishop Edwin H. Hughes meant by "the discipline of the pen."

Among other elements worthy of study, the message shows the value of a unifying theme, as a sort of symphonic refrain, which recurs at intervals, again and again. Also, the wisdom of using facts in accord with the unifying theme, all sorts of facts, except those that are hackneyed through overuse. In response to the revelation of God's grace in Christ and the Cross, "What saves a man is to take a step; then another step, ever toward Christ."

When will ministers and laymen learn that evangelistic preaching calls for ability and toil, never more so than today? How can the spokesman for Christ gain a hearing from the man in the street, who shies away from the local church? Surely by starting with him where he is, and then leading him to Christ along a

pathway that opens before him step by step. "I do not ask to see
the distant scene; one step enough for me."

STEPS THAT SAVE A MAN

"And Jesus saw him coming to him."—JOHN 1:47

A MAN NAMED Guillmet was flying a single-seater plane in
Southern France. He was caught in a blizzard and crashed high
in the French Alps. Critically injured in the accident, he managed
to drag himself out of the cockpit and find shelter under a wing.
The storm raged on for twenty-one hours. When the skies cleared
Guillmet began creeping down the mountain range. For sixteen
hours he moved inch by inch along the slope until at last he was
found by a searching party.

After lingering close to death for many days, he began a slow
recovery. Newspaper men were allowed an interview. One of them
asked: "How were you able to keep yourself alive during the
twenty-one hours while the blizzard raged on the mountain, and
the sixteen hours while you were creeping down the trail?"
Guillmet made this reply: "I knew that if my wife thought I was
alive she would know that I was trying to get back to her." Then
he added these words: "What saves a man is to take a step; then
another step."

The Bible tells of many men and women who, when first we
see them, have little to stir our admiration. But as their story un-
folds, and faith in God claims their lives, they become different
persons. They show the meaning of the words: "What saves a
man is to take a step; then another step."

Nathanael is such a one. When first we meet him, Nathanael
is sitting under a fig tree. He is cynical and doubtful. Philip

comes to him with face alight, saying that they have found Him of whom Moses and the prophets spoke, Jesus of Nazareth. "Can anything good come out of Nazareth?" Nathanael asks with a sneer. His attitude is disappointing. He is not a person from whom we expect much. But Philip is not discouraged. He extends an invitation, "Come and see." Then Nathanael takes a step. His decision cannot be counted as a major change in attitude. But it is a step in the right direction. "And Jesus saw him coming to him."

From that moment the picture of Nathanael grows brighter. We see him taking further steps in the right direction. He accepts the invitation of Jesus to follow Him. Then Nathanael is named with the twelve disciples. After the Crucifixion and the Resurrection he is telling the Good News far and near. In the end he dies a martyr to the faith. Tradition has indicated that he was killed in Egypt by those who were trying to destroy the Christian faith. Nathanael is only one of many whose lives are pictured in the Bible, about each of whom it can be said: "He took a step; then another step."

I. A STEP TOWARD CHRIST

All of us face moments when we need to take a certain step. For many the most important step in life is accepting Jesus Christ as the revelation of God's love. For others it is the step that unites us with the fellowship of the Christian Church.

Certain advances are necessary for those who are already Christians. For many of us the step we ought to take is toward a deeper life of prayer, a closer walk with God. Some of us need to decide to read the Bible regularly. Others among us should take the step by which our money and material goods become a part of our dedication. Some of us need to take Christ into our family life, our social life, and our business.

The joy of Christian living begins when it can be said of a man, a woman, or a youth: "Jesus saw him coming to him." What saves a man is to take a step; then another step.

II. A STEP AT A TIME

Why do we not become the men and women we know we ought to be? In our finer moments we are aware that many of our thoughts are unworthy of a follower of Christ. Our lives are a poor reflection of the One who walked the Galilean Road. We are mere shadows of the courageous, faithful, and triumphant persons we know we ought to be, and feel we might become. Why are we not what our hearts tell us we should be? Perhaps the distance seems too great from the person we now are to the person we see in our dreams. If we could reach perfection in a single instant we should all attain it. But it seems so far. Yet what saves a man is to take a step; then another step.

In the account of the successful ascent of Mt. Everest, the highest peak in the world, the author told of camps that were established at various heights along the trail. Each camp included a tent, a cooking stove, food, and blankets. The camps were placed at 10,000 feet, and at each additional 4,000 feet. "We never could have reached the summit if we had thought of it as a single climb," concluded the author. "We were able to reach our goal because we went from camp to camp."

Charles Lamb was an accountant in a business firm. One day he returned home to learn that his twin sister Mary, while mentally unbalanced, had slain their parents. Friends urged Charles to put Mary in an institution, but he chose to give up his position in order to care for her. The sacrifice had its reward, for he began to write, and achieved fame as one of England's outstanding authors. Through twenty-seven years Charles Lamb cared for his sister Mary. Usually she was a gay companion, but frequently she lapsed into periods of black despair. Charles never left her alone. When Mary died, friends inquired how he had been able to keep going under the continuous strain. He replied:

> I could not have kept on for a year, or even a month, if I had thought of it as a year, or a month. I was able to endure it because I took the days one at a time, happy when Mary was happy, and seeking God's help when she was disturbed.

We are not expected to reach the heights of faith and character in a single moment. God counts upon us to move step by step toward the heights. The direction is important. It should be said of us: "Jesus saw him coming to him."

III. A STEP IN FAITH

Many of us need to take a step in faith. Too often we postpone a decision to accept Christ as Saviour and Lord because we feel that we cannot accept all the doctrines of the Church. For the simplicity of God's love seen in Christ we have substituted systems of thought formulated by theologians. Often the so-called theology that troubles us is of little importance, and has no foundation in the Bible.

A student at Yale University was actively opposed to the Christian faith. He was usually in the center of a group discussing religion, and he was always ridiculing Christ and the Church. A friend who was disturbed by his attitude asked what he had against Christianity. "I can't stand all the doctrines," he replied. "What doctrines bother you?" inquired the friend. "Well, take the doctrine of the Immaculate Conception," he said. "I could never accept a ridiculous belief like that!" His friend explained that belief in the dogma of the Immaculate Conception is limited to the Roman Catholic Church; that the dogma is less than a hundred years old; that it is not mentioned in the Bible; and that it has nothing to do with the birth of Jesus, but that it deals with the supposed manner of His mother's birth. The student had based his opposition to the Christian faith upon ideas that did no more than reflect his ignorance.

The Christian faith at heart is not difficult to understand. It begins with belief in God as the Creator of the universe and as the Sustainer of all life. God's character is centered in love and concern for all His children. It continues with belief in Christ as the revelation of God, the Way by which a man finds pardon for his sins, and meaning in his daily struggle. The Christian faith includes belief in the Holy Spirit as God's continuing Presence in the world, with belief in the Bible as the unfolding revelation of God, and the key that tells us how to live. The whole is climaxed by faith in the life everlasting.

When men have tried to understand what these beliefs mean they have often gone far afield. Doctrines have been formulated to justify the foundation of a church organization. Minor teach-

ings of the Bible have been expanded far beyond their importance, to the exclusion of other and more essential truths.

Jesus Christ is the central Figure in the Christian faith. All the
other beliefs of Christianity are dependent upon what He said
and did. We are not called upon to accept all Christian dogmas
at one moment. It is enough at first to take a step in professing
faith in Christ.

We must admit that to have faith in Christ raises problems
for some who want to be honest in their thinking. You may
declare that you cannot accept the Virgin Birth and the Divinity
of Jesus, but you think that Jesus was the greatest Man who has
ever lived. If you feel so, take a step in accepting Him as the
greatest of men. Let His love of people and His courage in the
face of persecution grip your life. Your whole outlook will be
changed if the heroism of Jesus becomes a daily challenge to
make your life like His.

You may declare that you cannot accept the miracles of Jesus
as described in the Bible, but you think that the teachings of
Jesus are the greatest that humanity ever received. You are convinced that the world would be a better place if men adhered to
His instructions about how we should live. If you feel so, take a
step in accepting Jesus as the Master Teacher. Follow daily His
way of living.

Any earnest seeker who accepts Jesus the Man, or Jesus the
Teacher, will make a wonderful discovery. If you come to love
the Jesus who lived in ancient Palestine, and if you follow His
teachings day by day, you will soon take another step. You will
know that He is the Son of God. You will become a witness to
His Divinity.

We need faith in order to live. Our span of life is too brief to
wait until all the mysteries have been cleared before we profess
faith in Christ. Let it be said of you: "Jesus saw him coming to
him." Then like Nathanael, you will find yourself taking further
steps until the full meaning of the Christian faith becomes known.
What saves a man is to take a step, and then another step, toward
Jesus.

IV. A STEP IN TRUST

Many of us need to take a step in trust. Our worries and fears stem from our unwillingness to turn our lives over to God. We take refuge in physical health or in material goods. We are confident that we can control the world by a full use of our powers. But we constantly fail. We toss sleeplessly at night. We worry about what the future may bring. We fear what may lie ahead.

Fear reflects a lack of trust in God. Indeed, it does more than that. It indicates an empty faith. Whatever may be the religion of such a person, it is not the triumphant faith and confident assurance that Christ demonstrated during His earthly life, and that He now offers to His followers.

A woman came to talk with me about her problems. Her husband had passed away three years before, leaving a business that was close to failure. Several bankers had advised her to dispose of the business, but she had insisted on continuing, even though bankruptcy seemed inevitable. Her children were not following her instructions. Instead of yielding to the pressure of their mother, and doing what she wanted, they insisted on finding their own occupations. Her health was poor, and the finest doctors had recommended an operation. Each time, instead of following their advice, she turned to another doctor.

I listened patiently to the recital of her woes. Then I said quietly: "It seems to me that your greatest need is to learn to trust God." The woman bristled in anger. "I do trust Him," she replied indignantly. "Please forgive me for speaking bluntly," I went on. "You attend church each Sunday, and you give regularly to your church, but your faith ends at that point. The finest bankers have advised you to dispose of your business, but you refuse to listen to their counsel. You have tried to dominate your children, refusing to let God lead them where He wills. You have gone from doctor to doctor, hoping to find one who will say what you want him to say. You don't trust God. The only person you trust is yourself."

Many of us are unhappy because we have shut God out of our lives. If the Christian faith means anything it promises that God will guide and lead those who seek Him. We can be sustained each day by His love and care. But a life of trust cannot be realized without effort. We have too much confidence in our own wisdom and strength to be willing to yield our problems and cares to His direction.

Take a step in trust! Decide today to learn what it means that "underneath are the everlasting arms." Turn over to God the burdens that seem so overpowering. If you now take a first step in trust, in days ahead you will find it easier to take still other steps. Like Nathanael learn to walk each day with the Master. What saves a man is to take a step; then another step.

V. A STEP IN DEDICATION

Many of us need to take a step in dedication. When Peter was confronted by the needs of a man who was lame he did not wait for a future hour when he could give the man all that he desired. Peter said, "Such as I have, I give." At the moment he did not realize that what he had to give was the Lord's answer to the deepest need of the other man's life. It was enough that Peter responded with what he possessed.

While riding through West Virginia on a train I listened to the conversation of a young woman and her aunt. The young woman spoke of her plan to be a missionary in the foreign field. I was deeply moved by the indications of her dedication. Then the train slowed to a stop in a town that showed signs of poverty. A group of children were picking up pieces of coal. "Why do they allow such dirty children to play along the tracks?" asked the young woman.

I was saddened by the realization that this college student was talking about the dedication of all her future life to God, but she had no awareness that the dedication of herself should begin here and now. If she was insensitive to human need about her near at home, there could be little value in what she thought was the greater and more glamorous offer of her life in the future. "And Jesus saw him coming to him." He wants what we have to offer now. He pleads for our hearts now. He yearns to claim our loyalty now.

We often despair about the future of our world. We look hopefully for God's intervention in the affairs of men. We speak for vently about the Second Coming of Christ. Surely the future is in the hands of God. Our part is to be faithful to Him in our day. We may not have power to change the world, but we can be honest and upright in character at the place where we live. We can use what we have, in order to further God's purposes as revealed in Jesus Christ. We can tell the Good News of Salvation to everyone we meet.

Our span of life is brief. Judgment is at hand. The hour has struck to take a step in dedication. However small may be your gifts of talent and of money, this is the time to offer them to God.

"And Jesus saw him coming to him." When Nathanael took the first step toward Christ, he began the journey that ended in heaven.

The Master is pleading with each of us to come to Him now, and to accept His promises. What saves a man is to take a step, and then another step, ever toward Christ.

III. With Christ Near His End

14. James McGraw

James McGraw, Church of the Nazarene. Born in a parsonage, Peniel, Tex., Oct. 25, 1913. Educated, Nazarene College, Bethany, Okla. (B. Th.); Texas Christian University (A.M.); University of Kansas (candidate for Ph.D.). Pastorates (1936-39, 1949-52). Professor and assistant to president, Nampa College, Ida. (1946-49). Professor of preaching and pastoral ministry, Nazarene Seminary, Kansas City, Mo., since 1953. Books: Men Who Met Jesus, radio sermons (1952); The Holiness Pulpit—sermons (ed. and comp., 1957).

Here the professor chooses a text and phrases a subject that should appeal to people over the radio, as well as elsewhere. Both text and subject he uses as the focal point for facts about the washing of the disciples' feet. In churches that follow the Christian Year, even partly, such a message would fittingly lead up to celebration of the Sacrament on Maundy Thursday. At any other season, especially in a week-day evening service preparatory to Communion on the coming Lord's Day, such a message would prove timely.

In the House of God almost everyone present has used a towel before coming to church, and will use another after he goes home. How many of these lay friends have ever thought of the common towel as a present-day symbol of truth and duty that lie close to the Cross? Thank God for this aspect of "our Gospel, a gift of God to the imagination"!

CHRIST AND HIS TOWEL

"Jesus . . . laid aside his garments; and took a towel, and girded himself; . . . and began to wash the disciples' feet."
—ST. JOHN 13:3-5

WE HEAR MUCH these days about following Christ. From the pulpit come frequent challenges, from the hymnal many reminders, and from the New Testament numerous examples. Each of them presents the ideal of thinking and feeling, living and loving, like the Lord Jesus.

It thrills us when we think of following Him as He speaks to friendly multitudes who seem eager to hear Him preach. It appeals to our desire for aggression when we think how we may follow Him as He drives money-changers from the Temple. It would gladden our hearts to stand among the cheering throng who welcome Him into the Holy City, where they hope to crown Him as their King.

But more than all of this, and in keeping with our desire to share the suffering and reproach He endured on the way to the Cross, we need to follow our Lord's example as He takes a towel and girds Himself, that he may wash the disciples' feet. Behold Christ as the Man with the towel! In the average church today the furnishings most needed may be towels and basins for the washing of others' feet. Oh, not literally, as some have supposed, but in a deeper and far more meaningful way, the way of the Spirit, the Spirit of Christ. To be a Christian means to be like the Christ of the towel.

A good, long look at the Master as John portrays Him here should help us to see wherein we need to follow in His footsteps today. From His example let us see first of all—

I. THE DIGNITY OF SERVICE

Christ with His towel shows the dignity of service. Washing one another's feet! What could bring out more dramatically the spirit of Christian service? It does not ask, "What can I get out of this or that?" Rather it pleads, "Here, let me help."

Jesus saw dusty feet. The Christlike follower of the Nazarene is quick to see the needs of his brothers, one by one, and to sense their inner feelings. Like those disciples in the Upper Room, however, we may become so busy with thinking about our own little burdens that we may feel no concern about the needs of others. Our minds may be so filled with our own selfish thoughts that we do not notice the weariness and hurt of the man with whom we have been rubbing shoulders for months or years.

So our own grimy feet feel tired! Does this mean that we should devote our strength and energy to pitying, even pampering ourselves, while we close our eyes to the needs of others? Do we forget that there may be someone next door, or across the street, who bears a load heavier than we have ever known? No, not if we follow the Christ of the towel. He never became so preoccupied with His own weariness that He failed to see the tired, dusty feet of His friends. Such service as the Master rendered in the Upper Room calls for willingness to look around us and see what our neighbors need, whether they live across the street, or beyond the seven seas.

However menial and lowly the task appeared, Jesus found no hesitancy in undertaking any work that needed to be done. He did not shrink or recoil from any task that might have seemed humiliating. Washing another person's feet may call for bending the knee, lowering one's position, and if you please, deflating the ego. Even so, all of this shows a spirit like that of Christ with His towel. The Christlike follower is eager to perform any task that is lowly, more than when it carries prestige. Whatever the human need, he willingly accepts any humiliation that accompanies service in meeting that need.

When Jesus dignified the giving of service by washing the disciples' feet, He demonstrated how such usefulness demands the giving of oneself. With His hands, His time, His energy, and

His skill, He gave Himself to the performance of this menial task. You see, it is not Christlike to toss another person a quarter, with a friendly word, "Go and get yourself a shoeshine." That may be a courteous gesture, but often a gesture is not enough. Jesus gave Himself. He did not merely "help" a good cause. He did the kind act, and He did it directly for the persons in need.

A certain father known to me learned this truth too late. To his son the father had given all the things he thought the son wanted. These gifts included sums of money, a first-class education, good clothes, and a sports car. But that father never had given his boy what the lad wished most of all, a father. With his other gifts the father had not given himself. That son's life ended in tragedy. Too late the father learned how he had failed in rearing his only son.

Would that many Christians might learn this lesson about their relationship to Christ, as well as their loved ones! They readily make "the same subscription to the budget as last year." Perhaps they increase the amount to help finance the new organ. They may feel that they are doing nobly to support God's work so generously, if not sacrificially. But have they learned from the Christ of the towel what it means to give themselves for Him in service?

Behold the only begotten Son of God with a towel! He took that towel and used it because He had come from God to act as the Servant of men. According to our text, the Incarnate Son of God, "knowing that the Father had given all things into his hands, and that he was come from God, and went to God," took the towel to perform a menial task. Thus He has revealed God as truly as when He later died on the Cross. By His dramatic deed in washing grimy feet He has forever removed any stigma that men associate with service. His example helps us understand that to see the needs of others, and then to give ourselves in service, means to be like Him, and like God His Father.

II. THE GREATNESS OF HUMILITY

Contrast the Man with the towel in His hand, stooping to serve, with the disciples, who have been quarreling about which of them would become greatest in His Kingdom. Remember that

He had come from God, and that He would soon return to the
Father in glory. On the night before the Lord Jesus was to die,
how it must have grieved His heart to hear the disciples disputing
about their prospective rank in the service of the One who recog-
nizes no rank, encourages no promotion, permits no jockeying
for position, and sees no equality of spirit greater than the desire
to meet the needs of others by engaging in lowly service.

And yet those dearest earthly friends of our Lord refused to
render each other a needed service. To what extent are we like
them today? In many a local church there is seeking for honor,
thirst for praise, lust for power, contentious demanding to have
one's own way, and worst of all, adolescent pouting when one
fails to get it. What a shame and a tragedy among those who
profess to love and to follow the Christ of the towel!

How would we have arranged for such a washing of feet, or
any corresponding deed of usefulness? How would a representative committee approach the problem? "No one must ask Peter,
James, and John to do this menial task, because seniority exempts
them. Judas cannot serve, because he already has a much more
important post as the treasurer of the apostolic band." And so on
with Matthew, Andrew, and the others. Why not hire a Gentile
to come in and render this service for us? It is beneath our dignity, and we have in the treasury money enough to pay someone
else."

Careful, men! We are forgetting one of the most important
lessons that Christ has taught us. We are behaving like the
Pharisees, who were not content to pray in private lest someone
fail to see how "holy" they were. They gave alms and other
contributions with so much fanfare that no one could overlook
their so-called generosity. The Master told them that they had
done good to be seen of men, and that they had already received
the reward they sought. Then He told the disciples, as He now
tells us, "Whosoever of you will be the chiefest, shall be servant
of all" (Mark 10:44).

The importance of rank? Position? Honor? In the Kingdom
of the One who teaches that true greatness consists in the desire
to serve the needs of others, such aspirations have no place. In
the eyes of our Lord the least of all persons is worthy of His

love, His time, and His help. In the Upper Room He taught this truth more dramatically by action than anyone else could have done with a thousand words. After Saul of Tarsus became a Christian he must have learned this lesson well, for he wrote to the Romans that the Christian way means "in honor preferring one another" (12:10), and to the Philippians, "In lowliness of mind let each esteem other better than themselves" (2:3b).

To follow the example of Christ with the towel in His hand means to rejoice in the success of others. It calls for freedom from the unholy passion for praise from men, and leads to a holy aim to be worthy of praise in the sight of God. To attain such Christlikeness today, we need the infilling and the empowering presence of the Holy Spirit. So did those early disciples. Before the Day of Pentecost they thought in terms of rank, position, and protocol. But after the Holy Spirit descended upon them with power, they witnessed to the Resurrection of the Lord Jesus, and "great grace was upon them all" (Acts 4:33b). And so when our hearts are ready for God to dwell in us, and when the Spirit comes to empower us for Christlike living, "great grace" may be upon us. Then there will be in our hearts no place for the petty pride that makes the people of the world want to seem bigger and stand taller than their neighbors.

From the example of Christ with His towel we learn the dignity of service and the true greatness of humility. Let us also observe—

III. THE BEAUTY OF LOVE IN ACTION

In the midst of human need love never stands idle. Immediately it goes into action. When the Lord Jesus saw those grimy feet of young men who had walked with Him through busy city streets and over rough old country trails, He wished to help them feel refreshed and comfortable. Throughout three years of public ministry He had loved them with a love like that of heaven. And now in face of what must have seemed like secondary need, once again He translated divine love into human action. Christlike love always works this way. Not only does it lead us to see the needs of those nearby. Love also impels us to meet those needs at once, and gladly.

Do you wish to see the meaning of Christlike love in action?

Listen while the Master describes the Samaritan who kneels in the dusty ditch to wipe the blood and dirt from the face of a Jew who has been beaten, robbed, and left to die. One by one, others have seen the poor fellow, and then "passed by on the other side." They may have pitied him, shuddered a little, and even wiped from their cheeks a tear or two. But they did not have the sort of love that leads at once to action. The Samaritan had such love, and he did everything in his power to show that love by deeds. He gladly gave up time, energy, money, and credit. He may even have risked his life, and all for the sake of an unconscious stranger who belonged to a "hated race."

James, the brother of our Lord, has caught the spirit of love in action. In his epistle he shows how ridiculous and hypocritical it seems "If a brother or sister be naked, and destitute of daily food, and one of you say unto them, 'Depart in peace; be ye warmed and fed'" (2:15,16). Christlike love, says the Apostle, cannot be so empty and hollow as to mouth meaningless words, while never stretching out a hand to meet the need of a person in distress. Love goes into action immediately. You can give without loving, but you cannot love without giving. This axiom of the Christian life applies not only to the giving of money but also to the giving of understanding, affection, and sympathy. It likewise results in practical service.

> Alas, for the rarity
> Of Christian charity
> Under the sun.

The Christ with a towel in His hand! Take a long and loving look at Him as He serves others, as He humbles Himself, and as He shows the meaning of love in action. Not only look at Him. Dare to follow Him, in "loving deeds of service free." Follow this Christ of Galilee as John Wesley began to follow Him, immediately after his heart had been "strangely warmed" at the meeting in Aldersgate street. To the day of his death at the age of eighty eight, Wesley's fruitful ministry brought him endless opportunities to be served, to be praised, and to become wealthy. But he insisted on remaining humble, immune to flattery, and free from greed. After the probate of his will the executor reported that all the possessions Wesley left behind were "a silver spoon, a frock, and the Methodist Church."

The same principle holds true of men who never have become famous. For example, take one of the missionary heroes among Nazarenes. In Germany at an old "Peniel" Harmon Schmelzenbach once caught a vision of "the smoke of a thousand villages" where native people in South Africa never had heard the name of Jesus Christ. Because of tears that burned his cheeks whenever he thought of those dark folk who never had heard the preaching of the Cross, he could not keep on at home with his books. So he burned out his life while proclaiming the drama of redemption in Swaziland. For twenty-nine years as a missionary pioneer, with never a furlough to go home for rest, who can wonder that he led to Christ five thousand Swazis?

Our world today needs many more men and women to follow the example of Christ with the towel in His hand. Eager for every opportunity to serve, faithful in performing every task that comes to hand, however lowly the work may be, remember that in the service of Christ there can be no premium on prestige, no yearning for applause, no seeking after preferment. May your love for Christ, and your Christlike love for others, find expression in deeds as well as words. In the name of our God, while you speak much about the Lord Jesus, by His grace become more and more like Him, the Christ with His towel.

15. Ralph G. Turnbull

Ralph Gale Turnbull, United Presbyterian. Born, Berwick-upon-Tweed, Scotland, Mar. 3, 1901. Educated, University of Aberdeen (B.A.); University of Edinburgh (M.A.); University of Manitoba (B.D.); Princeton Seminary (Th.M.) D.D., Whitworth College, Spokane, Wash. F. Phil. Soc., London; F.R.G.S., London. Pastorates in Great Britain, Canada, and Philadelphia (1934-49). Professor of homiletics, Western Seminary, Pittsburgh (1949-54). Pastor, First Church, Seattle, Wash., since 1954. Author of 16 books, including: The Gist of the Lesson (1954-59); The Seven Words from the Cross (1956); Jonathan Edwards, the Preacher (1958); Sermon Substance (1958); Devotions of Jonathan Edwards (1959); A Minister's Obstacles (paper reprint, 1959).

The following sermon has to do with a matter everywhere to the fore of late. Unlike others who preach about peace of mind, this pastor deals with the matter Biblically, in the light of a royal text from the Upper Room. The materials have to do with the doctrines that undergird all Christian preaching of solace and hope. Such pulpit work concerns what William James used to term "comforting faith," over against a pulpit appeal for "fighting faith," on the part of those who should put on "the whole armor of God."

In form the sermon consists in a topical use of the truth in the text. To such topical use of Biblical truths no one familiar with the history of evangelical preaching ought to object. Clarence E. Macartney, for instance, preached topically nearly all the time. He used to insist that in the history of the Church almost every well-known sermon has been topical in form. He might also have said that in the wrong hands this way of preaching has many pitfalls, including monotony, shallowness, and secularism.

175

So let us thank God for the range, the realism, and the relevance of the peace that Christ has in Himself; the peace that contrasts with the sham brand that the world offers; the peace that He stands ready to give every believing heart, right here and right now. Doubtless this is why the sermon closes with the idea of relevance. Through this golden text the living Christ is speaking now, in the present tense. "Do not preach mainly about the historical Christ," says James Denney. "Preach about the living, sovereign Christ." Amen!

THE PEACE THAT CHRIST OFFERS

"My peace I give unto you; not as the world giveth."
JOHN 14:27

THESE WORDS from our Lord tell about the Gospel of Christ's Peace. In a world with all sorts of vested interests, He confronts us men with His Gospel. In it He offers us peace with God, peace with others, and peace for every believer. Since Christianity is Christ, it means in part His way of peace, for one and for all. But His gift of peace divine cannot come until by faith we receive Him, and appropriate His grace.

What then is this peace that Christ offers? What is the peculiar and distinctive fact about the peace that He gives freely in the Gospel? Remember that His Gospel means vastly more than good advice, or worldly-wise counsel. As our Peace Giver the Lord Jesus offers a desperate soul the best of "good news." His Gospel here is an offer from the divine Physician to succor the poor and the blind, the lame and the deaf, as well as the maimed, especially in mind. It is the offer of the divine Architect to rebuild and restore lives that have been broken and blighted. The Gospel of peace is the offer of the divine Shepherd who promises to care for His sheep, safeguarding them from peril, and supplying their every need.

The Gospel of God's peace is uniquely different, above all, because in it He offers and gives Himself. With Himself He gives the riches of His grace, here and hereafter. The gifts of the world, at best, are transient and passing. They may bring enjoyment for a season, but then they perish. Everything on earth, however beautiful and good, has its limits in time, and bears within itself the seeds of its own death and decay. But our Saviour offers us Himself and His peace; His gifts will endure forever. Thus the word peace sums up the essence of all His gifts. "My peace I give unto you; not as the world giveth." This is His legacy to His own. When the Saviour grants us His peace, by faith we find that His gifts are permanent and eternal in their range, in their realism, and in their relevance.

I. THE RANGE OF CHRIST'S OFFER

Consider how far-reaching is this offer of the Lord Jesus; how comprehensive, encompassing the whole of life. "Not as the world giveth, give I unto you." There is a range of interest that touches the entire gamut of our experience. For example, one of the most potent forces in life today is that of fear. Who can deny that for many persons today life is full of fears? Think of anxiety about things economic, about moral problems, about the life of young folk in a world full of lawlessness, about the future here on earth, and most of all, about what lies beyond. So it is manifest that one of the chief roots of men's troubles today is fear.

In the presence of fear, Christ offers His peace. "Fear not. . . . Fear not them which kill the body, but are not able to kill the soul: but rather fear him which is able to destroy both soul and body in hell" (Matt. 10:18). Consider also the sparrows, and God's care of them. "Fear not therefore: ye are of more value than many sparrows" (Luke 12:7b). Thus the love of God in Christ is able and waiting to cast out all unworthy fears. Fear has torment, but Christ's peace dispels anxiety.

"In the world ye shall have tribulation: but be of good cheer; I have overcome the world" (John 16:33). Think of all the fears and frustrations that we bear about with us day by day! And remember that through faith in Christ any one of us can conquer every fear. Instead of fear, through Him there comes peace.

Again, the closeness of life brings us into touch with all kinds of people. Have you ever thought how comprehensive is the range of Christ's offer to touch and bless all sorts of lives, with every shade of opinion and culture, economic position and social life, religious affiliation or no religious belief? Remember too that by His gift of peace, to those who believe and accept His offer, He divides men. "Think not that I am come to send peace on earth: I came not to send peace, but a sword" (Matt. 10:34). Thus He sets one person in a family over against other members. In the same home, shop, or camp, He may lead one person alone to bear the cross.

Why this division among men because of Christ? Flags may help to unite, treaties may unite, music may unite, and community interests may unite; but Christ says that He comes to divide. Even when He saves men, He sifts them. When He wins their allegiance, He winnows them. In the range of His power, as in the offer of His peace, He is the great Divider. Meanwhile where is peace? It is in the Cross of Christ, who reveals the grace of God and uncovers the sins of men. "I, if I be lifted up from the earth, will draw all men unto me" (John 12:32). Without distinction and without exception, he appeals to men. Through His Cross the Lord surmounts every barrier of race and color and tongue. Through His Death Christ opens up the way to peace.

All the while this One longs to become known as the Good Shepherd. "When he saw the multitudes He was moved with compassion on them" (Matt. 9:36). That is the mark of the One who succors. His compassion shows the range of His feelings for us all. He has loving concern for one lost soul, as well as for a crowd, like a lot of "sheep without a shepherd—fainting, scattered." Are not these the marks of the drifting world today? False religions, debasing cultures, tyrannical despotisms, and racial chains show men's need of peace. Christ's offer of peace is for us all. His Gospel of peace is for you in your need. No one can go outside the reach of His power to save and bless with peace. His offer awaits your acceptance. Only in the outreach of the Shepherd is there peace.

II. THE REALISM OF HIS OFFER

Think also about the realism of His offer. No one else has so touched life in all its depths. Others have tried to be saviors and leaders of men, but no one else has laid bare the actual needs of men so realistically as Christ. The same kind of realism is characteristic of the Book that brings His message, and calls for our study. The Bible is the one Book of the ages with true realism. It is not romantic literature dealing with theories and with unreal life. It is never afraid to speak the truth, and it never glosses over anything that needs exposure to sunlight.

As children in their transparency of thought speak without qualification, so the Bible deals with life. It tells about the drunkenness of Noah, the lies of Abraham, the deceit of Jacob, the immorality of David, and the hypocrisy of Ananias. The Bible likewise records the terrors of the crucifixion, which the Son of God endured because of our sins. Holy Scripture smooths over nothing sad, and makes no attempt to hide what we ought to see, whether it be good or bad. The teaching of Christ is like that in its realism. When He promises to give peace, He does it frankly in face of all the worst in the world.

The peace that Christ offers is totally unlike the so-called peace that the world tenders. In a time of sorrow the peace that the world holds out is only a patched-up substitute. The world may offer the encouragement of a slap on the shoulder, with a word about being brave, and a murmur about "bad luck." But when the Saviour offers His peace, think what He gives! How real and how true! By His promises of truth and by the comfort of His presence, Christ assuages sorrow and quenches grief. "There is a balm in Gilead, to quench the sin-sick soul." This peace is the gift of God. It passes all understanding. What realism!

Again, consider the realism of what Christ says about the worth of a man's life. "How much is a man better than a sheep?" "What shall it profit a man if he shall gain the whole world, and lose his own soul" (Mark 8:36)? This is the sort of realism that the world blinks at, and refuses to heed. But these are the terms on which

Christ offers Himself and His peace. No one else talks this way. In what seems to us sternness, He speaks with realism that brings us to Himself. In this experience He gives us peace.

The Lord Jesus is equally realistic about forgiveness of wrongs. "Lord, how oft shall my brother sin against me, and I forgive him? till seven times?" "I say not unto thee, until seven times; but, until seventy times seven" (Matt. 18:21,22). So you cannot deal with evil lightly, whether it be a sin against God, or ill-treatment of brother by brother. Neither can anyone find forgiveness cheaply or easily. Christ teaches that a man's forgiveness of a person who does him wrong ought to be like God's forgiveness of the former man's sins. What realism!

Christ is against sin. On the Cross He alone has dealt with sin as God would have sin dealt with unto its death. Today sin lies at the root of all the ills in human life. Men may boast about their freedom, but everywhere they are the bond slaves of sin. As our Lord has told us, out of the heart come the things that defile. How realistic is His way of cleansing the heart so that life will be pure! Every person who has been truly converted has during this experience felt the realism of Christ in dealing with sin. For the first time he at last has faced the reality of living. Through forgiveness Christ gives His perfect peace. What blessed realism!

III. THE RELEVANCE OF HIS OFFER

Christ's offer of peace likewise has relevance to all of human life and destiny. Because of its influence over morals and conduct, His peace may become the most important factor in life. It is relevant to our needs because it is peace through the Gospel. The relevance of the Gospel appears supremely in the Death and the Resurrection of our Lord. Even in the midst of our weakness and seeming defeat, the Gospel message brings us power and assurance. For the day of evil, here is good news. For the day of ordeal, here is new strength. For every dark and cloudy time, here is new-born hope. For the mightiest struggles of life, here is courage to conquer. Thus the Gospel stands ready to make all things new. What blessed relevance!

When a man is born again, there is a new creation. Then the

dynamic of God's grace begins to cleanse the affections and restrain the passions; to refashion the desires and buttress the will
for moral endurance. In His tender of peace Christ does not offer
us immunity from the temptations and moral risks of life, but
He does offer us power to meet and conquer them all. He alone
can restore the bankrupt life to decency and to the beginning of
better things. He alone can deal with the disabilities of a crooked
character, canceling its evil deeds and creating new springs of
desire. Thus He offers you a holy, happy, and healthy life,
wherein you may live as a child of God, and not merely exist as a
slave of sin. What relevance!

In Christ's new creation, there is peace. The readjustment has
come, bringing peace with God, peace with others, and peace
within. And yet there are those who question whether or not
Christ's offer has to do directly with the needs of our day; whether
or not His Gospel can touch and change life as it is now. Ah, yes,
in our time Christ's offer of peace is relevant for all the deepest
needs of men. It may be that there has been much progress in
society, but still our so-called civilization is a sort of closed system,
richly endowed of God with much that is good, but with resources
used in the service of the devil. In this tragic age our generation
knows much about many things, but it has failed in moral and
spiritual strength.

Just here our Saviour comes with His offer of peace. In the
Gospel He shows that things material can never satisfy the desires
of men, and that their souls need His power to lift them up to a
higher plane. As with the soil on a hillside farm, the erosion
of modern life has eaten into society, and has worn away much
that used to seem solid and fertile. If we would attain to the
fullness of life, we need to accept His offer of restoration. In oneness with Him there is the presence and the power of God. "This
man shall be our peace" (Mic. 5:5a).

Remember that when Christ offers us peace He offers Himself.
To us as believers the Person of Christ is ever central and supreme.
He and His Gospel can never be out of date, never behind the
times, never out of touch with human needs. We may talk much
about our problems, but that word does not appear in the New
Testament, or in the Old. In Christ there are no problems; He

has translated them into opportunities. Through His Death and
Resurrection, and through His union with believing souls, He
has wrought the way to the solution of all the religious, political,
and social issues of our age, and of every age. What relevance!

In this holy light we ought to become committed. Surely we
cannot escape from Christ, and from His claims. In Him, and in
Him alone can we find wisdom, strength, and courage to face all
our problems, and find His solutions. This way of serving Him
can never prove easy. His peace often comes through a sword in
the soul. His freedom comes through our submission. His life
comes to us through our sacrifice. In His Death and Resurrection
He releases for us powers beyond the dreams of men. Thus He
forgives our sins, crowns our lives with love, and gives us eternal
life. What relevance!

When the Holy Spirit indwells the new man, the peace of
Christ comes into the heart. Then He lives anew in the life of
the believer. Thus by faith you will find Him indispensable to
your soul, and far more than adequate for every situation. This
is why you ought now to receive Him in His fullness, and thus
enter into His peace. You will find that His peace, unlike any
other, brings you God in Christ. Then you will sing with Horatius
Bonar:

> I hear the words of love,
> I gaze upon the blood,
> I see the mighty sacrifice,
> And I have peace with God.

16. J. Marcellus Kik

Jacob Marcellus Kik, Reformed (Dutch) Church in
America. Born in the Netherlands, Dec. 24, 1903.
Reared in Grand Rapids, Mich. Educated, Hope Col-
lege, Holland, Mich. (A.B.) Princeton Seminary, and
Westminster Seminary, Philadelphia (Th.B.) Pastor in
Canada and the States (1930-56). For 14 years a religi-
ous radio service, and edited the magazine, Bible
Christianity. Associate editor, Christianity Today since
1956. Books: The Narrow and the Broad Way (1934);
Matthew Twenty-Four (1948); Revelation Twenty
(1955); Ecumenism and the Evangelical (1958).

Unlike most pulpit work today, the sermon that follows deals
frankly and fully with sin. According to friendly observers from
overseas, even conservative ministers in the States do not sufficiently stress "the dark line in God's face." About the interpretation of certain sayings, such as the "cry of dereliction," rev-
erent and thoughtful men differ, but concerning the black facts
themselves, who dares to keep silent? Who can translate the
message of Gethsemane and Calvary into a present-day "philosophy" of "sweetness and light"?

The form of the message accords with the spirit and "tone
color" of the text in its own background. The spokesman for God
wishes us to feel that we are now with the Saviour in the Garden,
and that we must not fall asleep. Where another would seek for
an illustration from the cup of Socrates, this man knows that
nothing on earth can begin to show what the Redeemer endured,
even before "the day of the Cross."

The sermon begins with a text that embodies a figure. Then
the minister translates his figure into terms of fact. Wisely, he
never lets us lose sight of the cup, and of what it should mean to
us now. If like many of the fathers we gave ourselves more often

*to such "faithful preaching" about sin and sacrifice, there would
be more iron in the blood of those who listen, and more power
in those who by faith enter into the fellowship of Christ's sufferings.*

THE CUP OF GETHSEMANE

"O my Father, if it be possible, let this cup pass from me:
nevertheless, not as I will, but as thou wilt."

ST. MATTHEW 26:39bc

THE CUP OF GETHSEMANE speaks to us about the agony of
Christ in the Garden, agony that He endured because of our sin.
Unconcern about sin characterizes the present generation. The
enormity and heinousness of sin do not weigh upon the soul, or
prick the conscience. Men openly flout the law of God. Trans-
gressors exhibit callousness to the fact that they are affronting
our holy God. This common attitude toward sin may in part be
the fruit of liberal preaching, which has come from many pulpits
during the past few decades. Because the pulpit has minimized
sin, the people have minimized sin. Academic theological circles
have recently awakened to the seriousness of sin, but this concern
has not yet reached the pew, or the man in the street. The impress
of twentieth century preaching still appears in a people indifferent to sin and its consequences.

How different from the scene in the garden, where our Lord
accepted the cup full of sin! Alas, the pulpit has minimized sin
by diagnosing it as a disease, easily cured by a better environment
and improved culture. In order to eliminate sin, it would seem,
all that men need is a few moral lectures by the minister and a few
firm resolutions by the sinner. Thus sin has been minimized by

denying the need of atonement, and by teaching the universal fatherhood of God, as sufficient to remove sin from the earth. As for the hereafter, it has been declared, the God of love will never condemn a soul to hell.

Anyone can test himself, to see whether he has fallen a victim to such preaching. Let him ask whether he feels that his sin deserves condemnation to eternal hell. Of course many people know that they have sinned, and that they deserve some type of punishment. But surely their sins do not deserve the eternal wrath of God! They are sinners, but not sinners deserving hell! Anyone with this attitude toward the hereafter has accepted man's estimate of sin, and man's estimate of sin falls far short of God's appraisal.

THE CUP IN THE GARDEN

God's evaluation of sin appears dramatically at Gethsemane. In a certain sense we may well hesitate to enter that garden, and there behold the agony of Christ. No human mind can begin to fathom the anguish of our Saviour, nor can any human tongue adequately describe what took place in that garden. Nevertheless, it is the cup of Gethsemane that gives us more than a glimpse into the enormity and heinousness of human sin. For this reason we must enter into the garden, and there think about the cup.

After the Last Supper Jesus with three disciples retired to Gethsemane. Upon entering the garden He began to be sorrowful and sore troubled. Then He said to the disciples, "My soul is exceeding sorrowful, even unto death: tarry ye here, and watch with me." Drawing apart by Himself, He prayed, "O my Father, if it be possible, let this cup pass from me: nevertheless, not as I will, but as thou wilt." Upon returning to the disciples, He found them asleep. He pleaded with them to keep watch so that He would not have to bear His agony alone. Again He prayed, "O my Father, if this cup cannot pass away from me except I drink it, thy will be done." Once more He found the disciples asleep, and urged them to remain awake. A third time He prayed, and so earnestly that His sweat became as it were great drops of blood falling to the ground. Then the mob burst into the garden and seized our Lord Jesus.

The cup that caused such agonized prayer must have contained something unspeakably awful. That cup filled Him with amazement. It caused Him to feel sore troubled. It brought on His soul the most deadly sorrow. It started blood to pour from His brow. So awful was the cup that Jesus pleaded with His disciples to watch with Him, so that by companionship they might alleviate His anguish. This loathsome cup caused Jesus to cry out three times, "O my Father, if it be possible, let this cup pass from me." What, then, did the cup contain?

THE CUP FULL OF SUFFERING

The cup, of course, was a symbol of the sufferings that awaited Christ on the Cross. To understand in part the depth of those sufferings we must know something about the Person of our Lord. Jesus was truly God. He had the attributes of God. This truth our Lord revealed through His miracles, in His teachings, and by His omniscience. At the same time He was truly Man. He had a real body and a reasonable soul. Except for sin, His body did not differ from ours. He hungered and felt thirst. In body He grew weary. As someone has stated, "He was capable of being bruised with stripes, torn with scourges, pricked with thorns, pierced with nails, transfixed with a spear."

Part of the cup that Jesus had to drink was the most excruciating physical anguish. Of these bodily sufferings the Psalmist writes: "I am poured out like water, and all my bones are out of joint: my heart is like wax; it is melted within me. My strength is dried up like a potsherd; and my tongue cleaveth to my jaws; and thou hast brought me into the jaws of death. . . . They pierced my hands and my feet" (Psa. 22:14-16). Physical affliction, however, was but a small portion of the cup that confronted Jesus in Gethsemane. Truly, any human soul would shrink from enduring the terrible agonies of crucifixion, but others have suffered in such fashion. The cup of Christ stood for anguish far more intense than physical pain.

To appreciate the awfulness of that bitter cup we must realize that it symbolized sufferings of soul. Jesus possessed a human soul, free from sin. His soul was moved as other souls are moved. Has your soul ever been stirred with pity? His more! Has your soul ever been stung with unjust reproaches? His more! Has your soul ever been taunted with bitter mockery? His more! Has your soul ever been sick through the venomous hatred of evil enemies? His more! Has your soul ever been deadened by the ingratitude of those whom you have benefited? His more! Has your soul ever become faint through the treachery of a trusted friend? His more! Thorns pricked His brow, but reproach and mockery penetrated His soul. Nails pierced His hands and feet, but desertion and treachery by friends entered into His soul. The spear transfixed His side, but the venomous hatred of enemies pierced His heart.

Often we count the wounds on the body of our Lord, but we forget the far more agonizing wounds in His soul. According to the Book of Proverbs, "The spirit of a man will sustain his infirmities: but a wounded spirit who can bear?" (18:14). However, the wounds in the soul of Christ were but a portion of the cup that confronted Him in Gethsemane. Wounds like these are sufficient to make any human soul cry out, "O my Father, if it be possible, let this cup pass away from me." Yet there were sufferings of our Lord in Gethsemane far more intense; yes, infinitely more intense, than sufferings of soul.

Here we enter still more deeply into the mystery of Gethsemane. Here we find the reason for the amazement, the horror, and the deadly sorrow that possessed the soul of Jesus as He beheld the cup in the garden. Here we discover the reason for the sweat of blood. This reason the words of the prophet Isaiah reveal most clearly, "The Lord hath laid on him the iniquity of us all" (53:6c).

THE CUP FULL OF SIN

The cup from which the soul of Jesus shrank with horror was a cup filled with the sin of the world. In that cup were the guilt and the pollution of sin. In that cup He could see the totality of sin, with all its length and width and depth. Just think! The world's sin with all its length and width and depth! One may talk about the brutality of a Joseph Stalin. In that cup was the brutality of a thousand Stalins. One may shrink from the filthiness of a prostitute. In that cup was the filthiness of a thousand prostitutes.

The sin of atheism, of idolatry, of profanity, of Sabbath breaking, of disobedience to parents, of murder, of adultéry, of stealing,
of bearing false witness, and of covetousness—your sins and
mine—they were all in the cup that confronted Jesus in Gethsemane.

A person may well feel oppressed by the weight of his own sin
and guilt. But think about the weight of the whole world's sin
and guilt. All of that sin pressed upon the soul of Christ in the
Garden. As the soul of our Lord sank lower and lower under the
weight of the world's sin, He cried out imploring the Heavenly
Father to remove that cup. While God's love for the world kept
Him from removing the cup, He sent an angel to strengthen His
Son, whose heart was breaking under the terrific load of the
world's sin.

Becoming sin for sinful men, however, was but a portion of the
cup in Gethsemane. There He took upon Himself the sin of the
world, and in His own body He soon would receive the wrath of
God against sin. This truth is portrayed by the prophet Isaiah,
"We did esteem him stricken, smitten of God, and afflicted. . . .
Yet it pleased the Lord to bruise him; he hath put him to grief"
(53:4b,10a). As Paul writes to the Galatians, "Christ has redeemed us from the curse of the law, being made a curse for us."
Here we enter still more deeply into the mystery concerning the
cup in the garden.

THE CUP FULL OF WRATH

God, as it were, did not see His Son but rather saw our sin,
which Christ was soon to bear in His own body on the cursed
tree. In righteousness the Father forsook His Son, and permitted
Him to endure the just punishment for our sins. No wonder that
on the Cross our Lord was to cry out, "Eloi, eloi, lama,
sabachtani?" "My God, my God, why hast thou forsaken me?" In
His wrath against sin God deserted His Son who had taken upon
Himself the sin of the world. All this wrath against sin filled to
overflowing the cup that confronted Christ in Gethsemane. Who
can wonder that He cried out to the Father, imploring Him to
remove the cup full of wrath?

There was one, however, who did not desert Christ in Gethsemane, or on the Cross. That was Satan, the prince of darkness. What tortures Satan inflicted on our Lord at Calvary we do not know. But we can well imagine that the devil would tempt Jesus by insinuating that His death was all in vain. Undoubtedly the devil would point out that the world did not share His concern about sin, and did not desire Him as Redeemer. The bitter mockery of Satan and of those under his control must have caused the cup to overflow. All of this our Lord could see in His vision of the cup in Gethsemane.

THE CUP FULL OF MERCY

In Gethsemane, as on the Cross, one thought sustained the soul of our Dying Redeemer. That one thought was the will of the Father to save men from sin. When Jesus prayed, "Not my will but thine be done," He knew that through His vicarious sufferings on the Cross, the Father willed the salvation of untold multitudes. Not merely hundreds or thousands or even millions, but a multitude that no man could number, a multitude like the stars in the heavens and the sand on the seashore.

It was the love of Christ for sinners that sustained His soul as He beheld the cup full of sin, suffering, and wrath. He knew that the only way the just and holy God could forgive sin was through the atoning Death of His Son on the Cross. In submitting Himself to the will of the Father, Christ manifested His love for us sinners.

In the cup at Gethsemane we behold God's evaluation of sin. To the agonized plea that the Father remove the cup, God had to turn a deaf ear. Though His Beloved Son felt sore amazed, and sorrowful even unto death, God did not remove that cup. He well knew that it was filled to overflowing with sin, shame, suffering, guilt, and wrath. But so great was the love of God for us sinners, and so great was His hatred of our sins, that He allowed His Son to drain the cup to its last bitter dregs. So the cup of Gethsemane gives us at least a glimpse of how our sins appear in the sight of our holy God.

What is your evaluation of your own sins? Do you think that at the end of this life, when you approach the throne of God, you can glibly say to the All-Holy One, "I have sinned; please forgive me"? What! If the living God refused to heed the agonized plea of His Son, do you think that He will grant your plea? If the sight of the agony and the sweat of blood on the face of His dear Son did not move the Father to take away the cup, why should the Lord God give heed to you? Are you more deserving than His Son? Who are you that God should remove the cup full of wrath against your sin?

Ah, but remember the love of God! If you humbly kneel beneath the Cross, and acknowledge that Christ has taken the cup in your stead, then God will forgive your sin, freely, justly, and forever. At the Cross the holiness of God was vindicated, His justice was satisfied, and His love was manifested. The ground of your salvation is that in your stead Christ took the cup full of sin, guilt, and wrath. He did so in order that your sin might be forgiven, and remembered against you no more for ever.

Do not minimize sin, the sin of the world, or the sin of your soul, by thinking that sin can be forgiven without the Saviour's taking for you the dreadful cup. But rejoice in the marvelous love of God the Father and the Son, the love revealed in the cup of Gethsemane.

17. Myron J. Taylor

Myron Jackson Taylor, Church of Christ. Born, Good-
will, W. Va., Mar. 26, 1924. Educated, Johnson Bible
College, Knoxville, Tenn. (A.B.); School of Religion,
Butler University, Indianapolis (B.D.). Pastorates,
rural (1946-58); Boulevard Church of Christ, Toledo,
O., since 1958.

This minister appears here in part because of his youth. To be at
all representative, the volume needs to include sermons from
ministers in various age groups. This young man chooses a striking
text. The message about "A Hill with Three Crosses" rightly
follows the same order as a sermon that F. W. Robertson of
Brighton preached at about the same age, "The Three Crosses of
Calvary." However, the present interpreter got his message from
the Book, and not from the young rector in Brighton.

Why put first the central Cross? Because without it standing
out clearly in view, the other two crosses would have no reason
for appearing in a sermon. If like T. DeWitt Talmage either
young man had begun with one of the other two crosses, he
would have paved the way for anti-climax. In a sermon the climax
is psychological. In the pulpit, as in the Bible, "first" still means
most important, and therefore basic.

Why put toward the end the part about the penitent thief?
Partly because the sermon here follows the order of thesis, antithesis, and synthesis. Also, because the speaker wishes every unsaved hearer to repent, and every believing listener to feel so
thankful for salvation that he will ask his neighbor to accept
the crucified Saviour.

Such a choice of subject gives one reason for hope about the
ministry of tomorrow. In other days, if any editor had thought
of inviting a young pastor (while in a rural church not large) to

submit a sermon for possible inclusion in such a volume, one of us young dunces would have sent in an effusion about the current delusion that every day and in every way the world was growing better and better.

World War I soon punctured our gas balloons. Now it seems that World War II has led many young pastors to start preaching first and most about the Christ of the Cross. "Christ died for the difference between right and wrong." "The Hill with Three Crosses" shows God's attitude toward right and wrong. The two dying thieves make clear the two ways in which a sinner now responds to the appeal of the fountain once opened "for sin and for uncleanness."

> Dear dying Lamb, Thy precious blood
>   Shall never lose its power
> Till all the ransomed Church of God
>   Be saved, to sin no more.

A HILL WITH THREE CROSSES

When they were come to the place, which is called Calvary, there they crucified him, and the malefactors, one on the right hand, and the other on the left.   ST. LUKE 23:33

BEHOLD A HILL with three crosses! Usually we fix our attention on only one, but we ought to remember that there were three crosses. In our own recollection, as in the history of the world, the central Cross stands out alone. But a passerby on that first Good Friday would have carried away a different picture of the crucifixion scene. After walking by the Place of the Skull on that never-to-be-forgotten day, a visitor to Jerusalem would have reported, "Today I witnessed the crucifixion of three men."

"Three lonely crosses on a lonely hill!" What a sight to stir the hearts of men! In the center the Lord Jesus died because He was the Son of God. On either hand died a man because he was a thief. In some respects they all seemed much alike: three men with agonized bodies sagging on pierced hands; three men with raging thirst tormenting them amid heat and dust; three men as a naked spectacle for "scorn to point her slow, unmoving finger at." Those three wooden crosses were much the same, and so were the methods of torture. Ah, but what a difference among the persons on those three crosses!

A hill with three crosses! On the central Cross hung the body of the Lord Jesus. He died lonely, but not alone. According to F. W. Robertson, "There are two kinds of solitude: the first consisting of isolation in space, the other in isolation of spirit." Close beside Him hung the two thieves, neither of whom yet shared His fellowship with the Father, or His vision of a world redeemed. Both of them could share the anguish of the Lord's body, but only one dying thief was ever to know "the joy that was set before him."

"Three crosses on a lonely hill!" On each a man was dying. Each of them has its own distinctive lesson for us to learn today. On the central Cross the Son of God died for sin. On the one hand an impenitent thief died in sin. On the other hand a repentant thief died unto sin. Here is the Gospel in personal pronouns.

THE REDEEMER DYING FOR SIN

First look at the central Cross, on which the Saviour died for sin. This was the Cross of redemption, or as Robertson says, in "the dying hour of devotedness." When we gaze at the central Cross we feel almost ashamed that we belong to the human race, for we had a share in nailing Him to the Cross. In a sense we too spat in His face and thrust a crown of thorns on His brow. By our sins we also led Him to Calvary and left Him there to die "for us men and our salvation."

When we gaze on the central Cross we should look beyond it and up to God. On Calvary we behold so much of His self-revelation that we can receive only a portion of its meaning. As for its total message, that lies far beyond the mental capacity of man:

> For the love of God is broader
> Than the measure of man's mind.

Nevertheless, we ought to live beneath the shadow of the Cross, and thus enter more and more into its meaning.

Why else did the Apostle pen the following words to the Christians of his day? "I bow my knees unto the Father of our Lord Jesus Christ . . . that he would grant you . . . that ye, being rooted and grounded in love, may be able to comprehend with all saints what is the breadth, and length, and depth, and height; and to know the love of Christ, which passeth knowledge" (Eph. 3:14-19)? Here at the central Cross we behold divine "love in four dimensions." In its light from above we see that what took place on that central Cross availed not only for the penitent thief, but for everyone who repents. My friend, let it avail for you.

Someone may ask, rightly, "How could Christ die for me fifty-seven generations before I was born?" To such a wistful question there can be no final answer. How can we on earth enter into the deepest mysteries of God? But this much we know on the human level: any one of us today can reap benefits from the deeds of others who died before he was born. For example, have you ever thought about the use of anesthetics in a major operation? Can you imagine what such an ordeal would be like without the use of anesthesia? Then remember that the change to anesthetics came only a little more than a hundred years ago.

Even to read about old-time amputations and carvings of human flesh causes one to shudder. But today when the physician advises you to undergo surgery you can reply, "Well, at least I'll not feel it." Have you ever thanked God for anesthetics? Remember that they were discovered before you were born, and that they were discovered for you. When at length you face up to your sin as the deadly disease of your soul you will come to see at least a portion of what Christ Jesus did for you on the Cross. Then you will love to sing "Rock of Ages,"

> Be of sin the double cure;
> Cleanse me from its guilt and power.

On the central Cross God showed once for all that He takes our sins seriously. As Paul says, even though Christ was Himself without sin, God "made him to be sin for us . . . that we might be made the righteousness of God in him" (II Cor. 5:21). Without such a strong view of sin, the Atonement would be emptied of nearly all its meaning. When Jesus prayed, "Father, forgive them," by His death He was making possible the way by which that prayer could be answered. If Christ Jesus had not died on that central Cross, all the penitence in the world could not have brought that sinner to paradise. Our redemption consists in reconciliation with God, not merely in renunciation of the world. "God was in Christ, reconciling the world unto Himself." To believe in the forgiveness of sins without reference to the Cross would mean thinking that God does not take sin seriously.

On that hill of crucifixion everything had to do with that central Cross. So it ought to be in your heart and life. In that central Cross you can find power to shake your life to its very roots, and then to bring repentance. Here you can find God, not angry or hurt so much as grieved because of your separation from Him. Remember too that Christ died, not that God might begin loving you, but because He has always loved you. Behold in that Cross the act of divine love to overcome the sin on every side. Remember too that Atonement for sin requires perfect holiness and perfect obedience. Therefore, in that central Cross you can find your only hope for time and eternity.

THE THIEF DYING IN SIN

In the second place let us consider the cross on which a man died in sin. This was the cross of impenitence and rebellion. As a thief he had lived, and as a thief he would die. He had spent his life in taking for himself what others had earned by their toil. At death he would end his days still in rebellion against the laws of God and men, "having no hope, and without God in the world."

We may wonder by what pathway this man had come to his cross. Did he grow up in a pious home where his mother prayed that he would become good and useful? Perchance did evil companions lead him astray? Or did he come from a vile hovel, and learn to steal almost as soon as he could toddle? About such things we cannot tell, though we know that a vile home today tends to produce sinners. The sacred record has to do with his sin and impenitence, not with his heredity and environment. Hence we know that he was steeped in sin, coarsened by crime, and hardened by hatred, so that he persisted in rebellion against God.

On a wooden cross this man was suffering the penalty for his crimes. He was dying in sin. To the very end he remained impenitent and bitter. On the central Cross the impenitent thief could see the Lord Jesus and hear His prayer of pardon for those who had hounded Him to death. The poor wretch could look on the women who were weeping, and hear the mournful cry of the bereaved mother. Still he could mouth the foulest aspersions. Even in the hour of death his heart knew no softening; his lips uttered no word of regret; his cheek felt no tears of repentance and remorse.

Among the objects of his scorn, the chief one was Jesus Himself. "One of the malefactors which were hanged railed on him, saying, 'If thou be Christ, save thyself and us' " (Luke 23:39). Evidently he knew something about Jesus, but at two points he was mistaken. First, he addressed Jesus with an "if." "If thou be Christ." To approach Christ with an "if" means not to come in faith. With an "if" Satan had tempted our Lord three times early in His ministry. With an "if" the impenitent thief was joining in the chorus of enemies who had led Christ to the Cross, "If thou be the king of the Jews, save thyself" (Luke 23:37).

The second mistake of the impenitent thief was in trying to dictate terms of salvation. "Save thyself and us." He had vague ideas about the sort of salvation he wanted, and about the way it should be attained. He wanted to be saved from death so that he could go back to his thieving. Such a mistaken attitude is common today. Often the best of us forget that Christ has not promised to save us from our crosses. Through the Cross, by His Cross, but not from our crosses! "If any man will come after me, let him deny himself, and take up his cross daily, and follow me" (Luke 9:23).

Many today live in rebellion against God. W. E. Sangster tells of a mother who has lost her only child, a girl of six. This woman accuses God and declares war against heaven. In desperation she goes to the cabinet where the little girl kept her toys. Throwing open the door, the mother allows the toys to spill out over the floor. Waving her hands over them she sobs, again and again. This woman lives with an open wound that only God can heal, and she will not look up to Him. In her heart there will always be a scar, but there need not be a festering sore. Her burden is one of rebellion.

THE THIEF DYING TO SIN

On the third cross a man died to sin. This was the cross of repentance. He too had been a thief, and he knew that he was punished justly. But even at the dying hour he looked on the Lord Jesus, and his heart was "strangely warmed." Perhaps for the first time in all his life he began to see things in their true light.

First of all, in the presence of the dying Redeemer this other thief admitted the justice of his sufferings and death. Speaking to the other thief, this one asked, "Dost thou not fear God, seeing thou art in the same condemnation? And we indeed justly; for we receive the due reward of our deeds: but this man hath done nothing amiss" (Luke 23:40,41). How difficult it is for a stubborn heart to acknowledge its own sin!

This dying thief called on Jesus but he made no demands. However, he did humbly request a gift of mercy. "Lord, remember me when thou cometh into thy kingdom." This man dying to sin must have seen in the Lord Jesus something not of this world. He had watched Jesus being nailed to the Cross, and as he heard the strokes of the hammer he had seen the blood stream forth. But from those lips the dying thief did not hear any such curses as were customary on Calvary. Rather did he hear a prayer for pardon, a prayer that "shivered the sky and thrust itself into his soul," as nothing had ever done through all his years. "Father, forgive them; for they know not what they do."

In response to his own humble cry of faith the penitent thief received a promise infinitely precious. "Today shalt thou be with me in paradise." He found that in Christ there was hope for any man, no matter what he had done, if only he truly repented. He discovered that while Roman power had done all it could do, having nailed him to the cross, there was another throne, higher by far than that of Caesar. That higher throne was the Throne of Grace. Through the Christ of the Cross the penitent thief found access to the Heavenly Father who would extend mercy to the weakest and the worst of men. On the "day of the Cross" he beheld the fountain that has been opened "for sin and for uncleanness" (Zech. 13:1).

> The dying thief rejoiced to see
> That fountain in his day;
> And there may I, as vile as he,
> Wash all my sins away.

"There is joy in heaven over one sinner that repenteth." And there was joy in the heart of the dying Redeemer. Have you ever paused to consider what the conversion of the penitent thief meant to Christ on the Cross? Forsaken by the disciples and serving as the butt of mockery by rulers, cast out by leaders of the Church and spat upon by jeering mobs, the sinless Son of God hung there on the Cross, surrounded by howling mobs. Then suddenly there came this shaft of light, this flash of glory, when the dying sinner beheld His redeeming Kingship, and flung himself upon divine mercy. Once Christ had said, "I, if I be lifted up from the earth, will draw all men unto me" (John 12:32). Now at last He was lifted up, and the first of countless sinners looked to Him for pardon, cleansing, and peace.

Oh, the joy of the dying Redeemer, joy in the midst of His anguish on the Cross! Here is a lesson for each of us. Part of a man's work on earth he may do with strength and vigor, but much of it he may accomplish only "through peril, toil, and pain." As long as God has anything more for him to suffer, a man's work on earth is not yet complete. Through eyes full of agony the penitent thief first beheld the face of his Redeemer. Through suffering, accepted by faith and borne with patience, there are lessons that we can learn in no other way. If we would let Him do so, doubtless God would teach in those other ways, but all too often the stubborn heart refuses and resists. So God lets us suffer.

THE PERSON WHO SUFFERS TODAY

On the Cross the righteous will of God had to be revealed through the sufferings of Christ, and also through the sufferings of the penitent thief. The same principle holds true today. For instance, consider the sufferings that come through war. God tells us that war is unspeakably terrible, and that it is against His holy will. But the mass of people, with minds set on selfish gain and pleasure, treat lightly all His warnings against the sinfulness of war. They refuse to believe God, and to repent. It may be that blasted cities and mangled bodies will force into our minds the fearful truth about this form of sin.

And yet suffering never proves to be in vain if it leads to sincere repentance. Often it is the consciousness of defeat and frustration, of sin and suffering, that makes us aware how much we need God. When our self-sufficiency is fatally wounded, our pride is humbled, and our defenses are down. Then through the breach of our humiliation God leads us to repentance. The Cross of penitence is for you, and if repentance comes through suffering, then rejoice in that suffering.

Repentance during the last moments of life is by no means probable. But blessed be God, such dying repentance is never impossible! "There has been one Bible case of 'death-bed repentance' that no one may despair, and only one, that no person may presume." In the hour of greatest need the Saviour hears the cry of the worst sinner in the world. He is waiting to hear you now. Wherever you stand in the stream of life, whatever your surroundings and your sins, if in penitence and obedience you call upon Christ, He has promised to hear and to forgive. As an example you have the dying thief to whom the Blessed Lord said, "Today shalt thou be with me in paradise."

You can look to Christ with complete confidence. You can rest secure that He will meet every need, because His sacrifice for sin is complete. Once forgiven and cleansed, you need only surrender to Him, and live to do His will. Do not be led astray by those who tell you that after death you will need the cleansing of purgatorial fires in order to complete the work of Christ on the Cross. By faith He is all you need. "Ye are complete in Christ." If by faith you are in Christ, there remains no more condemnation for sins. Behold He stands before you now, your Friend and your Helper, your Saviour and your Lord. All this you learn anew beneath the shadow of that central Cross.

18. John M. Gordon

John Manning Gordon, United Presbyterian, grandson
of the well-known Boston Baptist, Adoniram J. Gordon. Born, Atlanta, Ga., Jan. 19, 1913. Educated, Col-
gate University (A.B.); Princeton Seminary (Th.B.).
Pastorates (1935-49); First Church, Lancaster, Pa., assistant (1949-52), pastor since 1952.

*The lay officers report that the dominie's sermons, already
strong, have kept improving of late. The minister gives the credit
largely to the people. Amid many other activities twelve "Home
Bible Study" groups, socially congenial, gather once a week to
study informally the passage from which he will preach on the
coming Lord's Day. Each group consists of twelve persons or a
few more, many of them young married folk, until recently not
actively concerned about such matters. Sitting in comfortable
chairs they engage in discussion, note-taking, and other such
procedures as one would expect from educated young adults
approaching by far the best of the world's "Great Books."*

*At morning worship these Bible students listen eagerly to find
out which part of their golden passage the minister will select,
and what he will do with it. Evidently the plan arouses, encourages, and sustains curiosity. "Now therefore we are all here
present in the sight of God, to hear all that you have been com-
manded of God" (Acts 10:33). With more than a hundred fifty of
the younger adults present to serve as leaven, the entire congregation doubtless feels a new concern about the meaning and value
of the Bible sermon. The pastor also feels a new sense of urgency
and joy in preparing to preach, and in delivering his message.
Such "cooperative" Bible preaching has untold possibilities for the
kind of blessing that always comes through intelligent use of
God's written Word.*

The plan is subject to no patent or copyright. If adopted else-where it would need to be modified, according to local conditions. In many places on Easter other things good in their way tend to give the preaching of the Gospel a limited place, often secondary, and that when more people attend than on any other day in the year. Under such conditions, with a host of "occasional hearers" not accustomed to doctrinal sermons, a minister could not deal thoughtfully with three major "dimensions of the Easter message." On the other hand, when people co-operate with their pastor in prior study of his Bible chapter, or other passage, they evidently come to church prepared to relish and digest the kind of strong pulpit fare that their grandparents enjoyed under H. P. Liddon or Robert William Dale, Adoniram J. Gordon or John A. Broadus.

THREE DIMENSIONS OF THE EASTER MESSAGE

"In fact Christ has been raised from the dead, the first fruits of those who have fallen asleep. For as by a man came death, by a man has come also the resurrection from the dead. For as in Adam all die, so also in Christ shall all be made alive. But each in his own order: Christ the first fruits, then at his coming those who belong to Christ. Then comes the end, when he delivers the kingdom to God the Father after destroying every rule and every authority and power."   I COR. 15:20-24

IF ANYONE PRESENT intends to sit back and challenge the speaker to prove that the Resurrection of Christ is a fact, not a fable, the speaker will have to disappoint that person. Though I too have had my share of questions and doubts about the miraculous element in the Bible, there seems to me to be conclusive evidence to show that Paul was right when he wrote (1) that if Christ did not rise from the dead Christianity would be foolishness; and (2) that He assuredly did rise from the dead.

If we do not spend time this Easter morning marshaling arguments for the Resurrection of Christ, it is not because we consider the question of historical fact unimportant, but because the time now is limited, and also because we feel that such matters are best considered in free, two-way discussion. If anyone with serious doubts and a reasonably open mind wishes to be assured that the Resurrection was a real event in history, he may telephone for an interview, or else let us lend him a book.

What we have time for this Easter morning is giving our attention to a convinced first-century Christian. Let us ask him what there is in the Gospel of the Resurrection that will make us better Christians, clearer in our thinking, and more courageous in our living. Taking as our text these verses from Paul's mighty Resurrection Chapter, our answer falls into three dimensions, sharply defined. In the word of the Apostle three stages, logical as well as chronological, speak to us in turn about the authority of Christ, the dignity of man, and the destiny of the world.

I. THE AUTHORITY OF CHRIST

"In fact, Christ has been raised from the dead." First let us be sure that we understand what the word "Resurrection" means as we read it in our Bibles. It is not to be confused with "immortality," which is a much more general and less controversial term. The New Testament does not settle for the immortality of our Lord: that His soul lived on after death, and that His name will always be enshrined in memory as that of a mighty prophet and teacher. The Resurrection applies specifically to His coming out of the tomb bodily, thus leaving that tomb empty, except for His grave-clothes.

That was His body transformed, with strange and wonderful powers, apparently new. Still it was the body of Christ. He could ask Thomas to touch His wound-prints. He could eat the fish that Peter had caught. His voice vibrated in their ears, not

only for a tantalizing moment, but for days that lengthened
into weeks, as He instructed them in the Scriptures. To talk
about the Resurrection of our Lord, as if it simply meant that
His soul lived on, is to use language inaccurately. His empty
tomb and His frequent, unmistakable appearances cleared up
completely any doubts the disciples had entertained about His
earlier predictions that He would be crucified and would rise
from the dead. On that first Easter Day they knew that they had
seen the Lord, not His ghost, but Himself.

So much for definition. Let us go on to declaration. The introduction of Paul's letter to Rome tells us that Christ "was declared to be the Son of God with power by the resurrection
from the dead." In the Greek this word "power" may often be
translated "authority." His Resurrection convinced His disciples
of His authority. If His body had remained in the tomb, they
might still have believed in His immortality, but little more so
than with any prophet or teacher of their past history. They
might have continued to believe in the coming Kingdom of
God, which earlier prophets had been foretelling from remotest
times, but they would have had no real assurance that it was
the King Himself who had visited and redeemed His people.

"We thought that it was he that should have redeemed Israel"
(Lu. 24:21). "Another prophet, another postponement! A prophet
indeed, but no Redeemer!" So the two Emmaus travelers feel on
the afternoon of the first Easter Day. But Jesus first convinces
them from Scripture that the Messiah-King had to suffer and
die. Then, as He breaks bread with them at the supper table, He
shows them the unique outcome of that predicted Death. He is
not merely another seer; He is the only Saviour. He is not a
martyr, but their Master! When He spoke from the Cross, "It is
finished," He was not announcing defeat, but triumph.

Some of us, I'm afraid, think of God as we think of a minister:
as a person to be respected, but not taken seriously, a rather
pathetic symbol of the way things might be if life were not so
strenuous. At times we ministers contribute to such an impression by representing God in an apologetic fashion. In our sermons
we say, "What a wonderful world this would be if everyone were a
Christian!" "How much better things would be if Christians

would give God a little more time, money, and attention!" Such plaintive, pessimistic pleadings with people to do God a few favors indicate that we ministers often raise the sort of question that recently came from a teen-age girl. In the Northfield School during a class on religion, according to Professor Rachel King, this girl asked: "Are we supposed to believe that Christianity is the way God wishes things were, or the way they are?"

Was Jesus only an idealist who ran into the brutal facts of life, and showed us once again how impractical it is to be a saint, or even a nonconformist? If He had remained in the tomb, we might still wonder. But since He did not, since His body did not remain there after Easter morning, since He was "declared to be the Son of God with power by the resurrection from the dead," we can accept Christianity as the realism of God.

You recall an incident early in our Lord's ministry. Facing a man who was paralyzed He said, "Your sins are forgiven!" Then His critics whispered one to another. "Words are cheap," they sneered. Reading their thoughts, Jesus answered, "that you may know that the Son of man has authority on earth to forgive sins, 'Rise, take up your pallet, and go home.'" That was no stroke of luck, no feat of magic. That miracle showed the kind of authority He then had, and still has.

Whether or not we recognize His divine authority makes all the difference in the way we respond to the various words that He speaks to us through the New Testament, whether words of comfort or of command. Do His words merely tell us the way God wishes things were? No, they announce to us how things are. Christianity is God's realism. Do you accept Jesus Christ as your final Authority in this world and the next? If not, give heed to the Easter message, and especially to this first dimension, which is the declaration of Christ's authority. Notice also—

II. THE DIGNITY OF MAN

"Christ the first fruits, then at his coming those who belong to Christ." It is clear from our text, and clearer still from the chapter as a whole, that in the thinking of Paul the Resurrection of our Lord was inseparable from the later resurrection of Christian believers. "Christ the first fruits"—a characteristically Hebrew figure of speech. In Hebrew worship a farmer would bring to the Temple the first ripening stalks of grain, as a thankful forecast of the total harvest yet to come.

In this passage the Apostle's reasoning is not about the question of whether or not Christ rose from the dead. Because of first-hand experience, that was an indisputable conviction of the New Testament. Paul wrote this chapter primarily to counter the influence of Greek speculative philosophy, which said, "The body is unimportant. At death, like a husk it is going to be discarded. Christ's Resurrection is only a parable about the transmutation of man's soul." "Wait a minute," says Paul. "Of course it is a kind of parable, but it is also a glorious prophecy of what shall be when Christ returns."

His resurrection body, Paul is saying, serves as a guarantee of resurrection for our bodies. It is also an illustration of what our resurrection life will be. The Bible does not tell us much in detail about our future life, doubtless for the same reason that one does not inform a little child about international diplomacy, brief him about the ways of business, or delineate for him the bliss of married life. But two things the New Testament does clearly affirm for our comfort.

One is that for the Christian the life to come will mean to be with Him. "Let not your heart be troubled: ye believe in God, believe also in me. In my Father's house are many mansions: if it were not so I would have told you. I go to prepare a place for you. And if I go and prepare a place for you, I will come again, and receive you unto myself; that where I am, there ye shall be also" (John 14:1-3).

The other affirmation is that for a Christian the life to come will mean to be like Him. "Beloved, now are we the sons of God, and it doth not yet appear what we shall be: but we know that, when he shall appear, we shall be like him; for we shall see him as he is" (1 John 3:2). These promises all clearly assume that in the final Day I shall still be I, and that you will be you. Not reincarnation, but resurrection, is ours to expect.

"For we know that if the earthly tent we live in is destroyed, we have a building from God, a house not made with hands, eternal in the heavens. Here indeed we groan, and long to put on our heavenly dwelling, so that by putting it on we may not be found naked. For while we are still in this tent, we sigh with anxiety; not that we would be unclothed, but that we would be further clothed, so that what is mortal may be swallowed up by life"(II Cor. 5:1-4).

Let us freely grant that there are obvious difficulties in using the Resurrection of Christ as an example of what will be our future experience. The most obvious, perhaps, is the fact that only a scant three days passed between the time He died on the Cross and the hour when His body left the tomb. According to the common reckoning, only about forty hours elapsed. With Him it was the identical body that was transformed, and came triumphantly out of the place where it had been laid. For us it is not to be the literal rising from our coffins, else what would be the plight of those who have been cremated, or lost at sea?

An interesting observation about the New Testament miracles comes from George Macdonald. "The miracles of Jesus," he writes, "were the ordinary works of His Father, wrought small and swift, that we might take them in." Well said! In five minutes the miracle of the loaves accomplished what the farmer and the miller now take a year to do. In forty hours the miracle of our Lord's Resurrection demonstrated what will occur for us at the end of history. The Resurrection telescoped time in order to show us what God intends to do for us when time issues in eternity.

The real problem about the resurrection of our bodies is not, I feel convinced, one of mechanics. The problem is in our own mean minds, in our perverse prejudice against the Bible teaching that our bodies are to be temples, not prisons. Sometimes we have a like prejudice against the home church, even such a lovely temple as the one in which we worship today. On the brightest morning of spring we may grumble, "Do we have to go to church?" To our confused minds the very church attendance that is meant of God to give us wings may seem like a weight to hold us down.

The trouble of course is sin. Sin is the rebellious self-centeredness that perverts so many of God's noblest gifts. In one of his books C. S. Lewis has a striking allegory about a man on earth as he appears to those in heaven. This man's spirit carries perched on his shoulder an ugly, leech-like lizard, which represents his body, burdensome and degrading. Then by a supreme and terrific act of will he lets the Lord's good angel get his hands on that lizard. It screams and dies. Immediately in its place there is a tremendous white, winged horse, upon which the man leaps and rides out over the universe. This allegory, also, telescopes things. The surrendering of our wills to Christ may come through a lifelong process. The transforming of our bodies from dead weights into soaring wings is likewise a process that begins when we are born again, and will not be complete until the Resurrection Day.

Such is the prospect: a body like unto Christ's own glorious body, with wonderful enhanced powers, and all with complete responsiveness to the command of our spirits. The Resurrection of Jesus Christ gives us an inkling of what we shall be: spirit and body, perfectly wedded, gloriously partnered. So instead of hating our bodies, and looking on them as enemies, we may cherish for them the loftiest hopes. Like the little boy striding along beside his older brother, a star athlete, we are in close relation with the Living Christ. The little fellow may seem to be mostly head and stomach, with narrow shoulders and rubbery legs. Still he muses, as he looks at his brother, "That's what I'll be some day!" So he squares his shoulders, and starts to attain his dreams.

The ancient Greeks, who seemed to gloat in the physique beautiful, inwardly despised their bodies. The early Christians, who were other-worldly in outlook, often felt that godliness was more important that bodily exercise. Nonetheless, they believed in the nobility and preciousness of the entire human person. The Greeks saw only the temporal, but the Christians also had a glimpse of the eternal. They longed, not to be unclothed, but to be clothed upon.

Here is good news for the ill, the crippled, the unattractive, and even those of us well equipped physically, who wish we could be much more skillful and versatile with body and brain. Some day we shall be, for we shall share with Christ in the bodily benefits of the Resurrection. Such is the potential dignity of man, with sinless spirit and flawless body, indivisible, according to the design of God, as He has shown in the Resurrection of Jesus Christ. Note once again—

III. THE DESTINY OF THE WORLD

"Then comes the end, when he delivers the kingdom to God the Father after destroying every rule and every authority and power" (v. 24). In English as in Greek we have two quite different ways of using this word "end." It may mean the termination, the finish, the ceasing of existence. Or it may mean the object, the purpose, the goal towards which we aim, as when a worldly man says, "The end justifies the means." "To this end was I born," says Jesus, in speaking of His life purpose. "The end, everlasting life," is Paul's way of describing the destiny of God's children.

There are the same two ways of thinking about the end of the world. For some it is the cessation of all life and meaning in our planet, with its final transient denizens either scorched or else deep frozen, a grim outcome that scientists tell us may be after a million years or more! But for Christians, as for the Bible, the end of the world means "the one far-off divine event, to which the whole creation moves," the Commencement Exercises when our adolescent world will be graduated to a higher level of constructive maturity.

To be sure there are in every school some for whom the entire course seems to be purposeless. "Dad, bless his heart, is paying the bills. Since he contributes generously to the alumni fund, I'm not likely to be expelled. Let us eat, drink, and be merry now, because after Commencement the picnic will be over, and at best there will be nothing ahead but the gloomy necessity of earning a living!" We have, I'm afraid, hosts of people whose balancing of time and eternity is like that. "Heaven, if there is such a place, sounds frightfully dull. The Kingdom of God, if it ever arrives on earth, is going to be a sort of endless Puritan Sabbath when the blue laws that Christians have been trying to foist upon us gayer folk will all be enforced!" For many persons the end of the world, if not the end of existence as we know it, means the end of life as we like it.

But the message of the Resurrection, as Paul here applies it to the destiny of the world, is exactly the opposite. Listen again to the words that conclude our text: "Then comes the end, when he delivers the kingdom to God the Father after destroying every rule and every authority and power. For he must reign until he has put all his enemies under his feet. The last enemy to be destroyed is death." Listen also to the cosmic expectation in Romans: "The creation waits with eager longing for the revealing of the sons of God; for the creation was subject to futility, not of its own will but by the will of him who subjected it in hope; because the creation itself will be set free from its bondage of decay, and obtain the glorious liberty of the sons of God" (8:19-21).

When by man sin entered the world, a monkey wrench was thrown into the machinery of the world. When Jesus died upon the Cross the whole creation was shaken to its foundations. Men saw and almost felt the gross darkness. They paled as the earth shook. There were strange tales about the apparitions of dead men and of angels. The curtain of the Temple was ripped from top to bottom. These are not fantastic embroideries; they are appropriate concomitants of the Christian conviction that the Death of Christ meant cosmic tragedy. Contrariwise, His Resurrection meant a cosmic triumph. From one end of the universe to the other there were shouts of joy and symphonies of praise, the sort of exultation that John heard in his vision on the Isle of Patmos, and wrote down in the Book of Revelation:

> Then I looked, and I heard around the throne and the living creatures and the elders the voice of many angels, numbering myriads and thousands of thousands, saying with a loud voice, "Worthy is the Lamb who was slain, to receive power and wealth and might and glory and blessing!" And I heard every creature in heaven and on earth and under the earth and in the sea, and all therein, saying. "To him who sits upon the throne and to the Lamb, be blessing and honor and glory and might for ever and ever" (Rev. 5:11-13)!

The echoes of Patmos sound forth in the mighty music of Handel's *Messiah,* with its hallelujah upon hallelujah, like bank upon bank of cloud-like majesty. Write all of this off as ecstatic speech and poetic fancy, if you will, but to me it is the best answer, in fact, the only answer, to the scary headlines of our atomic age. From beginning to end the Bible talks about God's plan for His universe. "Behold I create new heavens and a new earth, in which dwelleth righteousness," says the Lord. The new heavens and earth will be as much better than the old as the resurrection body is to be better than the one that we now wear. There is no need to fear the annihilation of mankind. No need to quail when evil strides rampant over the earth, and flashes through the air. The Resurrection of Christ foretells God's final triumph, in which His own shall have a glorious part.

These are three dimensions of the Easter message. It speaks of Christ's authority, of man's dignity, and of the world's destiny. Whether this holy day will be to you a message with these dimensions, or merely a time for religious nostalgia, tinged with spring fever, depends on whether or not you have walked with Jesus as a learner, and at length have yielded to Him as a disciple. It was through no accident, and no historical evasion, that His Resurrection appearances were only to disciples. Today those who are committed to Him morally and spiritually are those who see in Him eternal realities. If you are now willing to do His will, you shall know the Resurrection doctrine, that it is of God.

19. Philip E. Hughes

Philip Edgcumbe Hughes, Church of England. Born, Sydney, Australia, Apr. 4, 1915. Educated, University of London, (B.D.); University of Capetown, S. Africa, (M.A., LL.D.). Formerly Vice Principal, Tyndale Hall, Bristol; Lecturer in Theology, University of Bristol (1947-52); Secretary, Church Society, London (1953-55). Now Lecturer, Parish of Mortlake, London. Member, learned societies. Books include: Revive Us Again (1946); The Divine Plan for Jew and Gentile (1949); Platonism and the New Testament (1950); Scripture and Myth (1956); The Biblical Doctrine of Baptism, by Pierre Marcel (transl., 1953); in preparation, commentary on II Corinthians, International Series.

The sermon about "The Reforming of a Skeptic" was preached this year at the International Reformed Congress in Strasbourg, France. Back of the message lies the experience of one who has worked in university circles and understands the doubts of many a thoughtful, educated man today. The nature of the assembly in France doubtless led to the choice of subject, and influenced the treatment, especially at the end of the sermon. The discussion throughout shows how a present-day Christian scholar meets an intelligent skeptic on his own ground, and deals with him in the light of Holy Scripture. In other circles, at least on our side of the water, a pastor may have to follow a less difficult course. Still he can learn much from this sermon. So can the layman who often wonders how to deal with a case of honest doubt.

The London divine turns at once to a Bible case. Instead of confusing the picture by looking at a procession of Bible characters who voiced skepticism, the sermon deals with only one case. Unlike most American preachers, this man follows the Bible, which seldom employs confusing plural pronouns in describing one person. Even though Thomas was a twin, he did *his own doubting. In dealing with him our Lord did not once say "we." He had no doubts. The discussion at Strasbourg delved down deep into the folly of the skeptic's practical philosophy, his blindness in ignoring facts in the Bible, and his way of escape by coming face to face with the Risen Christ.*

Thank God, it is still intellectually respectable to believe in the Resurrection of our Crucified Lord, and therefore in His Deity!

THE REFORMING OF A SKEPTIC

"My Lord and my God!"—ST. JOHN 20:28

THIS FAMOUS testimony of St. Thomas is essentially the confession of a reformed skeptic. I mean that up until this moment his view of Christ, and consequently his confession of Christ, has been faulty. Despite the fact that during the preceding years of our Lord's ministry Thomas had been a member of the privileged inner circle of twelve disciples, and had witnessed His mighty deeds of grace, the previous confession of this young follower has been inadequate.

According to the flesh (II Cor. 5:16), Thomas had known Christ intimately. But he had not yet by faith penetrated to the truth revealed in the Master's words and actions, yet veiled by His human form, the truth of His theanthropic Person as the Messiah. This disciple's view of Christ, accordingly, needed reform, and the principles by which it was reformed were precisely identical with those principles that led to the mighty Protestant Reformation of doctrine and worship in the sixteenth century.

Thomas is the natural skeptic of this world. Like most skeptics of every age, no doubt he prided himself on his caution and sense of detachment. Even when his close friends and fellow-disciples brought him the joyful news that Jesus had risen from the dead, and had shown Himself alive to the other disciples, Thomas withheld belief in their testimony. "Except I shall see in his hands the print of the nails," he declared, "and put my finger into his side, I will not believe." To most people, as to Thomas, this attitude would appear to be reasonable, even commendable. Does not the old saying affirm that "seeing is believing"? Why then should anyone condemn young Thomas for refusing to believe what he had not seen?

THE UNREASONABLENESS OF THE SKEPTIC

In fact the attitude of Thomas is anything but reasonable. It is unreasonable, first of all, because it involves the assumption that he himself is the center of reality. What he himself has not yet perceived he dismisses as unreal. What he has not yet experienced he cannot regard as authentic. In effect, if not in purpose, he is an "existentialist." His world is a world of subjectivity. The only truth he admits is that of his own limited experience. Inasmuch as historical facts and doctrinal propositions are objectively defined, and outside himself, to him they lack significance and authority. Even the contemporary testimony of eyewitnesses well known to him cannot claim his belief. For him the only valid history is his own experience: "Except I shall see . . . I will not believe."

The indefensibility of this position becomes clear when we remember that God the Creator, and not man His creature, is the center of all reality. By his very constitution as a creature formed in the image of God, every man ought to know that God alone is the supreme and all-embracing reality. But someone may object: "Man is no longer as God created him; he has fallen away from God and into sin." That is true, but still man has not by constitution ceased to be a creature of God. Though marred by sin, the divine image in man has not been deleted, and can never be effaced. Indeed, the very sin whereby the image of God has been marred is precisely the revolt of man against the conscious and constitutional knowledge of his own creature-hood.

In its essence sin is the rebellion of the creature against the Creator. It is insubordination and insurrection, involving at its heart repudiation of the creature-Creator relationship. Sin is not merely ignorance of the truth; it is suppression of the truth. Sinful man knows the truth about God, but wickedly rebels against that knowledge, and even seeks to destroy it (Rom. 1:18-32). He wishes to be as God (Gen. 3:5), to usurp God's place at the center of reality, and to escape from the objectivity of God. Man would escape into the stronghold of his own subjectivity, which exalts itself against the knowledge of God. In doing so he plumbs the very depths of unreason and folly.

THE SECOND ERROR OF THE SKEPTIC

The attitude of Thomas is unreasonable because it assumes that he himself is the center point of reality. It is unreasonable, also, because he wishes to make himself the final judge of what is possible and what is not. To maintain a thoroughgoing subjective position the skeptic finds impracticable, because he cannot deny that there is an objective world outside and beyond himself. He observes that, quite independently of himself and his presence, the objective world displays an unmistakable regularity and orderliness. Even the stoutest skeptic cannot gainsay such universal commonplaces as the sequence of day and night, summer and winter, seedtime and harvest, birth and growth. On the innate presupposition that this world is an ordered whole he is able to discover nature's "laws," and in some measure to harness its forces. This ability is in itself evidence that the image of God is still a dynamic reality of his constitution.

However unintentionally, skeptical Thomas here represents the "natural man" (I Cor. 2:14). He knows that this whole world system functioned before his birth and that it will continue to do so after his death. To him this consideration seems humiliating. By way of compensation he seeks to assert himself in the face of this objective world, to which he belongs, but which is independent of him. His self-assertion takes the form of attempting to superimpose his subjectivity upon the world's objectivity.

Having placed himself, as he supposes, at the center of reality, and looking on himself as God, it remains for him to assign the limits of possibility. To do so he must assume that there is in the world nothing incomprehensible to him. The natural order, he argues, is governed by certain fixed and discernible laws, in terms of which, when once discovered, every event and every fact are fully explicable. In his eyes this objective natural order of things is the sacrosanct domain of science, within which there is neither place nor need for the concept of God. It is a closed system, with man, not God, at the controls.

But what of death, that unavoidable frustrater of all human ability and self-adequacy? Does not death, by its awful inexorableness, and by its extinction of every faculty, sit in judgment upon every pretension of man to self-sufficiency? Death is indeed the supreme problem and the insurmountable obstacle of the "natural man." It is the point at which his proud subjectivity is laid low and annihilated. In the face of this black objectivity, how is he ever to assert himself? How can he impose his subjectivity upon that by which it is terminated?

At most, the skeptic can but adopt the pathetic and irrational existential device of "passionately choosing" that over which he has no control: the inevitability of his own death; the final encounter with nothing and non-being. At least, he must "explain" death as a law of nature, and quite simply as part of the natural order. He must affirm his "knowledge" that dead persons do not rise to live again, that death is final, and that resurrection must be classified among the things that are impossible. Whatever its implications, this conclusion, if true, would rule out the possibility of a resurrection unto judgment. That is a possibility, more than any other, of which the "natural man" would like to be rid.

THE FOLLY OF IGNORING THE BEYOND

Things, however, are not so simple as the self-centered skeptic would like them to be. Even while he makes himself the center of reference, turn where he will, there is always the fact of a "beyond." He has taken the stand that to him all things are comprehensible, and that if given time he can understand all

things. But in fact he finds that there are many things he is
unable to comprehend and explain. His knowledge is limited.
His horizon is restricted. There are mysteries and "unknowns."
There is also the future, that vast beyond, subject to no laws of
nature, ungovernable by men, and unpredictable. To the human
eye, the "beyond" is the domain of chance, in which anything may
happen.

Thomas the skeptic, however, does not flatly deny the possibility of anything so "abnormal" as a resurrection. He is willing
to affirm that death is a part of the closed natural order of
things. But at the same time he is unable to disengage himself
from his own inner subjectivity, and from the mysterious "beyond" that encircles and stifles his would-be self-sufficiency. Suppose, after all, that he should happen to see the risen Jesus. Then
in accordance with his subjective principles, he would have to
admit into the sacred pantheon of his authentic experiences even
resurrection from the dead.

There is always a chance, the "natural man" argues, that the
apparently impossible may take place. The sequence of events in
history, he thinks, is not predetermined, but is subject to fortui-
tous and unpredictable collisions of entities and interactions of
circumstances. In other words, he feels compelled to find in the
universal system an aspect of openness. Has he not learned from
"modern science" that in the remote and unexaminable past
life originated from lifeless matter by a million-to-one chance?
Is he not instructed that ever since the far-distant beginning life
in all its wonderful and ordered variety has developed and ad-
vanced by random mutations, which fit into no pattern and
obey no laws? Therefore it seems that the supposed impossibility
of a resurrection must become a possibility.

Thus the "natural man" postulates a world that is both closed
and open: closed to intervention "from above," or "from without"; but open to the unknown future within. In his endeavors
at any cost to preserve a picture of the universe as a self-contained
system of which he is the center, the skeptic is dogged both by
contradiction and futility. He has projected a world of both
fixed laws and sovereign chance, in which possibility and impossibility are both absolute and relative concepts. In short, he is

unable either to be consistently subjective or consistently objective.

Inconsistency and contradiction, indeed, are characteristic of the thinking and the whole position of fallen man. Unfortunately, the same holds true of many professing Christians, who to a larger or smaller degree permit unscriptural modes of thought to control their outlook. As a professing Christian the modern Thomas has little option but to attempt to rationalize the inconsistency of his position by taking refuge in the irrationalism of dialectical theology. He tries to adopt a simultaneous "Yes-and-No" attitude foreign to the teachings of Christ, and subject to the warnings of Paul (II Cor. 1:17-20).

THE BLINDNESS OF THE SKEPTIC

Let us consider how seriously Thomas' appraisal of the situation was at fault when his fellow disciples reported to him that they had actually encountered the risen Christ. It should be sufficient to recall that even while Thomas was withholding belief in the Resurrection, Christ nonetheless and in fact was alive from the dead. Therefore Thomas was totally wrong in the conclusion to which his thinking had led him. His wrongness was due to his having failed, quite inexcusably, to take into account certain important facts well known to him. They were facts, we may presume, which he had no conscious intention of ignoring. This indicates how easy it is for the mind even of Christ's follower to be conditioned by the thinking of the "natural man."

Among the facts that Thomas at this point overlooked, the first and the most fundamental was the fact of God. As the Source and Ruler of all life and knowledge, God, and not finite man, still less the fallen individual, is the center and the key to all reality and all possibility. Apart from the acknowledgment of this basic truth there can be no correct understanding of things in their total significance. Not only does the whole created order bear the impress of the divine pattern, and show the purpose of the divine mind. All things, whether in their origin or in their future, are subject, not to unpredictable chance, but to the sovereign control of Him who "worketh all things according to the counsel of his will" (Eph. 1:11). This sovereignty is displayed in the inescapable fact that both in time and in history He who is sovereign as Creator is sovereign also over His creation as Redeemer and as Judge of all. All philosophizing that fails to build upon this essential fact, as the only legitimate foundation for a proper understanding of things, is doomed to inconsistency and contradiction.

Again, Thomas failed to take into account the fact of Christ. This was a fact that he was particularly well placed to appreciate. During the period of our Lord's public ministry Thomas had been His constant companion and favored friend. Day by day this disciple had witnessed the unblemished perfection of the Master's Person, heard His sublime teachings, and watched His marvelous works. The life of Thomas, with the lives of countless others whom he knew, had been blessed and enriched by the goodness and the grace of the Lord Jesus. By first-hand experience this disciple knew Christ to be unique. Thomas was aware that the uniqueness of Jesus could be explained only in terms of One who had come from God, and who was, as Christ consistently declared Himself to be, one with the Father. It was to questioning Thomas in particular that Jesus had affirmed Himself to be what no mere man could ever become: the Way, the Truth, and the Life, as well as the sole Mediator, to know whom was also to know the Father (John 14:15-17).

Yet Thomas culpably ignored this supreme and unparalleled fact of Christ. The disciple ignored the explicit and repeated instruction of Him whose word was unfailingly accompanied by the power of truth; the teaching that He had power both to lay down His life and to take it again (John 10:17); that He would not only be put to death, but also be raised from the dead the third day (Matt. 16:21). Thomas even ignored the fact that with his own eyes he had witnessed the Lord's raising of others from the dead (cf. John 11; Luke 7:11-18). Reason no less than experience should have caused Thomas to believe that He who had so evidently shown Himself to be the Prince of Life could not be overpowered and held captive by death; that He who was the Way, the Truth, and the Life must needs rise again from the dead, just as He had foretold. But Thomas chose the foolish, proud way of doubt and skepticism.

THE FACT OF SCRIPTURE

Once more in his reasoning the skeptic failed to find a place for the fact of Holy Scripture. He was familiar with Scripture, and accepted it as the veritable Word of God. But, like many a professing Christian today, Thomas behaved inconsistently. He acted as though his faculties of thought and reason were not subject to the authority of God's Word. The present-day skeptic all too readily displays a preference for the verdict of the "expert," who with "scientific" solemnity assures him that death cannot be followed by resurrection.

Inasmuch, however, as Holy Scripture is the Word of God, it should be authoritative for the Christian in every aspect of his existence: in his intellectual activity as well as his worship; in his reasoning as well as his morals. He is to "bring every thought into captivity to the obedience of Christ" (II Cor. 10:5). Christ's own obedience to Scripture as the authoritative Word of God is so obvious as to need no demonstration. The fact that the Death and Resurrection of Christ were indeed "according to the Scriptures" (I Cor. 15:3) was overlooked by Thomas. But in this case, as always, in the face of every contrary pronouncement by some "expert," the truth of Holy Scripture has prevailed. With equal appropriateness our Lord's rebuke to the two disciples on the road to Emmaus might have been addressed to Thomas: "O foolish one, and slow of heart to believe all that the prophets have spoken: ought not Christ to have suffered these things, and to enter into his glory?" (Luke 24:25).

THE CONVERSION OF THE SKEPTIC

Eight days after Thomas rejected the testimony of his fellow disciples, the risen Lord appears again to the little company while they are meeting together behind closed doors. This time Thomas is with them. The Lord invites the skeptic to prove for himself the reality of the Resurrection by placing his finger in the nail prints and his hand in the spear wound—the very tests that he demanded a week before. Then the Lord gently rebukes him for his unbelief. At last Thomas realizes the extent of his stupidity. By the logic of faith his eyes are opened to see what he should have known all along without any doubts.

Now that his eyes were open to believe, no practical demonstration was necessary. Like many of us (thank God!) the heart of Thomas was better than his head. When at last both heart and head were in harmony, he bowed before the living Saviour and uttered the simple but fundamental profession of faith that was henceforth to be the strong fortress of his life: "My Lord and my God!" This then was the confession of his reformed faith.

Thomas saw and believed. His personal encounter with the living Christ made overwhelmingly clear to him that his reasoning hitherto had approximated that of the "natural man," and had led to altogether false conclusions. When face to face with the risen Lord, he stood self-convicted of culpability in refusing to believe until he had seen, and inexcusable disregard of crucial facts that were fully known to him. There was not a single word that he could utter to justify his former attitude of doubt.

The exclamation of Thomas, "My Lord and my God," was the confession of a contrite as well as a believing heart, the acknowledgment that even without seeing he ought to have believed. Then he heard Christ pronounce a blessing on all who have not seen and yet have believed. By faith such disciples prove that to believe is to see, not with the physical eye, but with the inward sight that penetrates beneath the outward appearance and enables the faculty of reason to view things in their correct proportions.

In our twentieth century we have no more excuse for unbelief than Thomas had. We are confronted with precisely the same facts that confronted him: the fact of God, the fact of Christ, and the fact of Holy Scripture. To ignore or make light of these facts leads inevitably to false conclusions and disastrous inconsistencies. We too may encounter the risen Christ, but not according to the flesh, for He is now the ascended Lord. Indeed, we may now encounter Him in a far more real and intimate fashion: inwardly, not outwardly; by faith, not by sight; much as the early Christians and all subsequent believers have come to know Him.

Like Thomas, we may come to know Him not as another

entity outside the believer, and distinct from him, but as the Divine One who is ever with us, as we are ever with Him; Christ in us and we in Christ. This intimate and transforming experience, however, takes place only when by faith the believer beholds Him as the One who has been raised from the dead, still bearing the prints and scars of His suffering and crucifixion. Like Thomas, whenever any one of us beholds Him as the only Saviour and Lord, who vicariously bore our sins and their punishment, and then rose from the grave in the power of an endless life, one feels constrained to cry out with Thomas, contritely and in the deepest faith, "My Lord and my God!"

THE CONFESSION OF THE REFORMED FAITH

Dear brethren, we are assembled here at this Congress to consider together a vital and very practical question: "How should we today confess our Reformed Faith?" The foundation on which we build our thinking and our conclusions must unfailingly be the simple but absolute confession of Thomas: the unreserved homage and adoration of Jesus Christ as our Lord and our God. This confession, let me remind you, is far more than a declaration with the lips; it is a confession of the life.

This great dynamic principle of all our faith must display itself in action. Otherwise our confession would be empty and impotent, and certainly not a Reformed confession of faith. Christ, risen and all-powerful, must be seen by the world as the Lord of every department and relationship of our existence. He alone is Lord of all knowledge as well as Lord of all being; Lord of nature and Lord of all history; Lord of the present and Lord of the future; Lord of the powers that are seen and Lord of those that are unseen. He alone can be our supreme and absolute King of kings and Lord of lords (Rev. 19:16).

As we shall delight to confess and praise Him throughout the ages of eternity, let us delight to confess and praise Him here and now. As citizens of many nations, speaking various languages, let us now adore Him with the ascriptions of praise that we shall unitedly give Him in the everlasting glory of heaven: "Thou art worthy, O Lord, to receive glory and honor and power, . . .

for thou wast slain, and hast redeemed us to God by thy blood out of every kindred, and tongue, and people, and nation" (Rev. 4:11; 5:9).

May our Heavenly Father unite and bless us all according to His perfect will and purpose as we seek to proclaim to this generation our Saviour and Master Jesus Christ!

Now unto the King eternal, immortal, invisible, the only wise God, be honor and glory for ever and ever. Amen (I Tim. 1:17).

20. Roy H. Short

Roy Hunter Short, Methodist Bishop. Born, Louisville, Ky., Oct. 19, 1902. Educated, University of Louisville (A.B.); Louisville Presbyterian Seminary (Th.B., Th.M.). D.D., Kentucky Wesleyan University; LL.D., Florida Southern University. Pastorates (1922-35). District Superintendent (1935-41). Pastor, St. Paul's Church, Louisville (1941-44). Editor, "Upper Room" (1944-48). Bishop since 1948, now in the Nashville area. Secretary, Council of Bishops. Author, many articles. Books: Your Church and You (1942); Evangelistic Preaching (1956); Evangelism Through the Local Church (1956).

The sermon about "The Salvaging of Souls" begins with matters of human interest and concern. As a peripatetic preacher the Bishop may often have to address a throng of strangers who look up to him with veneration, and perhaps with a sense of unreality. Before he comes to the heart of his message he may feel it wise to establish a spirit of rapport. Evidently he wishes everyone present to know that the Bishop himself is deeply concerned about salvaging.

Is this the way to preach now? Yes, one way. In addressing a convention of young persons, all of them strangers, many a clergyman has made a similar approach. In our day worthy preaching from the Bible assumes countless forms. All of them are alike in these respects: (1) the minister strives to meet a specific need in the hearts of those who hear: (2) he singles out a certain passage inspired of God to meet this need; (3) he prepares a message in keeping with the interests and capacities of the hearers; (4) all the way through he looks to the Spirit in prayer.

The present sermon has to do with the risen Lord's way of salvaging the soul of Simon Peter. In recent times this sort of *pulpit work has become know as "life situation preaching." Here the life situation is that in the closing chapter of the Fourth Gospel, which is the most personal of the four. It tells most about Christ, and about Him in dealing with men and women, one by one.*

More and more the reader feels that Christ now stands ready to salvage the soul of any person who like Peter has failed in loyalty to Him, and of everyone else in need of being reclaimed. So let us thank God for everyone who preaches about Christ as the divine Salvager of the soul.

THE SALVAGING OF SOULS

"When the morning was now come, Jesus stood on the shore, but the disciples knew not that it was Jesus."

ST. JOHN 21:4

AT VARIOUS LOCATIONS on the bed of the sea, sometimes beneath many fathoms of water, lie buried the slowly rusting hulks of once-proud vessels that used to sail the mighty deep. Long ago somehow came disaster, and they went down laden with their precious cargoes of gold, silver, and other treasure. Today one of the most interesting callings on earth is that of trying to salvage the cargoes of these sunken vessels, and in some cases even the vessel itself.

On the slope of Mount Vesuvius in Italy once stood the proud city of Pompeii. In 79 A.D. the mighty volcano belched forth fire and molten rock, so that the city was buried in lava, in some places to a depth of sixty-five feet. For long centuries the very site of Pompeii was overlooked, but in 1763 the work of excavation was begun, to lay bare the outlines of the ancient city, expose to modern eyes the pattern of its daily life, and recover all that remained of its ancient treasures.

Since 1861 the work of restoration has been carried forward by the Italian government. Every year thousands of visitors from all over the world find it a most rewarding experience to witness these fascinating endeavors to salvage the remnants of a civilization suddenly destroyed and then long forgotten.

In the quaint land of Holland one of many charms is that of a country built up largely by the process of salvaging. Much of Holland is made up of land that the Dutch have slowly reclaimed, as for centuries they have patiently pushed back the restless sea.

THE SALVAGING OF SOULS

Such attempts at salvaging have added significantly to the wealth of the world. They capture our imagination, and challenge us never to despair or give up hope of recovering that which has been lost. But there is another kind of salvaging, far more glorious than any of these, which have had to do with material things, many of them precious. This other kind of salvaging goes on at countless points almost everywhere. It is the salvaging of souls, each of them more precious in the sight of God than all the material treasures of earth.

The work of salvaging souls is carried on by the humble rescue mission located on some street where the sponsors of lost men believe and sing:

> Down in the human heart, crushed by the tempter,
> Feelings lie buried that grace can restore;
> Touched by a loving hand, wakened by kindness,
> Chords that were broken will vibrate once more.

Salvaging is also the work of the chapel set up in the name of Christ at some far corner of earth's remotest bounds, in what we usually call a mission field. There the glorious light of the Gospel shines out in the darkness, and thus becomes a continuing demonstration of "how far a little candle sends its beams." Salvaging of souls is the work of any church anywhere, whether on the main avenue, on a side street, or on a rural hillside where a chapel has been true to its holy calling. All of this work has to do with the salvaging of precious human lives, lives that have been stained with evil and crushed by sin, lives that have been lost to God and to goodness.

To this work of salvaging our Lord gave Himself continually and gladly, saying, "The Son of Man is come to seek and to save that which was lost." As He went about over Judea, Samaria, and Galilee He was always seeking to do one thing. In His great love He was seeking to rescue the lost sheep of His Father and bring them back safely to the shelter of the fold. That was the driving force behind every sermon He preached, every personal interview He held, and every long night He gave to agonizing prayer. That was the ultimate explanation of the Cross, for His Death on Calvary was the one final deed by which He made forever possible the saving to the uttermost of all who believe.

Because our Lord gave Himself so completely to the work of salvaging during all the days of His earthly ministry, we are not surprised to find Him at the same task between His Resurrection and His Ascension. Quite naturally the first objects of His concern were the men who had companied with Him for three years. When the terrible day of the Cross came, they had not proved so strong as in their early protestations that He could always count on their loyalty.

Of the twelve, one betrayed Him. Others in fear forsook Him and fled. And perhaps saddest of all, one denied Him, even with oaths, declaring that he never had known Jesus. And now in His great love the Risen Lord continues to seek and to save them, even as He has been seeking to save them from that first glad day when they left their all to become His disciples. Once more He seeks to set them upon their feet and to establish their goings. He gives them yet another chance to prove their loyalty, and He encourages them to be steadfast unto the end. This too is the salvaging of souls.

In the closing chapter of his immortal Gospel, John vividly describes these efforts by our Lord. All of the eleven are the objects of His solicitude, and especially Simon Peter, whom He has loved so much, and who has sinned against Him so grievously. In like manner, everyone who reads the striking record in this chapter may, if he will, see a picture of the Master's concern for his own redemption. Likewise he who reads may hear three pertinent and penetrating questions that the Master asked the disciples there by the side of the lake.

No matter how grievous his sin, or how deep his shame, if any one of us with all his heart gives satisfactory answers to these three questions, there is hope for this man. As He seeks to do in us His divine work of salvaging, the Lord asks us the same questions today as He did with those disciples long ago. In the answers that we now give Him lies the reason for our hope. If we are truly conscious of our need, and if in love we turn to Him, Christ our Redeemer will help us.

THE SENSE OF NEED FOR CHRIST

It was a needy group of men whom Jesus found that morning beside the sea. All night they had toiled at fishing, and they had taken nothing. They were hungry, and they felt discouraged. When Jesus came to them and asked, "Children, have you any meat?" they acknowledged their need as they answered, "No." Then the Master Himself made possible for them a shore breakfast, and urged them to be His guests. "Come and dine."

"Have you any meat?" This same question the Lord Jesus continues to ask all of us whom He would salvage and save for God and for goodness. The question is most pertinent, for basically it asks us whether or not we feel a sense of need. Until we do feel such a sense of need, even Christ Himself cannot do anything for us.

Sooner or later most of us learn that we do not actually have the meat we seem to have. Often we are surrounded by things, and we become satisfied. By and by one after another of us says to himself, "I am rich, and increased with goods, and have need of nothing." But sooner or later life teaches us how wrong we have been. Coming to realize the emptiness of those things for which millions of men live, at last we awaken to the fact that "Man shall not live by bread alone," and that "A man's life consisteth not in the abundance of the things which he possesseth."

Moreover, sooner or later most of us come to see that with all of our striving we cannot save ourselves. We cannot forgive ourselves. We cannot blot out the stain of our sins. We cannot break the shackles that bind us. Within ourselves we cannot find the strength that we need to face the storms of temptation that assail us. Above and beyond ourselves we need some Power that makes for righteousness.

When for any one of us the hour arrives of recognizing his need, then for him there is hope. Only those who to themselves and before God acknowledge their need can hope to find mercy and grace to help when such divine succor is needed most. When a man can honestly sing and pray,

> Nothing in my hand I bring,
> Simply to Thy Cross I cling,

that man is on the way to the place where Christ can make of him a new person. Then he can sing, most sincerely,

> Just as I am, without one plea,
> But that Thy blood was shed for me,
> And that Thou bidd'st me come to Thee,
>   O Lamb of God, I come, I come.

Christ the Redeemer will help us if in love our hearts respond to His love. On that morning by the shore there was a second pertinent question that Jesus asked, a question that He continues to ask of every man, "Lovest thou me?" Originally He asked this question of Simon Peter. In fact, with some slight variations He asked Peter essentially the same question three times.

The Master's heart must have leaped with gladness when the truly repentant disciple replied most earnestly, "Thou knowest that I love thee." Notice these two words, "Thou knowest." For his shameful failure and miserable denial of his Lord, Peter has no defense. He makes no excuse for himself. But he does protest that, whatever the explanation of what occurred by night in the garden, he now loves the Lord. With all the intensity of his soul Peter declares, "Thou knowest that I love thee!"

And Jesus does know! He knows that in a crucial hour Peter's love has failed, but He also knows that this love has not suddenly died. Full well He knows that the love kindled on the altar in the heart of the fisherman one morning, and fanned into a living flame through years of companionship with Christ, has not in one quick moment completely passed away.

THE FAILURE IN LOVE FOR CHRIST

Here is a word of encouragement for all who have known Him, and in some rash moment have forgotten Him, and thus have brought grief to His heart, and bitter tears of shame to their own eyes. Not every sin of which we may have been guilty necessarily means that our love for Christ has died. Sometimes it means that only for the moment our love for Him has failed.

In a certain drama one of the leading characters proves unfaithful to his wife. Only once has the husband been untrue. When he comes back to her, with the utmost humiliation and shame, his wife holds his face in her hands, and in the spirit of forgiveness characteristic of love, she exclaims, "It seems so good to have you back again!" Then he replies, "I never really went away."

To suggest that when love fails it does not necessarily die must not give the impression of looking lightly upon sin, or upon the failure of love. Because of what once took place in the garden, Peter never afterward was exactly the same. That failure of love for Christ troubled him as long as he lived. Always when we do wrong there is a cost that follows inescapably. As Adam Bede said long ago, "There's a sort of damage, sir, that can't quite be made up for." Nevertheless, if there still is in the heart true love for Christ, there is hope for the man to be reclaimed, and those who are most like their Lord are always eager to take part in such a reclamation.

Once there was in Leeds a barber named William Shent, who was one of John Wesley's itinerant preachers. After several years of useful service he fell into grievous sin and was expelled from the Methodist Society. When John Wesley heard of the matter, he wrote the society a letter, reminding them how much William Shent had once meant to the Kingdom, and pleading with them to receive him back as a brother beloved, restoring him in the spirit of meekness, and considering themselves, lest they also be tempted.

Wesley knew William Shent, and knew that he loved the Lord. Wesley understood full well that while Shent's love for Christ had once failed, deep down in his heart that love still continued. The

Society did as Wesley suggested. William Shent was restored, and to the end of his days he was faithful to his high calling, being diligent and effective in the service of his Master.

To those who have known Him and have sinned, Christ asks, "Does this sin mean that your love for me is dead? Or do you still love me?" If we can answer, one by one, "Yea, Lord, thou knowest that I love Thee," then in His gracious goodness He pardons all our sins, and holds out the glorious possibility of further usefulness.

"Lovest thou me?" Not only does our Lord ask this question of those who have been His disciples, and then in some sad moment have forgotten Him. He asks it also of those who never yet have known Him as Saviour and Lord. Here is the second great question, upon the answer to which any man's hope for redemption must rest. The Lord has already asked the sinner if deep in his heart he feels the need of the Saviour. Such a sense of personal need is ever necessary, but it is never enough. The contrite sinner also needs to hear the Redeemer ask, "Lovest thou me?"

If any man in his sins feels his desperate need, and finds his heart responding with the first glad flush of love toward Him who on the Cross died for us sinners, then that man has taken the second step toward letting Christ do for him what He alone is abundantly able to do. In justifying the action of a sinful woman who broke an alabaster box and anointed His feet, Jesus told the striking parable about two debtors. And then He observed, "Her sins which were many are forgiven, for she loved much." The faith that leads to salvation and the love that rises up in glad response are so close together as to be scarcely distinguishable. They both spring from acceptance of Him who said, "I, if I be lifted up from the earth, will draw all men unto me."

THE CALL FOR LOYALTY TO CHRIST

Christ the Redeemer will help us if we seriously resolve to follow Him with utter abandon, and unto the end of life's way. This aspect of the matter appears in the third question He asked that morning by the shore of Galilee, "What is that to thee? Follow thou me." This question had come because of a trivial incident. The Master had called Peter apart from the group for personal conversation. As they walked away John had followed them. Then Peter, turning about, saw John following. Quickly Peter asked, "Lord, what shall this man do?" The inquiry gave Jesus an opportunity to say something more than was necessary for Him to tell this young man for whose future usefulness He was so much concerned.

So in mild rebuke the Master said to Peter, "What is that to thee? Follow thou me." What heart-searching words! How they ring across the years and come today to every follower of Jesus, as if he were the only Christian in the world! "What is that to thee? Follow thou me." Of every man who would follow Him the Master asks that he be marked by a noble determination of soul, and that he forget what the other man does, or does not do. Christ would have us not be discouraged by the other disciple's achievements and successes.

What the other person accomplishes is often so much more than we feel we can possibly accomplish that we fold our hands in despair. We are like the young man who heard Phillips Brooks preach, and was so much moved by the eloquence and power of the sermon that he went home vowing he would never preach again. He forgot that there are varieties of gifts and that it is just as important for the one-talent man to be diligent in the use of his one talent as it is for the five-talent man to be faithful in the use of his five talents.

Furthermore, He would have every disciple possess such determination of soul that he will not be disposed to find excuses because of the other man's failures. Often we do so, like the Pharisee of old, who concentrated his attention on the shortcomings of others and thus dulled his own sensitivity to sin.

Finally, our Lord would have every disciple possess such determination of soul as to follow Him, regardless of what others may or may not do. Like Joshua of old, let every disciple now say, "Choose ye this day whom ye will serve, but as for me and my house, we will serve the Lord."

On his thirteenth birthday Jonathan Edwards is reported to have written in his diary: "Resolved first, that every man should do right. Resolved second, that I will do right whether anyone else in the world does or does not."

This then is the third thing that Jesus asks of everyone in whom He seeks to do His redeeming work: the full commitment of self, and the determination to follow Him all the way, whatever the cost.

Today, as by Galilee of old, the Master is engaged in the salvaging of souls. Still He asks of men, one by one, "Have you any meat?" "Lovest thou me?" And "What is that to thee? Follow thou me." For everyone there is hope. No matter what one is, or what one has done, there is hope for everyone who confesses his need of Christ, responds to Him with a loving heart, and resolves to follow Him all the way. There is every reason for hope, because He is the tested and the all-sufficient Salvager of souls. He is abundantly able to save unto the uttermost all who come unto God by Him.

IV. With Christ
After the Ascension

21. Geoffrey W. Bromiley

Geoffrey William Bromiley, Anglican Church, Scotland. Born, near Bolton, Eng., Mar. 7, 1915. Educated, Emmanuel College, Cambridge (B.A., M.A.); New College, Edinburgh (Ph.D., Litt. D.). Pastorate (1938-46). Vice Principal, Tyndale Hall, Bristol (1946-51). Rector, St. Thomas's Church, Edinburgh (1951-58). Lecturer, Graduate School, New College, Edinburgh (1951-58). Professor, Fuller Seminary, since 1958. Books: Reasonable Service (1948); Ed., Zwingli and Bullinger, Christian Classics (1953); Baptism and the Anglican Reformers (1953); Thomas Cranmer, Theologian (1956); Sacramental Teaching and Practice (1957); Ed., Karl Barth's Church Dogmatics (transl., 1955 ff.); The Unity and Disunity of the Church (1958).

The following sermon was chosen to represent evangelical preaching abroad today. The message differs from our American pulpit work. The spokesman for his Lord assumes that after Easter church-comers still yearn to hear about Christ. Perhaps because the Ascension did not take place on a Lord's Day, many of us bypass the event, and ignore its meaning. Anyone who endeavors to prepare such a message will learn why Phillips Brooks declared that among all the important events in our Lord's mission on earth the Ascension is the most difficult to preach. See his message for "Ascension Day" in his Sermons for the Church Year (1910). See also James S. Stewart, "The Gospel of the Ascension," in The Strong Name (1941).

The Anglican divine treats the subject Biblically and doctrinally. The sermon consists in a saturated solution of New Testament truth about what William Milligan terms The Ascension and Heavenly Priesthood of Our Lord (1892). The sermon here brings out the relation between this high doctrine and three *others, two of which most of us neglect: the Atonement of our Lord, His Authority, and our Adoption. The method calls for confident affirmation and repetition of these truths about our ascended Lord. In every paragraph, and in almost every sentence, He stands out supreme, whereas many of us would glance at Him for a little while, and then talk about what the doctrine should mean to us.*

The sermon differs, also, in the paucity of contemporary allusions. The speaker evidently assumes that the saints find no one else so appealing as Christ, and no other facts so absorbing as those about Him. And yet the sermon holds my attention, and increasingly with every reading. The minister's own heart must have been "strangely warmed," for his words and sentences often flow with the surge of Gospel truth charged with feeling.

This way of preaching objectively, not subjectively, exalting Christ rather than our own problems, might not at first appeal to some who have become accustomed to American man-centered discourses. But surely the older evangelical way of preaching what the Bible stresses does satisfy the heart hunger of those who yearn to hear more about "the undiscovered bourn from which no traveler returns."

THE ASCENSION AND SESSION OF CHRIST

"Who, . . . when he had by himself purged our sins, sat down on the right hand of the Majesty on high."

HEBREWS 1:4

SET IN A PASSAGE that speaks about the self-humiliation and the glory of the Incarnate Son, this verse is a plain declaration of His Ascension and Session. The Son who came down from heaven in a movement of condescension has also returned to heaven in a movement of exaltation. He came forth from God on the way that led Him finally to the Cross. He has gone back to God on the way that began with the Resurrection.

When the Lord Jesus came to earth He was made a little lower than the angels. But even in His humanity He has been clothed with honor and glory (Psa. 8:4; Heb. 2:9). Having humbled Himself, even to endure death on the Cross, He has been highly exalted, and given a name that is above every name, that at the name of Jesus every knee should bow (Phil. 2:8-10). To the Incarnation as His coming into the world there corresponds the Ascension as His triumphant return to the Father in glory.

I. THE COMPLETION OF THE ATONEMENT

The fact that He has gone back to the Father, and has taken His seat on the divine throne, tells us clearly and simply of the Atonement that He has made, and the work of salvation that He has completed. According to the text, by Himself He has purged our sins. The work that He came on earth to do was that of reconciliation. An offering had to be made for sin, an offering that sinners could not make for themselves, and not for one another. Forgiveness had to be secured; the burden of sins lifted; the penalty paid; the stain wiped away; and the power destroyed. All of this tells why He came to our earth. "Behold the Lamb of God, which taketh away the sin of the world" (John 1:29).

In fact, He alone has purged our sins. He has done it Himself. He has done it once for all, and all sufficiently. He has done it in such a way that it need not ever be repeated or supplemented. Indeed, it cannot be reenacted or added to. Its fullness cannot ever be exhausted, or diminished. Its power and its efficacy can never be lessened or limited. From the heavenly seat that He has assumed He can now contemplate the mission that He fully and comprehensively discharged on earth, so that there can be no question of others being required to add to His work of redemption, or of Christ's being recalled from heaven to make good any defects or deficiencies in His work of salvation.

All of this means that the Ascension and the Session of our

Lord bring us a message of triumphant assurance. Our past may be ever so accusing. Our sins and shortcomings may be ever so sad and serious, even shocking. Our faith may seem ever so feeble. But over against all these shortcomings we may set the perfect work of redemption that the Son of God has completed on our behalf. He has actually made the Atonement. His blood avails to cleanse us from all sin (I John 1:7). At Calvary our sinful past was nailed to the Cross. However feeble our faith, the One in whom we believe is mighty. The efficacy of His finished work does not depend on the strength or the weakness of our response.

It is not our Christian life and our works that justify us in the sight of God, but the Death and the Resurrection of Christ for us sinners. Through all the trials and emergencies of life, through all the vicissitudes of faith and experience, through all the self-confidence or self-despair that may come to us, we know that Christ is now at the right hand of the Father, and that His work of salvation is done. It cannot be undone, and it need never be done again. To this completed work we can always return; in it we can always rejoice; from it we can always draw strength; and on it we can always rely. Neither in this world nor in the next shall we ever be thrown back on our own resources. What He has done for us He has done so fully and so well that we should give Him our unwavering confidence, and with rejoicing go through whatever life on earth may bring.

II. THE EXERCISE OF HIS AUTHORITY

The return of Christ to the Father does not only tell us of the Atonement that He has made. It also assures us of the authority that He has assumed and that He now exercises. When the Son had purged our sins, He took His seat at the right hand of the Father. This royal seat, while it indicates a holy mission accomplished, is never a place of inactivity and repose. The Session does not mean that Christ is ever unoccupied. It does not suggest that He feels no further concern for the humanity that He died to redeem. The heavenly seat of our Lord is the throne from which He rules both heaven and earth. It is the seat, not of inactivity, but of authority. It is the place of almighty power, of kingly rule, of omnipotent majesty.

As the heavenly Victor, the Christ who in weakness made the

Atonement for our sins now has taken His rightful place on
the throne from which He rules. All authority on earth and in
heaven has been given unto Him. Before Him every knee shall
bow. Indeed, He does rule today, though His Kingdom has not
yet been revealed in all its glory. He is the Lord of nature and of
history, the Head of the Church, the King in comparison with
whom the mightiest of earth's potentates must seem futile and
ephemeral. Nor is His reign a creaturely dominion, assailable
and transient, in scope restricted, and in duration impermanent.
It is the rule of God Himself,—unlimited, eternal and irresistible.

This means that the Ascension and Session of Christ bring us
on the one hand a further assurance of authority, and on the
other hand a summons to do His will. The assurance is that no
matter what may happen here below, Christ is Lord, and His
purposes will prevail. Sometimes it may seem that circumstances
are too strong; that the forces arrayed against the Gospel are
overwhelming. Both in our own lives and in the life of the
Church it may seem that everything is lost. Then we remember
that Christ is seated in the place of power. In His almighty
hands all things now work together for good, and they will ever
continue so to work, according to His purpose.

The path of duty may lead us, as it led Him, by way of the
Cross, but that is still the way to Resurrection power. Inimical
forces may grasp after world-direction, but they are subject to the
plan of our God, and they will set forward the dominion of His
Christ. The kingdoms of the world must become in fact what
they already are in God's will—the kingdoms of our Lord and of
His Christ. This is our assurance. The summons is to acknowledge His rule, to place ourselves under His authority, to give ourselves completely to the service of this King. It is not our will that
is to be done. It is not our kingdom that is to come. The seat of
power is not the throne of self-will and selfishness.

If in our own strength we contend for the Lordship of Christ
among men, we fight a losing and an exhausting battle. We spoil
our lives; we frustrate our service; we rob ourselves of peace and
plenitude. Since Jesus Christ is seated on the throne of power, to
Him we must come with our homage; from Him we must take
our marching orders. In our lives the world about us must see
that Christ reigns; that even in our weakness when we set our-

selves to do His will He causes us to triumph; and that when we obey the Lord we can do for Him all things that need to be done. If any Christian wishes to know the confidence and the triumph of Christ's rule, that believer must learn to obey. If we really believe that Christ rules, we have every reason to obey. When we obey, we know that the Christ who rules in our hearts stands ready to rule over the world.

III. THE ASSURANCE OF OUR ADOPTION

The Return of Christ to God the Father teaches us first that He has made the Atonement; second, that He now exercises all authority; and third, that He has secured our adoption. As the Son of God He came down from heaven to become the Son of Man. As the Son of Man He went back to the right hand of the Father to be what He had been from all eternity, the Son of God. In glorified humanity the Word once made flesh went back to God with all glory. In the Person of the Son, manhood was taken up into Deity. In the strictest sense this can hold true only of Christ, for among all the sons of men, of Him alone can we say that He is God. Yet because He is our Representative and our Substitute, the One who was made flesh for us, there is a real and precious sense in which through Him we also receive the adoption of sons.

As the living Word our Lord did not go back alone, for He accomplished that which He had come from heaven to do. As the firstborn among many brethren, He arose from the dead and ascended to the Father. With Him he has taken believers into the family of God's redeemed. Christ has even promised us places of power in the world to come. He has promised to make us "kings and priests unto God and his Father" (Rev. 1:6a). There we shall reign with Him in glory. But we can have no independent sonship or sovereignty. In ourselves we are not God's heirs or lords over His creation. But since we are in Christ, by virtue of His identification with us, we have the promise of new and glorious destiny and powers, not merely the prospect of being His creatures and His servants (Rom. 8:21).

The Ascension and Session of Christ bring us a thrilling message about the rich purposes of our God and the high privileges of those whom Christ has redeemed. When man fell into sin it seemed as though he had irrevocably forfeited his high calling of God in creation. But when the Father put forth His saving power in the Person of His Son, God did not merely restore man to his lost estate, but gave him a destiny far more glorious, that of being partaker in the divine nature (II Pet. 1:4). Surely it should thrill us to know that out of what seemed to be final disaster God could bring so wondrous a triumph. Surely it ought to humble us to feel that with all our unworthiness we should become the recipients of such heavenly and eternal honors.

"What is man that thou art mindful of him?" (Psa. 8:4). Who are we that God should deal with us so bountifully? In ourselves we are next to nothing, but for the sake of Christ we have all these glorious privileges. Yet we can feel no foolish pride in the overflowing of God's fatherly love for us sinners, because this work is all of grace. We cannot selfishly look forward to the consummation as any triumph of our own, for it is supremely His. But humbly and thankfully we can adore the wise and powerful grace that has planned and wrought for us this un-expected and unmerited favor. In the ascended and exalted Christ we find the guarantee that this grace is really ours, that we have received the adoption of sons, and that we are caught up with Him in that movement of Ascension to the family and the Kingdom of God.

IV. THE MEANING OF OUR ASSIGNMENT

This truth of a secured adoption leads us to the final and intensely practical lesson, that in the triumphant homegoing of Christ He has given us an assignment. Our true home can hence-forth be no longer here, but at the right hand of the Father, where our life is hid with Christ in God. In this world we can be only pilgrims, journeying through to the eternal city of which He has graciously called us to be citizens. As pilgrims on the way to the City of God, we too are engaged in a movement of ascent. Not only do we in holy expectation look for the coming again of Christ in glory. In the ascending movement of our going home to Him, we seek those things that are above. Climbing down from the false heights on which we human beings try to place ourselves, we try to scale the far loftier heights on which God would have us live in Christ.

The Ascension and Session of Christ first give us the calm assurance of His finished work, and then act as a spur to positive and constructive action. To us who belong to the crucified, risen, and ascended Lord comes the summons to accept and express our true citizenship, and to serve as colonists of heaven among the natives of earth. In our thoughts, our speech, and our actions God would have us enter into the victory of Christ. Though their setting must be here on earth, they should carry much of the sweetness and radiance of heaven. Our heavenly citizenship bids us tread in the way He has marked out, follow the directions He has given, rise up and do the works of God's Kingdom, and press toward the mark for the prize of the high calling of God (Phil. 3:14).

Unlike the men of Babel, we are not to build our own way up toward heaven. Rather do we begin with an open way, and a completed work. Through the valley of self-denial we are to rise up and follow where He has gone before, into the heights of the new life in Christ. Resting in the Atonement that He has made, obedient to the authority that He exercises, rejoicing in the adoption that He has secured, we take up the assignment that He has given. Thinking and speaking, working and praying, serving and conquering, we can no longer enjoy the humdrum and slothful life of earth, but we are caught up in the train of our risen and ascended Lord.

Ah, but do we take up this trail? Too often do we not prefer one that is earthbound, even downward? Do we not refuse or ignore the directions that come from the ascended Christ? Do we not even make His finished work of redemption an excuse for inactivity that shows unbelief and disobedience? Are we not convicted as well as called, convicted of dallying, stumbling, and falling on the upward pathway? Should we not constantly look to our ascended Lord, to receive from Him afresh the assignment to our heavenly pilgrimage? With the assignment let us receive anew the assurance that for us He has climbed the holy hill, that He now sits at the right hand of the Majesty on high, and that as on eagles' wings we shall be borne yonder, to share His kingdom, His power, and His glory (Heb. 2:10).

22. O. A. Geiseman

Otto Albert Frederick Geiseman, Lutheran, Missouri
Synod. Born, Sioux City, Ia., Aug. 8, 1893. Educated,
Concordia College, Milwaukee (A.B.); Concordia Seminary, St. Louis (Th.B.); University of Chicago (M.A.);
Chicago Lutheran Seminary (S.T.D.). Pastorates (1915-
22); Grace Lutheran Church, River Forest, Ill., since
1922. Lecturer, Concordia Teachers College, River
Forest (1939-41). Staff, Chicago Lutheran Radio Hour
(1939-41). Winner, Pulpit Digest Sermon Contest
(1938). Author 12 books, including: Consuming Love,
life of Adoniram Judson (1920); Make Yours a Happy
Marriage (1946); For Peace Within (1948); Old Truths
for a New Day (two vols., 1949, '50).

This pastor represents a branch of Lutheranism strongly conservative in doctrine and quite aggressive in action, especially
in radio and television. In other days many a Missouri Lutheran
sermon dealt first and at length with the Law, and then at equal
length with the Gospel. Over the radio Walter A. Maier appealed
to hosts with his two-headed sermons, but in varied forms. The
present message embodies the same evangelical beliefs, but in a
fashion different from that of old. "Today is not yesterday."

Much evangelical preaching lacks the note of "apostolic optimism," whereas people still long to hear with Bunyan "the
sound of the trumpet in the morning." The present discourse
does not ignore or minimize the sin and woe of the world today,
but still the pastor voices a note of joy, hope, and triumph. So
did Spurgeon, John McNeill, and many other evangelicals of
yesterday excel as "happy preachers." Not everyone may agree
with some of this sermon's details about forms of social betterment, but everyone should rejoice in the Gospel as Good News
from God.

Notice also the custom here of dealing with Christian doctrine *as it concerns the human beings in church. After all, is there in the Bible, or in Christian experience, any such truth as the work of the Holy Spirit without direct reference to men and women with flesh and blood? And yet we often make truth about God and His children seem abstract and impersonal. It surely is not so with the dominant illustration here, about two Christian noblewomen who refuse to despair about the future of the evangelical movement, even behind the Iron Curtain. "Wherefore lift up your hearts"!*

EXCITEMENT AT PENTECOST

"They were all amazed and marveled."—ACTS 2:7a

THOSE OF YOU in the house of the Lord will observe that we of the clergy now wear red stoles. Red is a most exciting color. It represents life, blood, and fire. This color is particularly appropriate today, because on this Pentecost Sunday we commemorate a most exciting event that took place in Jerusalem more than nineteen hundred years ago.

Jesus our Lord had promised that after He withdrew His visible presence, He would send on the disciples the Holy Spirit. On the fiftieth day after His Resurrection this promise found its exciting fulfillment. At a room in Jerusalem the disciples were assembled to wait for the Spirit to come, they knew not how. When He came, a sound as of a rushing mighty wind filled the streets of Jerusalem. The sound seemed to concentrate at the place where the disciples were gathered. There the Spirit of God descended upon them in the form of fiery tongues, which indicated that something vibrant with power had come to pass, something of tremendous significance.

THE FIRST DAY OF PENTECOST

When the Spirit descended upon the disciples, exciting events followed one after the other. Immediately the disciples began to preach the Gospel. At that season multitudes of people had come to Jerusalem for the celebration of a great Jewish festival. So the disciples seized this opportunity to tell about Jesus as the Son of God, who had come to die on the Cross, so as to take away the sin of the world. Especially did Peter deliver a mighty sermon, which had tremendous repercussions.

On this first Day of Pentecost three thousand recruits were gained for Jesus Christ. At once their hearts and lives began to be transformed. People who previously had not believed in Jesus now put their trust in Him as Redeemer and King. Because the Holy Spirit came into their hearts and lives, they became an utterly new sort of persons. Now they often met for prayer. They began to gather round the Word and the Sacrament. Since their hearts had begun to experience the love of God through Christ, they began to express their love in their daily lives. Those who had abundance of food shared with those who had not. The entire situation must have seemed almost incredible, but still God placed on it the stamp of authenticity by allowing the apostles to perform miracles. How exciting!

If all of this had happened only once, as an isolated event nineteen hundred years ago, there would still be a sort of excitement that deserves commemoration. But what occurred on that day means all the more to us because Pentecost marked the beginning of a new era in the history of mankind. After the Death and the Resurrection of our Lord, Pentecost was destined to become the most exciting day in history. Soon the apostles would depart for various portions of the then-known world, to share with many peoples the Gospel of Jesus Christ. How exciting!

This crusading zeal found its most striking examplar in the Apostle Paul. Year after year he made long journeys, and wherever the way opened he preached the Gospel. Whether in a public market place, a private home, a rented hall, or a Jewish synagogue, he welcomed every opportunity to present the claims of Jesus Christ as the Son of God and the Saviour of mankind.

Not long after the days of the Apostles, their successors reached out into the lands from which came our own forebears: Germany, the Scandinavian countries, France, Spain, and England. Throughout the known world of those days the Gospel went like wild fire. Since then the movement has continued to spread. Herein lies the romance of Christian Missions. How exciting!

THE SPIRIT AT WORK TODAY

In our own day the activity of the Holy Spirit has reached something of a crescendo. To us it seems remarkable that after the first Day of Pentecost those early Christians gathered around the Word and the Sacrament. But what was true then still holds true today. Of this fact the splendid audience here today provides a fitting illustration. We may not feel any excitement in what we hear today, but we ought to know that apart from the continuing work of the Holy Spirit in Christian hearts we should not be here.

What we witness here is taking place around the world. You can go to any one of the continents or to the islands of the sea and the chances are good that you will find a place where the Gospel of Christ is being preached. It may be in a beautiful church, in a vast cathedral, or in a little chapel amid the jungles of Central Africa. Everywhere Jesus Christ is being preached and is being praised. It would be safe to say that never has there been a time on earth when the Spirit has gone forth in such mighty global fashion as today. This outreach has been due in part to the fact that we have at our disposal means of communication of which previous generations did not dream. By means of radio, television, and the printed page we can reach out into the utmost bounds of earth. So the Spirit of God, who caused excitement on the first Day of Pentecost, is to this day continuing His exciting work with unprecedented vigor.

What is happening here with us, and elsewhere round the globe, is taking place in regions where we may feel that nothing good can occur. Recently I had an opportunity to hear Countess Alexandra Tolstoi, daughter of the famous Russian novelist, and Princess Ileana, daughter of the Queen of Roumania and granddaughter of Queen Victoria. They were speaking to a large gathering here in a downtown hotel. Because of her station, like that of Princess Ileana, Countess Tolstoi certainly has had intimate and trustworthy contacts with people behind the Iron Curtain. She told us that in Russia on last Easter Sunday so many people wished to get into the Christian churches that it was impossible to admit them all. She reported that many persons who nominally belong to the Communist Party have been asking for holy Baptism. So you see that even where we may think the Spirit of God has no opportunity, He is now continuing His work of transformation.

THE EMPHASIS ON PRAYER

On the first Day of Pentecost the new converts to Christ began to stress the practice of prayer. If you wish to see how large a place prayer occupied in their daily lives, read the Book of the Acts, which a Bible scholar has called "the most exciting book in the New Testament." Read also the letters of Paul and Peter. Note that Paul tells his readers, "I remember you always in my prayers," and that he exhorts his friends, "Pray without ceasing." In like manner Peter bids the brethren, "Be sober, and watch unto prayer." In those days prayer was as vital for the souls of believers as breathing was for their bodies.

The two Christian noblewomen to whom I have referred both witnessed to the power of prayer. They told us that their own people, while behind the Iron Curtain, have learned to pray. Now they are praying as never before. They have lost all their earthly goods. Politically they have lost their freedom, and they can look forward to none. With virtually no hope for their lives here on earth, they have felt driven to their knees before God. According to one of their ministerial leaders, "We are living in the Book of Acts, and, oh, it is glorious!"

Wherever the Spirit of God is active in the human heart, there you find a person who prays. Like Luther and other Reformers, he not only believes in prayer; he prays. And then he serves. The early Christians not only prayed; they not only talked about Christianity. They also practiced it; they gave themselves in deeds of love. Such Christian prayer and Christian usefulness have always been marks of the Holy Spirit's indwelling presence and of His outworking power.

When Christianity moved out into the Roman Empire the new movement found itself in lands often plagued with all sorts of epidemics. It was not uncommon for some dreadful plague to wipe out an entire city or countryside. When an epidemic broke out, people who were able to flee would leave behind them the sick and the dying, and hurry away to the mountains, so as to escape the danger of being infected. But when those unbelieving pagans deserted their sick and dying "loved ones," the Christians remained behind and cared for those non-Christian neighbors in dire distress.

One day a Roman Emperor asked the Governor of Bithynia for information about the Christians. This ruler of a province in Asia Minor answered: "The Christians are a strange lot. They love one another." They also loved their fellow men, especially anyone in need. Even during the darker Middle Ages, when the spiritual life of the Church often seemed to be at low tide, the stream of Christian charity did not fail. Among those who withdrew from society to enter convents and monasteries, there were groups who continued to pray and to practice Christian charity. To the poor and the wayfaring these followers of the Lord gave food and lodging, with care in sickness. They also fostered such learning as existed in their day, and busied themselves with transcribing the Holy Scriptures.

THE DELIGHT IN GOOD WORKS

A few years ago some of us had the privilege of visiting the interesting city of Florence. There the guide pointed out a rather large house. Around the front of it ran a porch with an iron railing. At one end of the porch was an opening through the banister, and beyond it was a wire basket. For centuries the institution had been open there. In time of war or of peace, whether people prospered or suffered from poverty and want, that institution stood ready to care for wee foundlings. If some unwedded girl became a mother, under the cover of darkness she could take her babe and lay it in that wire basket. She knew that an order of sisters made it their life work to care for such little foundlings. And so today, whenever a heart is touched by the Holy Spirit, that heart responds with loving kindness to help anyone in distress.

In the history of the Christian Church such charity has always been practiced, and in our day it has risen to heights unprecedented. It would take many books to describe all that is now being done in the name of Christ, showing His concern for the weak and the helpless. Think of hospitals, orphanages, and homes for the aged; institutions for the blind, the deaf, and the feeble-minded; with places for the relief of those afflicted in various other ways. In every part of the world, wherever Christianity has gone, you will find such places of mercy. They all serve as manifestations that the Holy Spirit is still at work. On the other hand, where non-Biblical religions have prevailed, you cannot find such houses of mercy and such deeds of love. Out of Hinduism or Buddhism, Mohammedanism or Confucianism, or any other rival of Christianity, such fruits of the Spirit do not come.

You and I dwell in a land where Christian charity has even caused men of the world to engage in good works. Today almost every local community operates all sorts of charitable enterprises, such as a family welfare association. Every county makes provision for people in distress and not able to care for themselves. The state looks out for the unemployed, as well as for widows and orphans. The Federal government maintains a vast program of social security. However secular and imperfect such movements have become, they show the desire to carry out the pattern of Christian charity.

You see that what took place on the first Pentecost Sunday marked a new era, and made world history. In all our world today, the most significant history is being made by the Spirit of God. According to the women whose addresses I have reported, the world is in a bad way; it has all sorts of desperate needs. Those women told us, "These problems are not going to find their solution by war, or by the use of military means. There is only one solution, and that is the religion of Jesus Christ." Here are well-informed women, both of whom have been driven out of their homeland by atheistic Communists. These women know what it means to escape with their lives, while bereft of all their earthly belongings. Now they see no reason for hope through the use of national power. They find their hope in the transformation, the re-creation, of the human heart by the Spirit of God through the Gospel of Jesus Christ.

THE MEANING OF PENTECOST TO US

The coming of the Holy Spirit ought always to cause excitement, under Christian control. How exciting the experience is for you and me depends on the part we're playing. Those early Christians preached. Are we preaching? Both collectively and as individuals we ought to ask ourselves this question. Collectively, we're preaching the Gospel. We're trying to teach it in our daily school and our Sunday school, so that hundreds of boys and girls have an opportunity to learn about Jesus Christ. But are we preaching and teaching it as individuals? Is there in the world today any person who knows Christ because you've told him? Are you functioning as an agent through whom the Holy Spirit can carry on His work today?

Are we gathering round the Word and the Sacrament? Many of us are, as this audience makes clear. But on our church rolls there are names of persons who are not gathering round the Word and the Sacrament. They are falling by the wayside. They are letting the world lure them away from Christ. We should pray for them and feel for them a holy concern. We should invite them and urge them not to neglect their holy privileges, but to become active workers in the program of God's Holy Spirit.

In the past Christians have prayed. Do we pray? Oh, we do pray as a congregation. But are we praying as individuals? Many of us are, I'm sure. I have reason to suppose, however, that in our congregation there are homes in which there is no prayer; homes in which the children do not even learn to fold their hands and ask God to bless the food before they eat, or thank Him after they have eaten. When the Spirit of God is in your heart, you pray. If you are not praying, ask yourself whether or not you have received the Holy Spirit. If so, do you now daily enjoy a sense of His indwelling presence?

Where the Spirit of God is, there is love. Such love shows itself in countless ways. First of all it ought to manifest itself in our homes and in our congregational family. If we cannot live together in peace, if we cannot be kind, loving, and decent with one another, what is the use of our talking about world peace? We say that we are believers in Christ, and that the Spirit of God has changed our hearts, so that we now experience the love of Christ in our lives. If all of this is true, as we trust it is, then there ought to be adequate expression of Christian love everywhere in our daily lives. Love in the home, love toward our dear ones, and love toward our fellow men, whatever their race, color, or creed. Love to the neighbor across the street, and to the needy beyond the sea.

Here in the States we may not know many persons in need who are not being cared for by some community social agency. But this does not mean that there are not in this world, and in this community, persons in dire need of Christian love. If we knew how many babies are dying right now from lack of proper food and medical care, we could not sleep tonight. If we could see the suffering that people endure in every part of our world, our days might seem like chambers full of horror. Whether they are orphans, helpless old folk, inmates of a leper colony, or some other sort of lonesome unfortunates, they need our Christian love and care.

All about us are masses of people to whom the Spirit of God should manifest Himself through the love in our hearts. If so, our hearts need to be enlarged by the love of Christ through the Holy Spirit. Then they will open up and express that love through words and deeds of Christian helpfulness. So may it please the Spirit of God to come upon us in such fullness and richness that each of us, individually, and all of us, corporately, may serve as His agents to carry on the exciting work of Pentecost in promoting the work of God's Kingdom here upon His earth.

23. Cary N. Weisiger, III

Cary Nelson Weisiger, III, Presbyterian Church, U.S.A. Born, St. Louis, Missouri, Jan. 11, 1910. Educated, Princeton University (A.B.); Westminster Seminary, Philadelphia (Th.B.). D.D., Muskingum College, New Concord, O. Teacher, Allahabad, India (1931-34). Pastorates (1937-48); Mt. Lebanon United Presbyterian Church, Pittsburgh, since 1948. Round-the-world speaking tour, Mission Fields (1955). Trustee, various organizations. Guest preacher, colleges and universities.

The sermon about "The A B C of the Gospel" unifies the three main parts of a message that sweeps the gamut of redemption. As a rule a pastor speaking at home would deal with one of the three main parts. But now and again, for variety, he may feel led to survey vast areas. No matter how wide the scope, he can secure a clear, composite picture, provided he knows where to set the camera, and how to keep it there throughout the time exposure.

Structurally, the sermon follows a fairly novel way of arranging the parts. After the introduction, which focuses attention on the field of operation, first comes the thesis, which has to do with the primacy of God the Father. Then follows the antithesis, which relates to our part, that of sinning. Last of all, except the conclusion, comes the synthesis, where God's love and our sin meet at the Cross. In the pulpit no minister would employ these Hegelian terms, but at times anyone may find this way of preaching fruitful.

The materials come from two general sources, and only two. The warp consists of Bible truths, mainly from Romans. The woof includes a variety of human-interest allusions or references, all but one about today, and every one about a person, or persons.

A study of the ten or twelve examples would show this pastor's desire to make the Gospel clear and relevant to a wide variety of his friends in church. As the sermon progresses these examples tend to become more personal, even searching. One important section consists of "animated conversation" about a few hypothetical hearers, one at a time.

And yet the discourse does not seem anecdotal, or semi-secular. Even when the speaker refers to "depth psychology," he relates it to the Gospel. This kind of significant simplicity has nought to do with "simple simplicity," or silly shallowness. The Apostle warns us ministers not to let our "minds be corrupted from the simplicity and the purity that is toward Christ" (II Cor. 11:3b).

THE A B C OF THE GOSPEL

"The Gospel of God."—ROMANS 1:1C

THE BIBLE is the most influential book in the world. No other writings have ever exerted so much power over mankind. This is a fact that any impartial observer can easily verify. In the Bible no book has been more influential for conversion than the Epistle to the Romans. Through this book Augustine was converted, Luther was turned to Christ, and the heart of John Wesley was "strangely warmed." In the history of the Church these were hinge men. Because of their conversion experiences, doors swung open wide for new world epochs.

As a minister I owe much to Romans. After I had been out of the seminary half a dozen years, I realized that I had not developed any simple technique for explaining the Gospel in a personal interview. In the city of Augusta, Georgia, where I lived, I looked about for help. My eyes inevitably rested on a Baptist minister,

many years my senior, and then a pastor in that city. I knew
him to be a skilled winner of souls. So I went to him and explained my plight. Never in the seminary had I learned anything
so simple and so basic as that course in how to show another
person the way to become a Christian. My friend suggested a
little run of verses, and of course he chose them from the Book
of Romans.

So I memorized these verses, and many times I have had occasion to use them in personal interviews. "All have sinned and
come short of the glory of God" (Rom. 3:23). "For the wages of
sin is death, but the gift of God is eternal life through Jesus
Christ our Lord" (6:23). "For whosoever shall call upon the name
of the Lord shall be saved" (10:3). "I beseech you therefore,
brethren, by the mercies of God that ye present your bodies a
living sacrifice, holy, acceptable unto God, which is your reasonable service. And be not conformed to this world, but be ye transformed by the renewing of your mind, that ye may prove what
is that good, and acceptable, and perfect will of God" (12:1, 2).
What a succession of texts! Sin, condemnation, salvation through
the gift of God, calling upon the name of the Lord, and dedication to God, as through a burnt offering.

Now let us turn to this great book in the Bible. The theme of
the Epistle to the Romans is the Gospel. My text is a phrase
from the beginning of the first chapter, "The Gospel of God."
This theme dominates all the rest of the chapter. The Gospel
of God appears in verse nine, "The Gospel of His Son," and
later in the chapter, "I am ready to preach the Gospel"; "I am
not ashamed of the Gospel." Since we stand at the beginning of
the epistle, and I think it logical to have such a theme, my subject
is the A B C of the Gospel. Let A stand for Authorship.

THE AUTHOR OF THE GOSPEL

Long ago through His prophets God had promised His Gospel.
Through Moses the Lord had said that He would raise up unto
the people a prophet like unto Moses, and greater than Moses.
"Unto him shall ye hearken" (Deut. 18:15). Moses likewise
pointed forward to an altar and to a high priest greater than
the altar and the high priest of the ancient tabernacle. Samuel

declared that in order to be acceptable to God, religion must be of the heart; it must be spiritual. "To obey is better than sacrifice, and to hearken than the fat of rams" (I Saml. 15:22). David foretold a washing and cleansing for the broken and the contrite heart (Psa. 51). Isaiah beheld the glory of Christ and spoke of Him. Down through this long line of His ancient spokesmen, a line that included Jeremiah, Ezekiel, Daniel, and many others, God gave the promise and the purpose of the Gospel. The Hebrews did not think it up; they knew that it had come down.

In His Son, God caused the Gospel to become real and personal. According to the flesh, Jesus was made of the seed of David. According to the spirit of holiness, by the Resurrection from the dead, He was designated the Son of God with power (Rom. 1:3,4). That was all by the working of the Author of the Gospel; namely, God. Even those who receive the Good News do so because they are enabled of God. The application of the Gospel also goes back to the Authorship of God. From Him Paul received grace and apostleship, to bear witness to Christ. As the gift of God, the Roman Christians to whom he wrote had their fellowship in Christ. So that from beginning to end, with reference to its past, its present, and its future, we may say of the Evangel, it is all from God. It is promised of God, produced of God, and received by those who are called of God.

Often we speak of human beings as inventors. Such language must be relative. In the absolute sense, no human being can invent a single thing. The only true originator is God. Man's highest destiny is to think God's thoughts after Him. Whenever a person invents something that other people have never thought of, he is really discovering what God thought of in the beginning, and then put somewhere in His creation of the world.

All of this holds true in what we vaguely know as religion. Whenever in religion you get human invention you get distortion or negation, or both. For example, think about the art of painting. I am not much of an artist. The lowest grade I ever got at college was in modern art. That may account for my lack of appreciation for the phase of art called surrealism. A man paints on a canvas a face, puts on an extra nose, and on one side of the face a couple of extra eyes. Then he calls that art. I call it a monstrosity! I deem it a vain endeavor of man to create something absolutely new, for no man can do that. In religion when you get human invention you get a twisting or a denial of the truth. The only Author of spiritual truth is God. Therefore when we come to the Evangel our proper approach is to ask, "What does God say?" It is the Gospel of God. He is the Author. This is the A of the Gospel.

THE BACKGROUND OF THE GOSPEL

On the canvas of this first chapter in Romans the Apostle paints the Background of the Gospel, a background that is dark indeed, for it all has to do with sin. When we approach the subject of human sin, we have to reckon with far more than first meets the eye. In human personality, beneath what may seem to be a calm exterior and a smooth surface, there may be the awful workings of sin. From modern psychology has come a phrase full of meaning and suggestion, "depth psychology." The phrase rightly suggests that deep down in human personality lie vast hidden areas that are subject to violent storms. Out on the ocean, when all underneath is calm, mighty storms may rage on the surface of the deep. But in matters of human personality and sin the opposite often holds true. The surface of life may seem tranquil, but underneath may rage a terrible storm. Thus do countless persons endure their days and nights, passing through them with desperation known only to God.

As a boy I read a thrilling story about a man who dove down into the sea and there engaged in mortal combat with an octopus. As I read on I felt more and more fascinated and horrified. In my own body I could sense the chill terror of those encircling arms with their countless slimy suckers. To my intense relief, the diver was able to plunge his knife into the central, directing head of that octopus. So the diver escaped, unharmed. Something of the sort we ought to do with the devil. Down beneath the surface of men's lives, let us take the power of the Gospel, and use it to do combat with the sin that saps and destroys human beings made in the image of God.

Sin also has its open manifestations, which stand out in the latter part of this first chapter in Romans. Here Paul shows the length to which sin will go, and the detestable forms with which it works in human society. He points our gaze to three sorts of basic disturbances that sin causes in mankind. Disturbances in the relationship of man to God; disturbances within man himself; and disturbances between man and man.

The disturbances wrought by sin manifested themselves of old in three ways. One was perverted worship. Here you need only think of Sodom and Gomorrah, or Pompeii and Herculaneum, which exchanged the truth of God for lies, and for idolatry, which always debases. Again, there came perverted sexuality, wherein people exchanged the proper expression of marital love into unnatural relationships that channeled the creative urges of life into dead-end streets of lust and frustration. Thirdly, there were perverted human relations wherein people exchanged the proprieties of justice and mercy for ways of passion and violence. In those societies sin came to its bitter end. In the Revised Standard Version the final description of such sinners is summed up in these words: "foolish, faithless, heartless, worthless" (Rom. 1:31).

In that old world, where sin went on unrestrained, society lost its head and its heart. The modern world is no better. Have you with shame read a typical magazine article entitled "Sweden and Sin"? Have you with disgust kept informed about the recent increase of homosexuality in England? Do you read your own newspapers that mirror vices, and show how sin breaks out in the open, often erupting with volcanic force? Deep down where you cannot see it, sin keeps working so terribly that ofttimes you can watch its outworkings in shattered bodies, shattered nerves, and shattered lives.

Because of sin the shores of life are strewn with human wreckage. Here is a man in his early thirties, who ought soon to be getting into the very prime of life. He came from a family with wealth and every advantage, who could give him the best opportunities in business. Fifteen years ago he had sound health, a good mind, an attractive personality, and the brightest of prospects. But in the armed services he fell into perverted practices, which he has continued in civilian life. They have led to the complete shattering of his personality. Several years ago, utterly broken, he went to a mental institution. There he only partially responded to treatment. The physicians report that he will never again be able to manage himself, or even handle his money.

Does anyone here feel that I am overdrawing the picture? If so, I ask you to do this one thing: watch yourself. If you are careless about your soul, if you think that all this teaching about the dark background of sin is not relevant to you, watch yourself through these coming years. For if it is not checked, sin always gets worse and worse. It produces a deepening entrenchment of prejudice against God and the things of God, a hardening of the heart, with an increased grasping of the hand after the grosser things of life.

Sin is always sin. In human beings, one by one, and in human society, sin still rages. If Calvin Coolidge were here today, he would gain the impression that I am against sin. So I am. So is Paul. So is our Lord Jesus Christ. So is God our Father. So is the Holy Spirit. So is every Christian who has any discernment as to the root causes of all the disorders in the world today. In sin lies the dark background of the Christian Gospel.

THE CONTENT OF THE GOSPEL

Now we come to C, the Content of the Gospel. In imagination let us go from this place of worship into a classroom, and there let us take a test. Most of you have had a long course in the meaning of Christianity. You have come up through the Bible school; you have attended many services, and, God bless you, you have listened to many sermons. Of course you know what the Gospel is. Even so, let each of us take a pencil and a piece of paper. We shall imagine that Paul is writing on a blackboard the question that constitutes our test, "What is the content of the Gospel?"

The person next to you says to himself, "This is easy!" Then he begins to write: "The Gospel is a code; it's a set of rules; it consists of God's holy requirements. In the Old Testament these are found in the Ten Commandments; in the New Testament they stand out in the Sermon on the Mount, especially in the Golden Rule. We are supposed to live up to these requirements. To love God and love our fellow men, that's the Gospel!" When the paper is finished Paul takes it up, reads it, shakes his head sadly, and marks it with a big fat zero. Then he says to the writer, "You got only to the edge of the Gospel."

The person on the other side of you has even more confidence. He says to himself, "I'm going to put down the correct answer. I know that the Gospel is more than a code of laws, with commandments and requirements. The Gospel is a philosophy; it's an ideal; it's the noblest of all teachings. We're to try to aspire toward the realization of the fatherhood of God and the brotherhood of men. We are to follow such slogans as 'Hitch your wagon to a star,' 'Follow the gleam,' and 'Ever onward and upward.' That's the content of the Gospel!" This person too has flunked out in the test. He has reached only the fringe of the Gospel.

Think about the matter in terms of a church building. It has front steps outside and other steps inside. The building itself may represent the content and heart of the Gospel, which is a message of forgiveness and deliverance from sin. The front steps may correspond to the Law, the requirements of God. The inside steps may represent the ethical ideals that we strive to realize in our content. The front steps aren't the church; the inside steps aren't the church. The Law of God is not the Gospel; the ethical ideals aren't the Gospel. The Gospel is the Good News of what God has done in His Son Jesus Christ to secure for us sinners the power to keep the Law of God and to realize the ethical ideals of the Bible.

The content of the Gospel is Christ. The inspired record tells of Jesus as made flesh here on earth; as living among men, teaching them and doing many mighty works; as dying on the Cross for our sins; and as rising again in glory. The Gospel is the inspired record of how, when we receive Christ by faith, God accepts us as righteous, and says, "Now I give you my Holy Spirit with power to keep the Bible Law, and to realize in your own experience the ethical teachings of Holy Writ."

At the divinity school a professor once gave us this illustration. He said that mankind is like a criminal who has been condemned. Here is the poor convict in his cell. He has broken the law; he's doomed; he's going to be executed. To him comes the legalist, or moralist, the man who wrote that first test paper. Looking through the bars of the cell, he says to the poor fellow who will soon go to the chair, "Be good!" The convict looks at him with disgust. Then the idealist, the philosopher, comes to the cell, looks through the bars, and says to the convict, "You see that slit up yonder? If you stand in the right place and keep your eyes fixed up there, you'll see something of the sunlight by day and the stars by night." The convict replies, "That's very cheerful advice, but it's not going to get me out of the electric chair!"

Then the evangelist comes walking down the corridors of the jail. As he peers through the bars he says to the convict, "You're free! Your Lord has paid the penalty of your crimes. Now go out and with gratitude to Him keep the Law that you have broken, and realize the moral ideals of a true citizen." My friends, that would be good news for the convict. And that is good news for you. That is the Gospel of God in its content: Jesus Christ has set us free from sin. When by faith we receive Him as Redeemer and King, He gives us acceptance in heaven. He also gives us power on earth, both to live for God and to do what is right toward men.

If we know the Gospel, we have a twofold responsibility: to believe it and to share it. On the road to Damascus when Saul met the Living Christ, that sinner believed in Him and accepted Him. For Saul that road meant the beginning of God's forgiveness, favor, and power. Thereafter he could write: "I repudiate any righteousness of my own. I count it all as filthy refuse, that I may be found in Christ to have a righteousness which is of God in Jesus Christ" (Phil. 3:8,9). In like manner God asks us to believe in Christ and thus to accept the Gospel. The effectiveness of the Good News depends on God, not on you. He says, "By faith receive it; believe that through my Son you can have my favor, my forgiveness, and my power." Whether you are a Jew or a Greek, wise or unwise, the Gospel applies to you, and you, and everybody. If you have never before clearly understood the content of the Gospel, receive it now. Through Christ you are free. Now live in His power.

As Christians we are also to share the Gospel. That is why Paul wished to go to Rome, to Spain, and to regions beyond. He declared, "I am a debtor to the Gospel." "I am ready to preach the Gospel." "I am not ashamed of the Gospel." "I've got to go everywhere and tell this good news: 'You can be free, no longer a slave to Satan, no longer condemned because of sin. You may also have power, all the power you need; it's here for you in Christ.'" Thus the Apostle kept saying, "I must tell the whole world about the Gospel of God."

This way of living to proclaim the Good News may prove to be far from easy or safe. A prominent oil man, an ardent backer of Billy Graham, said to me that he did not wish Graham to go on a certain trip overseas. I asked the oil man why he was fearful. He replied, "Because the Communists hate Billy. Somewhere they could easily contrive an accident that would take his life." Even so, we have to reckon with the fact that Billy Graham is a Christian evangelist. Because he understands and accepts the Gospel, there is in him something that keeps saying, "Go, go, go!" He feels that he has to go, and that he never goes forth alone.

My friend, if you know the Gospel, and if you believe it, what of this compelling urge? In a little notebook do you have a prayer page where you list the names of persons who are not Christians, persons for whom you pray, one by one, and to whom you speak about Christ in terms of the Gospel? Do you have in your mind and on your heart a prayer page with the names of the unsaved whom you remember daily at the throne of grace? When did you last speak to some person about the Gospel? Not about the law, or about ideals, but about the Gospel! Or do you clam down whenever you have an opportunity to introduce Jesus Christ as your Savior and Lord?

What a twofold responsibility! First to believe the Gospel, and then to share the Gospel. By the grace of God learn to say with Paul, "I am a debtor." "I am ready." "I am not ashamed of the Gospel."

24. Helmut T. Lehmann

Helmut T. Lehmann, United Lutheran Church. Born,
Saskatoon, Saskatchewan, Can., Mar. 3, 1914. Edu-
cated, University of Saskatchewan (B.A.); Lutheran
College and Seminary, Saskatoon; University of Er-
langen, Germany, (Ph.D.). Pastorate (1939-43).
Teacher, Hamma Divinity School and Wittenberg Col-
lege, Springfield, O. (1943-44). President, Waterloo
College and Seminary, Ontario (1944-53). Senior Book
Editor, Muhlenberg Press, Philadelphia, since 1954.
Books: Heralds of the Gospel (1953): general editor,
Luther's Works, transl., vol. 31-54.

The sermon about "A Sense of Belonging to God" shows how an
evangelical preacher can use the truth of a royal passage from
Romans in meeting heart needs of "displaced persons" today.
According to statisticians twenty per cent of our families in the
States recently have been moving each year. In the city as well
as on the farm modern industry tends to create a host of "migrant
workers." Hence the pastor of a local church has an opportunity
to meet the needs of many "uprooted people."

The message here begins with a "psychological approach."
Before the minister sets forth his Bible truth he prepares the
way by appealing to the ever-present sense of wishing to belong.
He deals with the matter as it concerns a new church in a community that has sprung up almost overnight. He does not spend
time in sociological diagnosis and prognosis. The main body of
the sermon consists in a discussion from a viewpoint wholly
Christian. In order to guide in solving this present-day problem,
the minister points uprooted persons to the Rock of Ages.

Such a message shows that not all evangelical preachers ignore
the interests and the needs of the hearers today. Neither do these
ministers content themselves with administering soothing syrup

when a case requires a remedy that can reach down into the depth of the soul. Hence it seems that every pastor ought to seek and follow the guidance of the Spirit, so as to preserve a Biblical balance between the timeless and the timely, the contemporary and the eternal.

In a village community the wags used to insist that in the pulpit one minister had a good motor but poor transmission, whereas the man across the street had excellent transmission, but not much to transmit. If that be a correct statement, people thrive better under a man with a message than under one who has nothing but delivery. But why should not every evangelical preacher be "complete, equipped for every good work"? (II Tim. 3:17).

A SENSE OF
BELONGING TO GOD

"All who follow the leading of God's Spirit are God's own sons. Nor are you meant to relapse into the old slavish attitude of fear. You have been adopted into the very family circle of God and you can say with a full heart, 'Father, my Father.' The Spirit himself endorses our inward conviction that we really are the children of God. Think what that means! If we are his children we share his treasures, and all that Christ claims as his will belong to all of us as well! Yes, if we share in his sufferings we shall certainly share in his glory."   ROM. 8:14-18 (PHILLIPS TRANSL.)

IF YOU HAVE ever gone house hunting you remember some of the things you were looking for. The price had to be right, the lot a certain size, the structure of the house sound, and the location convenient. That word location had a meaning of much importance. You were looking for more than a lot and a house of brick, stone, or cedar siding. You wished to find a spot with certain advantages for you, your wife, and your children.

The location had to be near a church where both of you and your children could worship God and attend Sunday school. You wished your children to benefit from the religious and social experiences of Christian education. Your home had to be near first-class schools so that your boys and girls could make the most of what they have from God. It was your wish that the children be proud of their school. You also wanted to live in a community where as the years went by all of you in the family would develop a sense of belonging.

A GOD-GIVEN SENSE OF BELONGING

Because we are human beings the yearning to belong dwells in each of us. God made us this way. Our search for a place to live in a community shows a hunger for a sense of belonging. This is a healthy hunger. But because we are no longer what God wants us to be, our sense of belonging sometimes becomes twisted and bent. We want to belong to something because we fear isolation. We dread the destruction of the dignity that we feel we deserve. In our anxiety for the survival and development of the self, we are tempted to seek for ourselves, selfishly. We want tangible and visible evidences that we're worth something to ourselves and to others. And with this sense of belonging we also wish a feeling of security.

You may remember the surprise of a young minister at Levittown, Pennsylvania, when the members of the congregation complained about the cathedral chairs with which the church was furnished. There really was nothing wrong with the chairs, which were sturdy, practical, and comfortable. But still the people continued to complain. "At last I figured it out," said the minister in this new community. "The chairs moved. All the young people here have come from somewhere else, from upstate, Philadelphia, or New Jersey. Even though the distance isn't great, they have had to break with their old home ties. They are extremely eager for stability and for any signs of it. So I figured out a compromise. We fixed up kneeling stools so that they would hold the chairs firm. I didn't hear any complaints after that." (*The Organization Man,* by Wm. H. Whyte, Jr., p. 417)

Now that's stretching a God-given impulse a trifle too far. Yet behind all the search for secure belonging there may lurk a selfish desire for self-realization, dignity and worth, stability and security, all as ends in themselves. In so seeking the self we may destroy it. We may achieve the opposite of our goal. According to Paul, this kind of search means to live "according to the flesh," "according to nature," "according to instinct," "according to the world." Such a quest bears within itself the seeds of its own destruction. In seeking selfishly a sense of belonging, we may cut the umbilical cord that unites us with God and with one another. Inordinate fear of losing our identity works in us havoc, undermining our mental health, making us distrustful of our neighbor and unwilling to commit all our ways to God. Such fear is an expression of a slavish attitude. This all leads to bondage and imprisonment from which we can in no wise set ourselves free.

Freedom from fear of not belonging to someone or something cannot be had simply by "joining" an organization, however worthy. Yet some of us work feverishly at trying to fill up an inner void by joining a plethora of organizations. No one has ever yet conquered fear by fleeing from it. Freedom from fear comes through a sense of belonging to the human family as the household of God. This new kind of relationship to God and to one another is not something that we can produce or secure by drowning ourselves in an endless stream of activities or by using all the techniques approved by men.

A SENSE OF BELONGING TO GOD

Freedom through belonging to the family of God's redeemed children is not our achievement. It is the gift of God in Jesus Christ. In Christ Jesus the Spirit of the law of life sets us free from the fear that gnaws at the roots of our being while we struggle for the survival of the self. In the face of all the threats of change and decay He imbues us with a sense of being alive in God. In facing the kingdom of the world, the flesh, and the devil, Christ gives us an increasing sense of belonging to the royal reign of God. Into us mortals the Lord Jesus breathes courage to address God as our Father. Through Christ each of us can say with a full heart, "Father, my Father."

Such freedom was bought with a price. On the night of His

betrayal our Lord was on His knees in Gethsemane. Before Him lay the road to the Cross, betrayal by one of His disciples, denial by another, and desertion by them all. In that hour of anguish as He prayed "his sweat became like great drops of blood falling down upon the ground." In that hour of intense struggle with the devil, sin, and death, a prayer came from His lips: "Father, if it be possible, let this cup pass from me." In His last moments on the Cross the Lord Jesus uttered a prayer that He as a youth had learned to repeat every evening. This was part of a prayer psalm: "Into thy hands I commit my spirit" (Psa. 31:5a).

On the Cross when the Lord Jesus uttered this prayer He added the significant word, "Father." Through Christ's sacrifice for us on the Cross, He won for us sinners the right and the liberty to address God as "Our Father." Only because our Lord has won for us this freedom through his Death and Resurrection can we carry out His command to pray, "Our Father who art in heaven." In Christ, the Apostle tells us, "You have been adopted into the very family circle of God, and you can say with a full heart, 'Father, my Father.' The Spirit himself endorses our inward conviction that we really are the children of God. Now we have a sense of belonging to the very family circle of God. Think what this means!"

A SENSE OF HOLY VOCATION

Not long ago a group of laymen met to discover ways in which they could carry out their Christian responsibility in their different vocations. They listened to addresses aimed at clarifying their responsibility to God and to men. Much that was said was veiled in heavy language of theology. Weary of such highly involved discussions one layman got up and spoke, "Much of what we have heard seems to make God's claim on us complicated. Words like 'existential commitment,' 'ground of our being,' and 'the transcendent immanence of God' are not filled with meaning for most of us. Actually God's claim on us can be put into two short sentences. In Christ God says to us, 'I want you,' and 'I can use you.'"

God wants us! He does not look on us as unwanted children. He wishes us to have a sense of belonging to Him. He wants us so much that for us He gave Himself in the Person of His Son, who lived and suffered, died and rose again. Through His written Word God makes known to us here and now that He wants us just as we are. He wants us with all our frustrations and our aspirations, our failures and our achievements, our anxieties and our hopes. His wanting us now and always in His redeemed family shows His loving will for us. This is something for us to think about and to act upon. The contemplation of God's love for us ought almost to sweep us off our feet.

A SENSE OF A CALL TO SUFFER

Like the Apostle, however, we must check our enthusiasm. We know that we are not in heaven, not yet. Here on earth belonging to God's family means sharing in Christ's sufferings. For some of us this may mean suffering in body: illness, unemployment, financial or professional setbacks, and a host of other misfortunes that make us feel a strong kinship with Job. But sharing the sufferings of Christ is even more largely a matter of the heart; the suffering is inward. As children of God we have to live our faith without being able to prove to ourselves or to others that what we believe is true. We can witness to our faith, but we can't prove it. We have in our hands nothing tangible to tell us that our hope is not a delusion; nothing visible to prove to ourselves or to others that our faith is more than wishful thinking. As children in the family of God's redeemed we have no outward security, really nothing to cling to. Even the suffering that the predicament of Christian existence entails in a sinful world,—not even this can prove that what we believe is altogether so.

Neither does a sense of belonging call merely for acceptance of suffering as coming from the hands of God. Acquiescence to suffering may be only our normal response. We may say, "If that's the way it is to be, then there's little I can do about it." If we want to be a bit more pious about our lot we may say with wistful self-resignation, "The Lord's will be done," or something like that. Sharing in the sufferings of Christ goes much further than being simply semi-fatalistic.

To share Christ's sufferings in their height and their depth means to love God for the suffering that He sends, to praise Him for our afflictions, and to extol Him for our chastisements. "The Lord disciplines him whom he loves, and chastises every son whom he receives" (Heb. 12:6). When Job first heard about the tragic death of his sons and daughters he did not only say, "The Lord gave, and the Lord has taken away." Even sorrow, suffering, and death could not keep him from adding a word of praise, "Blessed be the name of the Lord" (Job 1:21).

In full view of earth's tragedy, the sense of belonging to God swept St. Paul off his feet. If you scrutinize a little more closely his description of this new relationship to God, you will find that he is groping after words to set forth the indescribable. Here in Romans eight, when he does get round to putting down on paper what he feels, the phrases come gushing forth like volumes of water on their way to the sea. If we're God's children we share in all God's treasures. All that belongs to Christ belongs to us. We are heirs of God, and co-heirs with Christ. The roots of all our fears and anxieties have been cut off. It's true! We really belong to God, and in Him we belong to one another.

To share in Christ's sufferings with a shout of praise unto God is part and parcel of the sense of belonging to His family. In this experience the Spirit Himself endorses our inward conviction that we are children of God. In other words, not through what we do but through what God does we know that we belong to Him and to one another in Him. This knowledge sets us free. He has liberated us from all dread of losing ourselves. Anxiety about lack of prestige, dignity, and worth may still be present, but it has lost its sting. Our neighbors and co-workers may seem like our competitors, but they no longer constitute a threat to our inner security. In the family and in the church, in the community, and at the daily task, we are free to love our neighbor. As Christians we can run the risk of loving our neighbor as ourselves, and more than ourselves, because we have a sense of belonging to the very family circle of God. Think what this means!

25. W. Stanford Reid

William Stanford Reid, Presbyterian Church of Canada. Born, Montreal, Sept. 13, 1913. Educated, McGill University, Montreal (B.A., M.A.), Westminster Seminary, Philadelphia (Th.B., Th.M.), University of Pennsylvania (Ph.D.). Various academic prizes. Teacher, McGill University (1934-51); Associate professor of history since 1951. Member, learned societies. Books: The Church of Scotland in Lower Canada (1936); Economic History of Great Britain (1954); Problems in European Intellectual History (1954); two others in preparation.

The message about "God's Feeble Witnesses" stresses the local need for personal workers. The sermon brings out three aspects of a "life situation" among church folk in worldly Corinth. The main divisions of the message come from the text in its setting. The stress falls on the fact that any believer can engage in soul winning.

This kind of sermon has what many an evangelical congregation desires today: a Bible message relevant to the spiritual needs of the hearers; a clear exposition of a passage written of God to meet such a need; and guidance in doing the will of the Lord as He makes it known in the passage.

In such a large, important field, no one sermon can deal with all the aspects. In response to inquiries about the way to do personal work, there could be a later sermon about the "life situation" in Acts 8:26-40, where a man on foot wins for Christ a government official riding in a chariot. When the next revival comes it will largely be due, we hope, to personal work by witnesses whom the world counts feeble.

GOD'S FEEBLE WITNESSES

"Ye see your calling, brethren, how that not many wise men after the flesh, not many mighty, not many noble, are called: but God hath chosen the foolish things of the world to confound the wise; and God hath chosen the weak things of the world to confound the things which are mighty; and base things of the world, and things which are despised, hath God chosen, yea, and things which are not, to bring to nought things that are: that no flesh should glory in his presence. But of him are ye in Christ Jesus, who of God is made unto us wisdom, and righteousness, and redemption: that, according as it is written, 'He that glorieth, let him glory in the Lord.'"   I CORINTHIANS 1:26-31

EVERY MEMBER of Christ's Church ought to be a witness for Him. Today, as at all other times, the crying need of the Christian Church is for witnesses. And yet when we face the opportunity to proclaim the Gospel to those who know it not, often we feel inadequate for the task. In our day and generation the Christian message often seems to be outmoded, outdated, and generally irrelevant. Consequently, in self-conscious weakness we refrain from speaking the word that God would place in our mouths.

That this is not a new problem is evident from what Paul says in this opening chapter of his first letter to the Corinthians. The members of that congregation lived in a city that was one of the most important, both commercially and intellectually, in the whole Aegean area. To many persons in such an environment the Gospel seemed to be mere foolish babbling. Apparently some of the Christians had attempted to meet the situation by trying to seem as intellectual as their pagan neighbors. But this sort of sophistication had resulted in nothing more than turning the simple message of the Gospel into an arid philosophical system.

Other believers, who did not have the ability or the training for that sort of thing, seem to have withdrawn into their shells. If so, they feared to bear testimony, because they felt that no one would believe. Hence the witness of the Church in Corinth was in grave danger of extinction.

This is the first problem with which Paul deals in his epistle. It is true, he says, that the Gospel is foolishness to those who do not believe, for they wish to judge everything in terms of their own wisdom and experience. The Jews want a sign from heaven, and the Greeks desire the philosophy of men. God, however, has chosen a unique method of bringing men to Himself. He has called feeble, powerless, apparently foolish persons to bear witness in a world of power and of learning. Through these feeble witnesses He would bring the men of this world to accept and acknowledge Christ as the power and the wisdom of God.

Now let us turn to our passage and examine what Paul has to say about God's feeble witnesses.

I. GOD'S CALL OF FEEBLE WITNESSES

First of all, and of fundamental importance, is the fact that God calls these feeble witnesses. So Paul begins by saying that the early Christians did not appoint themselves. It was God who determined that they should bring Christ to their world, and this must always be the case. No witness can ever be self-appointed, particularly in the service of God. In the Old Testament repeatedly we find determined attacks upon false prophets, who claim to speak for Jehovah, but who have not received His call to this high office. Likewise in New Testament times, as in subsequent generations, no one has ever had the right to set himself up as a herald of God, not unless first and foremost God has called him to this high office. Today to be a witness means to serve as God's herald. A herald can be a true witness for Christ only after he has received from God a call to this work.

Paul assures the Corinthian Christians, however, that if they indeed know Christ as their Saviour and Lord, they also have a call from God to tell others about Christ. The Apostle is not here writing his letter to a few select Corinthian leaders, such as the pastors and elders of the congregation. He is speaking to all of the believers in Christ, and pointing out that God has called each of them to bear witness. Even as the early Christians, when they were scattered abroad from Jerusalem, "went everywhere preaching the word" (Acts 8:4), so today witnessing is clearly the business of all those who are Christ's people. If indeed we know Christ as our Redeemer, it is our God-given responsibility, and our high privilege, to serve as His witnesses.

Right here we note that God's ways are not those of man. When man desires to make an impression on his fellows, what course does he pursue? For instance, when there is a campaign for some type of charity, a certain political action, or some other cause that seeks public support, the advocates of the movement seek to enlist the wealthy, the powerful, the influential, so that they will lend the cause their weight. In this way, the leaders hope, others will be interested and impressed so that they too will join the movement. This is man's way, for man ever thinks in terms of human wisdom and power.

When God chooses witness bearers, His way is wholly different. He calls those who are unimportant in this world—the weak, the poor, the foolish. As the Lord Jesus pointed out, it is only those who are willing to become like little children who can enter the Kingdom. In the early days of the Church the slaves seem to have given the Gospel a far more enthusiastic welcome than did the wealthy classes.

And yet we must not suppose that God never has called the wealthy and the highly educated to be His witnesses, or that He does not do so today. If and when He does so honor them, they too must realize that with all their wealth, and all their intellectual powers, they are utterly dependent upon Him. Even as they rely upon Him alone for redemption, so must they look upon themselves as His feeble witnesses. In their mouths the witness to the world will seem foolish.

Thus, whether we be rich or poor, wise or foolish, in the eyes of our world, we must continually remind ourselves that as Christians God has chosen us to be His witnesses, and that from the world's point of view we are silly, even moronic, in bearing testimony to such a simple Gospel. This is the high calling of every Christian. If this were all that the Apostle could say, however, his message would be disheartening. But he goes on to tell good news about our testimony for Christ.

II. GOD'S POWER FOR FEEBLE WITNESSES

In the second place the Apostle points out that with their call from God to be His witnesses, the Corinthian Christians have also received His power. The same truth holds good for us today.

The natural tendency—and one may even say, the sinful tendency—is for any of Christ's witness bearers to emphasize his own wisdom and power. By resort to argumentation, by appeal to the emotions, or by some other human means, he strives to lead men to accept the Gospel. Or else he goes to the other extreme, feeling that he is so foolish and so helpless that it is useless for him to open his mouth. In either case, alas, he is concentrating attention upon himself and his abilities, or lack of abilities. He is thinking about the effectiveness of his testimony, as though everything depended on his own powers.

As far as Paul is concerned, this way of thinking is vain and useless. Since to the unbeliever the Gospel is foolishness, neither by worldly philosophy nor by human power can the Christian convince him that the Gospel is true, and that its claims are valid. In sheer brain force the Christian frequently cannot equal the non-believer, nor is the believer able to adduce the sort of empirical "scientific proofs" that the non-believer demands. Even more basic, however, is the fact that the non-Christian does not even desire to believe the Gospel. The Gospel deals with him as a sinner, demands that he repent, and commands him to place his trust in Christ alone as Saviour. To all of this the unbeliever responds by laughing at the Christian's testimony. Feeling that the Gospel is outrageous in its claims, the man in view does not want "salvation." He will pay no heed to the believer's witness, and no one can change the outlook of such a determined unbeliever. If this be the case, what is the point in the Christian's endeavor to bear witness for Christ? Is it not utterly foolish? To this question Paul would reply, "From the world's point of view, yes!"

Nevertheless, the Christian must bear his witness. In love and in charity, as God gives him opportunity, he must be prepared to show men that they are sinners, and that their sinfulness is the source of their woes, both in mind and in body. Yet it can never be enough merely to condemn another man's sins. The

Christian also knows that in His sovereign grace Almighty God has provided a way of salvation through Jesus Christ. Therefore the Christian should always direct his testimony toward bringing men, one by one, to a living faith in Christ as the One who has paid the penalty for the believer's sins. Despite all possible ridicule and opposition, the Christian must ever bear witness to Christ, and to what He has done. With all the fervor and urgency of which he is capable, the believer ought to present Him as God's answer to all of men's needs.

Someone may object: "If men regard such testimony as foolishness, if they do not wish to be saved, what is the point in bearing such witness?" The answer is that through the mighty inworking power of His Holy Spirit God uses the testimony of His feeble witnesses, and makes their testimony effective for the winning of souls. For this reason God promised through the mouth of Isaiah: "My word . . . shall not return unto me void, but it shall accomplish that which I please, and it shall prosper in the thing whereto I sent it" (Isa. 55:11). In like manner Paul never grows weary of driving home the truth that Christian faith is worked into the heart of an individual, not by human wisdom or persuasion, but by the sovereign action of the Holy Spirit. "By grace are ye saved through faith; and that not of yourselves: it is the gift of God" (Eph. 2:8).

This is the power that lies behind the witness of the believer. Not his own testimony, not his own oratory, not even his own life, but the miraculous regenerating power of the Triune God is what brings an unsaved person to belief in Christ as Saviour, with obedience to Him as Lord and Master.

The Apostle, however, goes even further. In the passage now before us he writes about God's way of calling feeble believers to serve as His witnesses, and about His power ever behind their testimony for Christ. Then he goes on to unfold a truth even more glorious.

III. GOD'S TRIUMPH THROUGH FEEBLE WITNESSES

In the third place, the Apostle speaks about the triumph of God's feeble witnesses. Because the power of God makes the testimony of Christians effective, this witness eventually wins the victory. In truth he does not see coming to Christ immediately every person to whom he speaks. Indeed, the personal worker may not ever see some of them accept the Gospel. Herein lies the mystery of God's sovereign plan and predestination.

Nevertheless, as the believer continues to testify for Christ, he will see that even those who have most violently opposed the Gospel are brought to acceptance of Christ as their Saviour and Lord. Thus "God hath chosen . . . things which are not, to bring to nought things that are, that no flesh should glory in his presence" (I Cor. 1:28-29). Here is the triumph of God through His feeble witnesses, the triumph that brought about the submission of the mighty Roman Empire, and tamed the barbarian tribes of Europe; the triumph that in the sixteenth century curbed the vaunted power of the Roman ecclesiastical hierarchy; the triumph that throughout the world today is manifesting itself in hosts of humble hearts and lives who have been transformed through God's feeble witnesses.

In all such triumphs no one feels more astonished than the Christian witness himself. Ofttimes willingly and consciously, sometimes unwittingly and unconsciously, as in days of persecution, he has borne his testimony. In all cases he has rightly felt that with his own powers he could accomplish nothing. Then comes the hour when the recipient of that testimony suddenly beholds the light in God's Word, so that he repents, believes, and obeys the Gospel. Then the witness bearer gladly acknowledges that it is God alone who has wrought the miracle of redemption in the other person's heart. As a witness for Christ the believer has been a humble agent in the hands of his God.

Through the feeblest of the saints the Spirit of God brings to Christ as Saviour and Lord those who have been His enemies. Through humble witness bearers He brings into the fullness of His love and grace those who once stood outside His Kingdom. Through those who speak out for Christ, with words apparently ineffectual, the Lord God wins those whom He has called. Through feeble witnesses He has won the victory. "Thanks be unto God, which always causeth us to triumph in Christ" (II Cor. 2:14a).

The Lord works this way in order that no one may glory in himself, but that everyone may ascribe the honor to God. His witnesses have no right to glory, save in Him, or to take any credit to themselves. Neither should those who believe through Christian testimony take any credit to themselves, for apart from the power of the Holy Spirit, even the truth of the Gospel would have made no impression on their hearts and lives. For the effectualness of the Christian witness all the glory and the honor must go to Him who alone is the Lord and Redeemer of men.

Again and again Christian history has illustrated the truth of our text. In the Early Church God's feeble witnesses often came from among slaves and other social outcasts. Through such lowly agents, many of whom encountered persecution, torture, and death, the Church conquered large parts of the Roman Empire. During the Reformation Luther, Calvin, and other men on whom the Roman Church looked down, won for the evangelical cause large portions of Europe. In Victorian England such a scholar as William Robert Dale, of Carr's Lane, Birmingham, stood amazed at the overpowering effects of the Gospel as spoken by such an unlearned man as Dwight L. Moody. Likewise in our own century, with all its materialism, sophistication, and secularism, the Lord blesses personal work by countless inconspicuous saints.

For us this text from Paul is most practical. It means that day after day all through life each Christian as an individual should bear his witness to Christ as the Saviour of all those who come to Him through faith. Many times the believer may feel that his testimony is feeble, foolish, and ineffective. Still he is to continue bearing witness, knowing that he is not the one to decide whether or not his words will win a soul for Christ.

The Lord alone can make any such decision. He does so when and where He pleases. Our responsibility is humbly, clearly, and lovingly to show forth Christ, leaving the results of our witness to the hands of Him for whom we have borne testimony. "So then neither is he that planteth any thing, neither he that watereth; but God that giveth the increase" (I Cor. 3:7). This is the confidence and the joy of Christ's feeble witnesses, for in Him alone do they triumph.

26. E. N. Patterson

Eugene Nelson Patterson, Southern Baptist. Born, Stonington, Ill., Feb. 19, 1909. Educated, Howard College, Birmingham, Ala. (A.B.); New Orleans Baptist Seminary (Th.B., Th.,M., Th.D.). Graduate work, Union Seminary, New York; Oxford University, England; Temple University, Philadelphia (Th.D., pending completion of thesis). Pastor, (1935-45). Professor of Preaching, New Orleans Baptist Seminary, since 1945. Articles in theological journals.

The message about "The Gospel According to Paul" shows some of the reasons why during the past generation Southern Baptist churches have multiplied and increased more rapidly than those of any other major Protestant body. These brethren believe in preaching the Pauline Gospel, and that with apostolic fervor. Seldom do they tone it down or weaken it with water from man-made cisterns. When they cannot secure ministers properly trained, they use the best men at hand, but Southern Baptist colleges and seminaries are now sending forth hosts of educated ministers.

This kind of uncompromising pulpit work loses much of its sting when the hearers respect and like the pastor, or visiting professor. If they trust him as a surgeon of the soul they expect him to use the scalpel in every hour of need; and at other times to sound a warning against neglect of any sin-sick soul. It can be no accident that many of the local churches that appeal to hosts of common people do so by stressing the work of the pulpit, Sunday morning, Sunday night, Wednesday evening, and at other times, with Bible sermons full of Scriptural rigor. "If any man will come after me, let him deny himself, take up his cross, and follow me" (Matt. 16:24).

THE GOSPEL
ACCORDING TO PAUL

"Am I now seeking the favor of men, or of God? Or am I
trying to please men? If I were still pleasing men, I should
not be a servant of Christ.

"For I would have you know, brethren, that the gospel
which was preached by me is not man's gospel, for I did
not receive it from man, nor was I taught it, but it came
through a revelation of Jesus Christ."

GALATIANS 1:10-12

W HAT IS THE GOSPEL? When you hear the word, what first
comes to your mind? In the sermons and discourses of the Apostles,
you find that what they call the Gospel is closely related to Jesus
of Nazareth. In fact, it is easy to outline what they consider the
heart of the Gospel. In the earliest sermons that we have from
the Apostles, the Gospel stresses the fact that Jesus of Nazareth
was the promised Messiah. These apostolic preachers refer to His
life as He walked among men. They record His Death on the
Cross, His lying in the tomb for three days, and then His Resurrection.

Writing by inspiration the Apostles promise that some day
He is coming back to earth, this time in glory. In the light of
all the truths about Jesus Christ, these early preachers call on
men everywhere to repent of their sins and to have faith in
Christ, so as to be reconciled to God. In our day such apostolic
witness to the facts about Christ as the sinless Son of God has
became known as *kerygma*, which is the transliteration of a
Greek word that means preaching, or proclaiming, the Gospel.

In Paul's letter to the Galatians you find a number of references to what he terms the Gospel. These references appear
especially in the first twelve verses. Today we are singling out the
last three of the twelve. Here the Apostle has some striking and

important things to say about the Gospel that the Lord has called him to proclaim. These things ran counter to what many of his readers thought about the Gospel. So do the utterances of the Apostle run counter to many of our own conceptions about the Gospel today. So let us give heed to these words about the Gospel according to Paul.

I. NOT PLEASING TO THE WORLD

Paul's Gospel did not please the world of his day. In presenting it boldly he did not even try to please men, because he could not do that and still please God. Today this is fundamental to our understanding of the Gospel. It never has pleased the world, does not please the world today, and never will please the world in any age. In the life of almost every preacher there come times when he seeks to revise the Gospel so as to make it acceptable and even palatable to the world. But as he learns more about God he realizes that there is a vast gulf between the Gospel and the world.

The Gospel of Christ comes into direct conflict with many popular movements in our world. This has always been true. Christ was put to death because He would not compromise with evil. Many of the Apostles were put to death because their preaching of the Gospel was contrary to the opinions of their day. When you proclaim the message of Christ at once you touch on the question of human freedom, on race prejudice, on the liquor traffic, on divorce, and on every other moral problem that confronts our present-day society. Whenever a layman hears this Gospel he has to decide whether he will begin to obey God, or go on with the world. He has come to the parting of the ways.

The Gospel according to Paul puts many a person out of business. Before a man comes face to face with Christ, there may be in his heart a conflict as far as his work is concerned. But when once he hears the truth as it is in Christ, he may have to change his entire career. A former professional gambler told me how he had found Christ as his Saviour. He said that when he heard and accepted the Gospel of Christ he knew that he could not have Christ as Lord without giving up his way of making a livelihood. Through all the years since "the day of the Cross," the same has held true with multiplied thousands.

This Gospel still calls on every man to repent because of his sin, and people today do not want to repent. When a man lost in sin hears the truth as it is in Christ, he has to decide whether he will become a slave of Christ, or continue in his sin. If a person who believes in Christ takes it upon himself to tell another person that he ought to change his entire way of living, the normal reaction is for the hearer to tell the adviser that this is none of his business. But you cannot respond to God that way, because He is actively engaged in the business of redeeming lost souls, one by one. God still demands repentance for sin. Without repentance and conversion, without repudiating his own sins and then turning away from them to God, no person can become a Christian.

Christ still calls for the highest in the way of personal righteousness. It is true that in Him we who believe have perfect freedom, and that in a lofty sense we can do as we please. But every real Christian knows that his new freedom in Christ calls for his very best in personal righteousness. Since this Gospel comes into direct conflict with every person who is lost in sin, is it any wonder that such preaching does not please the world? There is no way to present this Gospel so that a person lost in sin can say, "I accept it," and then go on living in sin. "If any man be in Christ, he is a new creature: old things are passed away; behold, all things are become new" (II Cor. 5:17).

II. NOT PLANNED AS MEN WOULD PLAN

The Gospel according to Paul is not planned as any man would have planned it. A man would try to make it seem rational to the world. From the very beginning up to the present hour, man has tried to assay the Lord God in his test tube of reason. It still is the natural thing for one of us to say, "If I can not understand the Gospel, I will not believe the Gospel." But the very minute you make Christianity, or the Gospel, seem rational to the world, that minute the Gospel ceases to be Christian. For example, the Church has often tried to conform with the wishes of the world by asking man to leave his eternal salvation in the hands of the Church.

Any such appeal sounds plausible. "If you merely become a member of the local church organization, we stand ready to do the rest. We can even give you a formula, to show how the whole matter works. You join the church, receive baptism, and live in the church. That is all we require of our members." Throughout the ages so-called Christian churches have striven to make it reasonable and easy, painless and pleasant, to become members of the local church. By so doing, these would-be churches have gotten away from God's plan for salvation, which plan is the Gospel.

In writing to a worldly church in Corinth, Paul said, "We preach Christ crucified, a stumbling block to Jews and folly to Gentiles" (I Cor. 1:23). This is just as true in America today as when Paul wrote these words to the Corinthians. To the religious Jew of the first century, the Gospel was a stumbling block. Since he had a set of rules to live by, why did he need the power of God? When he heard the Gospel according to Paul, he felt that it did not make sense. Since he already had a religion made by men, he did not understand one that came from above. How true this is today! When a person has a religion of his own, without any reference to the power of God, he finds in the Gospel a stumbling block. Unless somehow God breaks through this barrier of a man-made religion, such a man will not believe.

The Apostle also declared that the Gospel seemed foolish to the Gentile. In terms of today, this points to the man of the world, who is not particularly concerned about religion of any kind. How true this is today! A man lost in sin hears that Jesus Christ came into the world and died on the Cross to save him from his sins. He learns that in order to come into right relations with the all-righteous God he must repent for his sins and then accept Christ as his offering, his sacrifice for his sin. To the man separated from God because of his sins, the Gospel sounds like the most foolish, irrational story that anyone has ever conceived. No wonder the man of the world, simply through reason, refuses to accept such a "foolish" story!

And yet to those of us who believe in Christ that so-called foolish story has become the wisdom of God and the power of God unto salvation. How little we mortals can understand about the ways of our God! How often we rebel against His plan for salvation, which plan is the Gospel! "O the depth of the riches and wisdom and knowledge of God! How unsearchable are his judgments and how inscrutable his ways!" (Rom. 11:33). There is nothing for us mortals to do with this God but to trust Him, to accept His Son, and to obey the Gospel.

III. A REVELATION FROM JESUS CHRIST

Paul declares that the Gospel came to him as a revelation from Jesus Christ. In the twelfth verse of the opening chapter in Galatians he makes a startling statement about the origin of his Gospel. He insists that he did not receive it from man, nor was he taught it, but that this Gospel came to him through a revelation of Jesus Christ. At first one may ask, "Did not Saul as a new convert study all of these things with men who believed in Christ? Since he was a highly trained Jewish rabbi, he must have known all about the Old Testament before he became a Christian. What then did he mean by this revelation through Jesus Christ?"

In order to gain light on the meaning here, let us turn to the First Gospel, where we find a supreme passage about the Church. Jesus is walking with His disciples, and He asks them a question. "As you go about your daily tasks what do you hear people saying about me? Who do people say that I am?" The disciples responded at once, saying that He was popularly supposed to be John the Baptist, presumably risen from the dead, or else Elijah, Jeremiah, or one of the other prophets.

Then the Lord Jesus made the question extremely personal. "But who do you say that I am?" As the spokesman for the apostolic band, Simon responded that He was the Christ, the Son of the living God. This was the testimony that Jesus desired. Immediately He told Peter and the other disciples that they did not get this tremendous truth from men, but that they had received it as a direct revelation from His Father in heaven. "Flesh and blood has not revealed this to you, but my Father who is in heaven."

This must have been what the Apostle meant when he wrote to worldly-minded Galatians that he had received the Gospel "through a revelation of Jesus Christ." The same principle holds true today. Apart from a personal revelation from God through the Holy Spirit, no man can know Christ as the Son of God, and his personal Redeemer from sin. For much the same reason a person can use all of his knowledge and ability in trying to explain the Gospel of Christ, and still he may fail. As Christians, and even as ministers, we do not present this Gospel in our own strength. There is an unseen supernatural power that always accompanies the telling of this Gospel. Hence the Apostle could declare, "I am not ashamed of the Gospel: it is the power of God for salvation to every one who has faith" (Rom. 12:1). In this Gospel today we still have the super-atomic power of the Lord God Almighty.

IV. THE GOSPEL FOR OUR WORLD TODAY

When one thinks about our world today, one may feel that as a Christian he faces a hopeless task. How can he ever teach any sort of religion, and above all this Gospel that runs counter to everything the world holds dear? But when a person has come into personal contact with the power of the Gospel, and by that power has himself been transformed, by faith he knows that it is still the power of God to every man who believes.

Today we need to rediscover what Paul learned long ago, and never forgot: that no one can reconcile this Gospel with the ways of the world. The Gospel never has been pleasing to the world, does not please the world now, and never will seem pleasant to the world of tomorrow. For this very reason we who preach must beware. In every way possible Satan strives to get us to turn aside from the Scriptures, and to "preach" anything else rather than the saving message of the Apostles.

Many times we feel tempted to try to make the Gospel of redemption seem rational to men of the world lost in sin. From Paul we need to learn that the Gospel begins to seem rational to a sinful man only after he comes to know Christ as his personal Saviour. When a man honestly and earnestly seeks God through Christ, he discovers to his amazement that all the while God has been seeking him. May every one of you here now have the experience that led the song writer to testify:

I stand amazed in the presence of Jesus the Nazarene,
And wonder how He could love me, a sinner condemned,
   unclean.
How marvelous! how wonderful! And my song shall ever be:
How marvelous! how wonderful! is my Saviour's love to me!

27. William C. Robinson

William Childs Robinson, Presbyterian, U. S. ("South-
ern"). Born, Lincolnton, N. C., Dec. 4, 1907. Educated,
Salem College, Roanoke, Va. (A.B.); University of
South Carolina (M.A.); Columbia Seminary, Columbia,
S. C. (Th.B.); Harvard University (Th.D.). Graduate
study, University of Basel, Switzerland. Pastorate
(1921-26). Professor of historical theology, Columbia
Seminary, Decatur, Ga., since 1926. Visiting lecturer,
Free Church College, Edinburgh; Union Seminary,
Richmond, Va.; Western Seminary, Holland, Mich.;
Institute of Theology, Princeton Seminary, N.J.; Ful-
ler Seminary, Pasadena. Member, learned societies.
Contributor, scholarly journals. Books: Christ, the
Hope of Glory (1945); Who Say Ye That I Am? (1948);
The Bread of Life (1950).

The author prepared the following sermon for delivery at the
fortieth anniversary of his being graduated from Salem College.
The message shows the rugged strength of the older Calvinism,
based on the theology of Paul. Before the spokesman states his
case, constructively, first he clears the ground. With the Apostle
he protests against theological systems built up from below, like
the Tower of Babel, and religions that rely on bases other than
Christ Jesus as crucified.

Biblically, the sermon consists in a saturated solution of inspired sayings from Paul, and in declaration of his doctrines as
the only way out of present-day muddleheadedness, as well as the
only hope for a world groping after God. The quotations come
from certain well-known authors, and from other sources far
from familiar, all of which show wide and careful reading. In
keeping with the content, the style often has a sense of life, motion,
and strength.

In a single message only an exceptional man, highly schooled in *his field, could present all these materials strongly, clearly, and cumulatively, and then make a spiritual application to the deeper needs of our day. Only an occasional congregation, at home in the Scriptures, and versed in theological lore, could relish, digest, and live by all these Biblical truths. On the contrary, if we had more preaching of this kind, as in Scotland of yore, and sometimes here in the States, we might now have hearers like the early saints, who seem to have understood the Epistles of Paul, even those to the Ephesians and the Colossians.*

PREACHING JESUS CHRIST AS CRUCIFIED

"I determined not to know anything among you, save Jesus Christ, and him as crucified."—I COR. 2:2 *(Translated from the Greek)*

THE CHRISTIAN FAITH is founded on a Person, not an idea. That Person, Jesus Christ, Paul presented as the Messiah, and proclaimed as crucified, as well as risen from the dead. On the other hand, ancients built the Tower of Babel in order to scale the parapets of heaven. Athens erected her altars to gods known and unknown. Modern man acclaims six mighty religions as good roads up the mountain to God. Today, as yesterday, men are pinning their hopes, not on Christ as a Person, but on intellectual principles, survival values, and ethical ideals.

For us men and for our salvation God came down to earth in the Person of His only Son. In utter self-abnegation the Lord Jesus came all the way from the realms of glory to the Cross of Calvary. He who was on an equality with God took the form of a slave. The Most High became the most humble. And yet because of that love and lowliness He still is the Lord. That Man, dying athwart the sky, beyond the walls of Jerusalem, is now the Lord of Glory (I Cor. 2:8).

In Jesus Christ, whose face we can see only with the eyes of faith, God has revealed Himself to us supremely. Thus the apostolic procedure is to portray Christ as crucified for our sins, and to pray that through this testimony from God the Holy Spirit will bring sinful men to saving faith. Through the preaching of the Cross, it still pleases God to save those who believe this message about His Son. As this Gospel is preached, God brings us into oneness with Christ Jesus and thus makes Him to become our wisdom, our righteousness, our sanctification, and our redemption.

Accordingly, this section of First Corinthians teaches us: first, how God does not reveal Himself; secondly, how the Father of mercies opens to us sinners the fellowship of His redeemed family; and thirdly, how He causes these truths of the Gospel to bear upon our daily lives.

I. THE REVELATION NOT FROM MEN

First, then, for our salvation God does not reveal Himself to us sinners through the wisdom of philosophers, through the height of places in the world, through the eloquence of orators, or even through His own majestic work of creation. To redeem the world from sin God makes Himself known supremely in Christ and His Cross.

The Jews looked for a Messiah who would without measure receive the blessings of God. The Jews also believed, "He that is hanged is cursed of God." Stumbling over the fact that the Lord Jesus did not present the portentous signs of a Messianic Warrior delivering Israel from her enemies, the Jews rejected the revelation that God made in the crucified Redeemer.

As the Law was given of God to convict the Jew of sin, school him in his insufficiency, and thus lead him to righteousness, where alone righteousness could be found, so was philosophy given to the Greeks as a tutor to lead them Godward. Only let us be sure that we carry the analogy through. In the words of Johann George Hamann, an evangelical divine in Germany two hundred years ago, "Was reason given to make us wise? Just as little as the

Law was given to the Jews to make them just. Rather, it was given to convince us of the opposite: to show us how irrational our reason is, that our errors may be increased through reason, as sin was through the Law."

Plato has some glimmering of the situation when he urges us to "lay hold of the best human opinion in order by it to sail the dangerous sea of life as on a raft, unless we can find a stronger boat, or some word of God, which will surely and safely carry us" (*Phaedo*).

Martin Luther understood that the world owes the Gospel a grudge because the Gospel condemns the wisdom of this world (*On Galatians*). Even when speaking about Genesis John Calvin begs us not to begin with the elements of this world, but with the Gospel that sets before us Christ alone, with His Cross, and then holds us to this point. Calvin says:

> It is vain for any to reason as philosophers on the workman-ship of this world, except those who, having first been humbled by the preaching of the Gospel, have learned to submit the whole of their intellectual wisdom to the foolish-ness of the Cross.

When the Apostle looked at the Christians in Corinth he saw that God had not called into His fellowship many who were wise according to the flesh, not many mighty, not many noble. Likewise through Jeremiah the Lord warns the wise man not to glory in his wisdom, nor the mighty in his power, nor the rich in his wealth (Jer. 9:23). And the Psalmist testifies that no man can give God a ransom rich enough to redeem the soul of his brother (Psa. 69:6-8).

According to the *Magnificat,* God lifts up the lowly in order to confound the mighty. According to the Apostle John, believers are born, not of the nobility of blood, not of the will of the flesh, not of the will of man, but of God (John 1:13). So in Corinth God chose the foolish things of the world to answer the wise, the weak things to shame the strong, the base-born and the things that are of no account, those that are not in order, to put to nought the things that are. Yes, it pleased God that the world through its wisdom should not know God.

Hence the Apostle did not set forth to meet the wisdom of his world with a torrent of his own oratory. To have fought the world with its own weapons would have meant to betray the cause that God had committed to him. And so today the Gospel is like a trumpet, "more powerful and penetrating when it does not follow the range of the [entire] scale, but keeps to one penetrating note." The Gospel is not a philosophy to be proved by the persuasive words of man's wisdom, but a message from God to be attested by faith and accepted in trust. The Good News of God's mighty acts for our redemption needs and admits only the plain, straightforward telling, and anything else would tend to empty the Cross of all its saving power.

Luther feels sure that in preaching one does not need to shout or cry aloud, because the effectiveness of the Gospel does not lie in the lungs of a man, but in the power of the Holy Spirit. Even though the world counts the Gospel weakness and folly, to those whom He calls, it is the power and the wisdom of God. Even though it be Paul the Apostle who plants, and Apollos the orator who waters, it is only God who gives the increase. Since the effectiveness of the Gospel is wholly from God, we may expect Him to honor only the message that He has given. According to Frederic W. H. Myers, in his poem, *Saint Paul,* that message is Christ:

> Christ! I am Christ's, and let the name suffice you;
> Aye, for me too, He greatly hath sufficed.
> Lo, with no winning words would I entice you,
> Paul has no honor and no friend but Christ.

In Christ and His Cross behold the power of Almighty God. The vast diamond-studded Milky Way is but as scattered dust from the chariot wheels of the Almighty. He who measures the heavens with a span, and comprehends the dust of the earth in a balance, even the Most High God, has revealed Himself for our salvation, not in His majestic might, but in the weakness of the dying Redeemer; not in His unfathomable wisdom, but in the "folly" of the Cross. Hence it is the Crucified One who alone is the Mediator between God and men, the only One through whom we can come to the Father.

Twenty years ago the "German Christians" insisted that the great issue then was theism against atheism, that the Nazis were believers in God and revivers of the national religion, and consequently, that church people should give fealty to Adolf Hitler in his leadership against atheistic Communism. In order to counter this effort to bypass Jesus Christ, the "Confessing Church" issued the Barmen Declaration: "The One whom we have to hear in life and death, and to obey, is Jesus Christ our Lord."

As college men, who seem to stand above some of our fellows by a grain or two of knowledge, let us not fancy that without the Gospel we can immediately comprehend the Almighty in His infinitude. Let us beware of the current hyper-intellectualism that presumes to describe God's ways of self-revelation as nothing more than symbols. Who are we that we should dare to classify the God and Father of our Lord Jesus Christ as merely a symbol for some phrase of man's making, such as "the ultimate ground of Being"? According to Hendrik Kraemer, in *Religion and the Christian Faith*:

> Biblical religion discloses God's self-disclosure, Jesus Christ, the Wisdom of God, which not only transcends and transforms, but also confounds and judges all human wisdom, ontology and theology not excepted."

II. THE REVELATION THROUGH PREACHING CHRIST

On the other hand, through the power of the Holy Spirit, who brings men into the fellowship of the Father, it pleases God to honor the preaching of Christ, and Him as crucified. According to First Corinthians, preaching means confessing as Lord this Jesus who has been raised from the dead on the third day. It means relying upon Him for the grace and the peace that the Church sorely needs. It also means looking forward to His revelation in "the Day of Jesus Christ."

In the first and the second chapter, however, preaching Christ means pre-eminently proclaiming Him as crucified. The Church has never found the supreme symbol of her faith anywhere but in His Cross. Since Luther met the Cross everywhere in the Scriptures, the Reformer declared: "When I listen to Christ, there is sketched in my heart a picture of a Man hanging on a Cross, just as my countenance is naturally sketched upon the water when

I look therein." Calvin too is certain that only through the preaching of the Cross will any man find his way back to God as his Father. So let us join with all the saints in a mighty chorus:

> Our glory, only in the Cross,
> Our only hope, the Crucified!

Paul preached Christ as crucified because at the Cross He consummated His work as Mediator between God and men. In God's holy majesty He is justly offended with our rebellious race. According to Heinrich Vogel in *The Iron Ration of a Christian* (transl., 1942), "Whoever thinks he can smile at God's wrath will never praise Him eternally for His grace." Without Christ, God and man are further apart than heaven and earth. But in Christ, true God and true Man, God and man are much more intimate than two brothers. In Christ, sun and moon do not come so near to us as God does, for Emmanuel has come to earth in our flesh and blood.

As Luther says, in commenting on Isaiah 9:1, God the Creator of heaven and earth became true natural Man; the eternal Father's Son became the temporal Virgin's Son. He became our flesh-and-blood Brother, one of us, standing where we stand, offering for us His perfect sacrifice, and thus representing us before God. As our Fellow, He became our Substitute, the Lamb of God who took upon Himself the sin of the world. He who knew no sin was made sin for us, that we might be made the righteousness of God in Him. On that Cross He was made a curse, that we might receive the blessing of God. Thus He satisfied for us the demands of the Law, averted from us the wrath of the holy God, and delivered all those who trust in Him, both from the thralldom of the devil and from the fear of eternal death.

"God was in Christ, reconciling the world unto himself" (II Cor. 5:19a). When His ambassadors preach the revealing, the reconciling, the crucified Christ, the risen Lord reaches forth through the hand of the Holy Spirit and draws us unto Himself. The Spirit takes of the things of Christ and shows them unto us. In us He works faith, and thereby He unites us to Christ in our effectual calling. The Son of God became Man. In Christ's atoning Death He suffered and endured for us, to avert the wrath of God from our world of sinners.

Under the Covenant of Grace, God the Father gave unto the Son, out of every nation and kindred and tribe, a mighty host that no man can number. Now God the Holy Spirit comes as the inward Teacher to open our hearts for the preaching of the Cross, to receive Christ Jesus as our Saviour and Lord. We may hold back, too weakened by sin to decide, and of course indecision is the first evidence of frustration. Then the Spirit places our hands in the riven side of the Redeemer and thus calls us into the obedience of faith.

The objective revelation of God in Jesus of Nazareth, proclaimed in the Gospel, and the subjective work of the Holy Spirit, by which we receive Christ in faith—these are the two hands of God, by which the gracious Father brings the penitent prodigal back to His own forgiving bosom. Here in His righteousness and His love, His wisdom and His power, God acts to save us sinners. The Gospel is not merely the proclamation of man's ideas. It is the mighty work of God, by which He snatches from the thralldom of Satan the victim of sin and death, and then transports him into the Kingdom of Christ, the Son of His love. Preaching Christ and Him as crucified is the Gospel, the power of God unto salvation. In the words of Martin Luther to the Duke of Savoy,

> The commencement of salvation and the sum of Christianity is faith in Christ, who by His blood alone, and not by our works, has made atonement for sin, and put an end to the dominion of death. . . . This faith is a gift of God, which is created by the Holy Spirit in our hearts, and not found by our labors.

III. THE PRACTICAL EFFECTS OF PREACHING CHRIST

Thirdly, the Apostle calls upon us to realize the practical implications of God's gracious action, both in our own faith and in our outward activities. Through this preaching of the Cross God has put us into Christ. Hence the Father says, "In Christ Jesus I have begotten you through the Gospel" (I Cor. 4:15). The very same Creator who once said, "Let there be light," has "shined in our hearts, to give the light of the knowledge of the glory of God in the face of Jesus Christ" (II Cor. 4:6). It is not our wealth, our wisdom, or our might that has made us Christians. It is something greater and far more wonderful than all of these. Hence our faith does not stand in the wisdom of men, but in the power of God (I Cor. 2:5). So every believer ought to sing with John Campbell Shairp, Scottish professor of poetry at Oxford:

> Let me no more my comfort draw
> From my frail hold on Thee;
> In this alone rejoice with awe,—
> Thy mighty grasp of me.

If we would know that we belong to God, let us find ourselves where God has graciously put us, in Christ Jesus. He is made unto us wisdom from God, and righteousness, and sanctification, and redemption. He has won all of this for us by His life of perfect obedience, and by His Death in our stead. He has revealed it all to us through His Word. He gives it all to us, makes us partakers of it all, through His Holy Spirit. To lay hold of Him by faith means to appropriate the wisdom, the righteousness, the sanctification, and the redemption, all of which come from God. To find ourselves through faith in Him means to see ourselves filled with His wisdom, clothed with His righteousness, liberated from the thralldom of Satan, and transported into the Kingdom of Grace. To have Him means to enjoy forgiveness, victory, peace, and the hope of glory!

However manifold our sins, we are washed, we are sanctified, we are justified in the name of the Lord Jesus Christ, and by the Spirit of our God (I Cor. 6:11). As we find our salvation in Christ Jesus, so the Apostle calls on us to begin all our thinking and our acting with Him. Intellectually, begin where the Lord has graciously put you. Begin where the light is brightest; that is, "the light of the knowledge of the glory of God in the face of Jesus Christ." In the bequest that led to the founding of our oldest university, John Harvard directed:

> Let every student be plainly instructed and earnestly pressed
> to consider well the main end of his life and studies: to

know God and Jesus Christ, which is eternal life, and therefore to lay Christ in the bottom as the only foundation of all
knowledge and learning, and see that only the Lord giveth
wisdom. Let everyone seriously set himself by prayer in
secret to seek Christ as Lord and Master.

The problems of life today are too great to be faced in the
strength of puny man. Only when we stand upon the foundation
that Christ has laid does God give us His power to meet the
issues of life. May we never turn away from His testimonies and
try the nostrums of men. Why should anyone forsake the fountains
of living water and resort to man-made cisterns that can hold
no true water of life? When we start with Christ as the foundation,
the Author of our faith, and the center of our experience, there
are blessings from God in every issue of life. But when one takes
up every popular project that culture offers, when one treats
"some great cause" as "God's new Messiah," before which one
relativizes Jesus Christ, everything is thrown out of order. For,
as the Apostle says, "Other foundation can no man lay than that
is laid, which is Jesus Christ" (I Cor. 3:11).

Some have taken as their primary concern total abstinence;
others, pacifism; still others, economic collectivism; and others
again, racialism. These men all treat Jesus Christ as secondary.
Thus one decides that all use of force is wrong, and that if in
cleansing the Temple Jesus struck anyone with the whip of cords,
[as of course He did not], then this man will have nothing to do
with Jesus. Another starts with current studies about the evils
of alcoholism, and concludes that Jesus did wrong in turning the
water into wine.

Then this man undertakes to make excuses for Christ, on the
basis of some kenotic theory. But Jesus Christ still is the Lord, the
Subject, who declines to serve as the predicate in any human
scheme of things. He is not a being who when He became Man
could cease to be God. He who for us men and for our salvation
became Man is also the living God. With Him as Absolute we
begin. Before the cultural program of secularism, pacifism, or any
other "ism," we do not apologize for Jesus Christ, or try to give
Him a secondary place.

Later in First Corinthians the Apostle warns us that no man

is speaking by the Spirit of God when he says, "Let Jesus be anathema" (I Cor. 12:3). Would Paul say that a man is speaking by the Spirit of God when he by-passes, relativizes, or corrects the Lord Jesus, in order to give the first place to some popular program? Positively, the Apostle adds that only by the Spirit can any man call Jesus Lord. We mortals do not merely take account of Jesus, and then fit Him into our man-made programs. Rather does He put us among His shock troops, with which He fights and wins His battles for God.

As we face the sundry issues and problems of our day, may God the Holy Spirit give us grace to call Jesus Lord, to recognize Him as the Absolute, the Beginning, the Foundation, aside from which no other can ever be laid. For when Christ is presented in all His full-orbed grace and glory, the Lord God touches hearts and lives, to save them from drink, from fightings, from selfishness, and from race prejudice. The Christian Church today has no commission to reverse the process. Take God's way, and His Holy Spirit blesses it. Try to reverse God's way, and the Church no longer remains God's ambassador; her preaching becomes the chaff of men, and not the wheat that brings the bread of God to the hungry souls of men. The ambassador of the living God preaches the Lordship of Jesus Christ, the Crucified.

V. With Christ
in Later Epistles

28. W. E. Sangster

William Edwin Robert Sangster, Methodist. Born,
London, June 5, 1900. Educated, Richmond College
(B.A.); University of London (M.A., Ph.D.). Pastorates
(1926-42); Westminster Central Hall, London (1942-
58). During World War II, charge of Shelter Welfare
(1940-45). President, Methodist Conference in England
(1950). General Secretary, Home Mission Dept., Methodist Church of Great Britain, since 1958. Many books,
including: The Craft of Sermon Illustration (1946);
The Craft of Sermon Construction (1949); Let Me
Commend [evangelism] (1949); The Approach to
Preaching (1951); Teach Me to Pray (1951); The Secret
of the Radiant Life (1957); Power in Preaching (1958).

According to Billy Graham this London minister is "the greatest
preacher of our time." Surely he is one of the most popular. What
ever his rank among the few most effective living pulpit masters,
his message, "How To Be Saved," calls for more than a casual
reading. The sermon grows out of the key verse in the epistles of
Paul. The content and the spirit are strongly evangelical, in keeping with the ideals and the practice of John Wesley. Hence the
sermon from London might have stood at the forefront of the
present volume.

In form the message has the sort of simplicity that appeals to
multitudes of eager hearers today, more than a few of them highly
educated and cultured. The simplicity comes in part from skill
and care in the choice of a single trail, and from refusal to turn
aside and follow other pathways. Passing by more than a few
opportunities to complicate the message by making Biblical
detours, this popular preacher fixes our gaze at once on three
words that stand out in his text. He might also have dealt with
the difference between the two prepositions. All of that the inter-

preter leaves to learned books, while he deals only with his three words, as keys to unlock the treasuries of redemption.

Simplicity likewise appears in the name of the sermon, and in the opening words. First the speaker associates his text with the preaching heroes of the lay hearers. Then he makes clear what he proposes to do in the sermon. The approach tells the hearer what to expect, and leads him to desire what the preacher intends to give. What else is an introduction for? Such common-sense pulpit simplicity is worthy of note chiefly because of its rareness.

Like simplicity marks the interpretation of the three dominant words, in their Biblical order. Note the choice of materials, both from the Bible and from life elsewhere. Note also the simplicity of the literary form. The sermon contains much evangelical Wesleyan doctrine, but seldom in a form abstract and impersonal. However, the speaker does not dodge any difficult word. If he finds it needful to explain and illuminate such an unfamiliar term as "imputation," he does so without apology. As a rule he gives the preference to ideas and words clear and interesting to persons not yet theologically minded.

This kind of pulpit simplicity without shallowness evidently brings much satisfaction to many of our younger ministers. It should also lead us older men to utter a Methodist "Amen!"

HOW TO BE SAVED

"By grace are ye saved through faith."—EPHESIANS 2:8

THIS WAS ONE of the great texts of the Evangelical Revival. Indeed, this is one of the cornerstones of all evangelical truth. It was Martin Luther's mighty watchword. If Spurgeon was suddenly called upon to preach, he found himself most forceful with this theme. Among John Wesley's famous forty-four sermons the first is an exposition of this sentence from Paul.

Let me take the text in hand my own way, as every man must give his own message. This evening I propose to examine this grand verse by scrutinizing in turn each of the three key words. If we can understand what Paul meant by each of these words, and what the evangelical preachers of all ages have meant, we shall find that, however the text has been neglected in recent years, this is still the marrow of the Gospel for those of us who believe.

1. THE WORD GRACE

"By grace are ye saved." What do we mean by grace? The old definition called it "the free, unmerited favor of God." On that definition I cannot improve. It means that at the heart of all true communion with God there lies this deep truth, that God Himself took the initiative. He loves us better than we can ever love Him. He loves us with a love that does not depend on any answering love of ours. We have not to earn His love, any more than we earned our mother's love. We have but to receive it.

Always the initiative is from God! When you first came to Him, if indeed you have come to Him, you came because He first drew you. The very faith by which you lay hold of Him is not of yourself; this also is a gift of God. Nor is it only in the beginning that your salvation is God's free gift. Every onward step you have made in your spiritual pilgrimage has been possible by some bestowing of His grace. Even the life of holiness, to which all the time He is seeking to bring you—the Christlike quality that He wants to repeat in all of His children—even that you have not to achieve but to receive. It is a gift of God.

I know very well that such teaching affronts the modern man, and that many people reject it. The man in the street rejects it tacitly. He may have had nothing to do with religion but whenever death is mentioned he thinks to himself: "Well, I've never done anyone a bad turn!" In his own mind he believes that not having been a flagrant sinner he can work his passage to heaven by the good turns that he has done. I know how our church fathers would have commented on that!

I don't know that any of them ever used this illustration, but I feel sure that something of the sort would have crossed their minds. They would have imagined a man in debt for perhaps half a million pounds, but refusing the help of any friend, and seeking to meet his liabilities by hoarding up his farthings, and coming at last to the audit with elevenpence-halfpenny to set over against a debt of half a million pounds!

There is in man something that rejects the idea of this free and generous forgiving. Of course it is pride, the deadliest of all the deadly sins. Bernard Shaw may in some things, I suppose, be taken as an example of the modern mind. He says, "Forgiveness is a beggar's refuge. We must pay our debts." So speaks the modern man, but, my dear friends, we cannot pay our debts. We shall never be able to pay our debts to God. As our spritual fathers saw so clearly, the only language that we can honestly use in the presence of our awful debt is this prayer:

> Just as I am, without one plea
> But that Thy blood was shed for me,
> And that Thou bidd'st me come to Thee,
> O Lamb of God, I come.

In response to this coming, the free, unmerited favor of God comes to us; cancels the debt; imputes the righteousness of Christ to sinners such as we are; and progressively, as we live with Him, also imparts that righteousness. Here again, the modern man feels affronted. "How can the righteousness of anyone else be imputed to me?" asks the critic. "It is His righteousness, not mine!"

You have heard, perhaps, about the little boy who was dull at school. He was not only dull with his lessons; he also left much to be desired in his conduct. One day he didn't go to school, and his mother said, "Why aren't you going to school?" He answered, "We've got a whole holiday. We've won a scholarship." Notice that he said, "We've won a scholarship." He could have done nothing about it. A lad as dull as he would have been incapable of winning such a scholarship. In the school a clever boy who concentrated had achieved that distinction. And yet, without hesitation, and no doubt with gratitude, the dull little lad reported, "We've won a scholarship"!

. This is only a simple example but I think it will help you to understand a little of what we mean by imputing righteousness. God permits the purity of Jesus to cover us. The hymn writer puts it like this:

> Jesu, Thy blood and righteousness
> My beauty are, my glorious dress;
> Midst flaming worlds, in these arrayed,
> With joy shall I lift up my head.

No wonder, then, that in all the rapture of a fine hymn Samuel Davies cries out:

> In wonder lost, with trembling joy
> We take the pardon of our God.

And Charles Wesley sings:

> Amazing love! How can it be
> That Thou, my God, shouldst die for me?

In addition to the imputing of righteousness, God likewise imparts it. When any penitent sinner first comes to Him, God imputes His righteousness. Then as we live with Him, He also imparts His righteousness, progressively. It is a part of the Holy Spirit's work to make us holy, too. He sets out not only to justify us, but to sanctify us, and all the time the whole work is by grace. Grace! The free, unmerited favor of God! The grace that today is flowing like a river! The grace to which any needy person in this building may turn with eagerness now!

II. THE WORD SAVED

"By grace are ye saved." Whenever we use the word "saved" some people at once think of hell or heaven. Being saved means to them just that: escaping hell; achieving heaven. But that is a very limited way to think of this term "saved." For instance, it puts the whole matter in the future. Now we are on earth, not in heaven, and we can be saved now. The Scripture says, "He that believeth on the Son hath eternal life." He has it here and now!

Salvation is not from earth, but from sin. It is deliverance not merely from the penalty of sin but also from the fact of sin. Those of you who are theologically minded may be thinking that I am confusing salvation and sanctification. Still I say that the outworking of salvation gives us deliverance from the sins of the flesh, and likewise from the sins of the mind.

Think of the men who have been hopelessly imprisoned by thirst for strong drink, and yet have been delivered from that bondage. Think of the men who have been eaten up with lust; whose heads, in the words of Montaigne, have been "merry-go-rounds of lustful images." Think of people in the grip of greed, who become as metallic as the coins they seek. All of these are victims of present sins, and from these present sins there is for each of them a present salvation.

Not only from the sins of the flesh! There is likewise deliverance from the sins of the mind. From jealousy, and all the canker that it brings; from gossip, and all the evil that it entails; from pride, the most subtle of sins. From all of these there is salvation, here and now.

Don't, then, think of salvation solely in terms of heaven. Think also in terms of a higher quality of life here on earth. In the light of Christ examine your own heart, and you may find yourself praying like this:

> O God, I am selfish. Too often other folk come second or third in my thoughts. In myself I have discovered jealousy. In the face of some temptations I am terribly weak. I cannot forgive people; I do not truly and deeply forgive. If they speak to me unkindly, hot burning words rush to my lips, and I want to sting them back.
>
> O God, it is hell to live this way at its worst. It must be heaven to be like Christ. If He can get me out of all this, and impart to me His quality of life, then I am saved, and He is my Saviour.

Have you this quality of life? When you think of Jesus, does the hunger for such a way of living come to you? Do you yearn to be like Him? This is what is in my mind when I think of your being saved. Once again I remind you of this simple truth: "By grace are ye saved."

III. THE WORD FAITH

"By grace are ye saved through faith." Like the word "grace" and the word "saved," the term faith is often misunderstood. Many people agree with the statement of the schoolboy, "Faith is kidding yourself to believe what you know isn't true." Even more elderly and serious commentators regard faith as primarily a matter of the mind.

There are many definitions of faith. No definition can be satisfactory if it confines faith merely to belief. That would make it merely the mental acknowledgment of some external fact, and would not include at its very heart the spirit of trust. This is the key-word of faith; it means to "trust." Faith is not merely an expression of belief. It is a venture of the whole personality in trusting One who is worthy.

Nor is it right to think, as some people do, that faith belongs only to religion. All life is by faith. When you board a bus, you have faith, faith that the driver knows his job. When you go to a restaurant for a meal you have faith, faith that the food is wholesome and well cooked. When you send your child to school you have more faith, faith that the teacher will not poison his mind.

Even science proceeds largely on faith. Contrary to the opinions of some people who haven't thought the matter through, no one can prove the great principles on which scientists proceed, such principles as the uniformity of nature and the conservation of energy. But in order to proceed at all, scientists must assume such basic principles. All business, too, is built on credit. The word "credit" is simply the Latin form of "trust."

If then we find faith everywhere else, should it surprise us to find it also in religion? In common life and in school, in science and in business, we find faith everywhere. But only in religion do we find it supremely. Just as in the scale of values nothing about a man is so precious as his soul, so the faith through which that soul can be saved must ever be the supreme expression of human trust.

Let me ask, are you conscious of your own need? At the same time are you aware of your weakness; of the pressure of your sins; of the dark problems in your life, and of your inability alone to grapple with them? Do you feel that you need the help of someone else? It is to such felt needs that the Gospel speaks about your being saved.

If you have never yet ventured on Christ, I plead with you to do so now. If you have already received a timorous faith, I urge you to venture on Him far more completely; to recognize that the real end of faith is to unite the person who believes with the Person on whom he believes; and that only as you are united with Christ through faith can you have the quality of life which is the sterling of eternity.

This is the glad, good news that the evangelists carried everywhere in the first century, and that their true followers have echoed in all the centuries since. Our Wesleyan fathers sounded it with tremendous power in the eighteenth century. In an age when most people had lost all hope, when they mistakenly thought that God was not there, or that He was not kind, the spokesmen for God came with the burning message that He was there and that He was kind; that by His free generosity men could be lifted into fulness of life, if only they trusted in Christ. This is still the heart of the Gospel. I sound it again, and with jubilation.

Nineteen hundred years after the Apostles first proclaimed this Gospel, and more than two hundred years after John Wesley first received it in his heart, I again offer you this Gospel: "By grace are ye saved through faith."

29. Harold L. Fickett, Jr.

Harold Lord Fickett, Jr., American Baptist. Born in a parsonage, Tucson, Ariz., Mar. 15, 1918. Educated, Baylor University (A.B.); Southern Baptist Seminary (Th.B.); Eastern Baptist Seminary (Th.M., Th.D.) Graduate study, Princeton Seminary. D.D., Wheaton College, Ill. Early pastorates (1937-43). U. S. Naval Chaplain (1943-54); Pastorates (1945-54); Tremont Temple, Boston, (largest Protestant church in New England), since 1954. Guest lecturer, homiletics, California Baptist Seminary (1950-54).

The message about "The Gospel of Divine Grace" comes out of "The Apostle's Creed" (Titus 2:11-14). The sermon begins with part of an old-time hymn, which sets forth this motif. Such a hymn consists in Gospel truth set to music. The four parts of the message come from successive portions of the Bible passage. The treatment is popular rather than scholastic, and suggestive, not exhaustive.

The local color has to do with, one by one, the sort of persons who occupy pews at Tremont Temple. Each example differs from the others in showing how the grace of God appeals to this person or that in our country today. Here and there the interpreter looks out into depths that no person can fathom, but as a rule he deals with his difficult passage simply and practically. According to university professors of English, "The art of exposition calls for ability to simplify and illuminate human experience." Exposition of a Bible passage does so in light that comes from the Spirit of God.

THE GOSPEL OF DIVINE GRACE

Amazing grace! how sweet the sound!
That saved a wretch like me!
I once was lost, but now am found;
Was blind, but now I see.

THIS HYMN from the dedicated pen of John Newton is dearly loved in evangelical circles. The reason is apparent: the song magnifies the wondrous grace of God. Among all the jewels that embellish the celestial crown, by far the most sparkling, the most majestic, and the most precious is this one of God's grace. Superlatives may describe the beauties of nature, the ingenuity of the scientific mind, and the productivity of modern industry. But all our superlatives fall far short of power to set forth a single facet in the jewel of God's grace.

The Apostle Paul was a product of this divine grace. During his lifetime as a Christian he had but a single purpose, one "magnificent obsession": to share the message of God's grace with everyone he met. In the course of his long service, many young ministers came under his influence. In various ways some of them endeared themselves to the heart of the Apostle. One of these was Titus. At the time when Paul wrote the epistle that bears the name of Titus, the young pastor was ministering to people on the Isle of Crete. Like Paul, Titus was an outstanding product of God's grace.

In the very heart of the letter to Titus, the Apostle deals with his favorite subject, the grace of God. In presenting "The Apostle's Creed," he writes with new vitality and vigor. Today his words literally cry out from the printed page:

The grace of God that bringeth salvation hath appeared to all men, teaching us that denying ungodliness and worldly lusts, we should live soberly, righteously, and godly, in this present world, looking for that blessed hope, and the glorious appearing of the great God and our Saviour Jesus Christ, who gave himself for us that he might redeem us from all iniquity, and purify unto himself a peculiar people, zealous of good works (Titus 2:11-14).

A careful analysis of this Apostle's Creed shows that he testified to Titus about, first of all, the fact of God's grace; second, the function of God's grace; third, the force of God's grace; and fourth, the future of God's grace.

I. THE FACT OF GOD'S GRACE

First, the Apostle bears witness to Titus about the fact of God's grace. "The grace of God that bringeth salvation hath appeared to all men." The grace of God was as real to Paul as life itself; as real as the air he breathed; as real as the fingers on his hand. He did not argue for it; he merely testified to it as a fact of revelation. Paul knew God's grace from two points of view: he knew it historically, and he knew it experientially

Paul was an erudite scholar. He was a careful student of Jewish history. In every epoch of God's dealing with His people, he could see examples of God's grace in undertaking for them, and in supplying their needs. At the Red Sea, in the desert, before the walls of Jericho,—the inspired record was ever the same. In grace the Lord God did for the Israelites what they never could have done for themselves. He won for them a victory over Pharaoh. He fed them with manna, and gave them water from the rock. He led them into the Promised Land. Yes, Paul was familiar with all of this, and far more. He knew the grace of God historically.

He also knew the grace of God from the viewpoint of his own experience. One day he was journeying on the road to Damascus, ostensibly to persecute Christians. In reality, he was traveling on a sort of toboggan slide down to hell. But by grace the Lord Christ revealed Himself to this persecutor of the saints. When the persecutor came face to face with Christ, the future missionary to the Gentiles cried out, "Lord, what wilt thou have me to do?"

Ever after that moment, when by faith he called Jesus "Lord," the future missionary knew the grace of God experientially. Ever afterwards, this experimental knowledge enabled him to be calm and tranquil in the face of difficulties, dangers, and even death. This same experimental knowledge of God's grace is what every man needs today. Without it life is filled with fears and frustrations. With it a person has the peace of God, and strength to do His will.

This truth came home to me forcefully a few years ago as I sat by the bedside of a saint ninety-six years of age, who was about to cross the river that separates this world from the next. I looked into her eyes and asked, "Are you afraid?" Her response was most assuring, "Pastor, there is nothing to fear when Christ is at your side." She knew the grace of God experientially. Do you?

II. THE FUNCTION OF GOD'S GRACE

In the second place, the Apostle testifies to Titus concerning the function of God's grace. It "bringeth salvation." Stated simply, the function of God's grace is to bring salvation to every man, woman, or child who believes. Elsewhere, also, the Apostle makes this truth crystal clear: "By grace are ye saved through faith, and that not of yourselves, it is the gift of God" (Eph. 2:8).

Grace must function in this way because sin is present in every life. In many churches today the tragedy is the absence of this emphasis in the pulpit. In the thinking of far too many contemporary clergymen the doctrine of sin, which alienates men from God, seems to be outmoded. The lack of emphasis on the fact of sin also has a baneful effect upon the laity.

A seminary president tells of a college sophomore who came to talk about Christianity. First the young man said to this Christian leader: "I don't want you to tell me that I am a sinner. That type of thinking went out with Aesop's fables. I wish to discuss Christianity intellectually. Are you willing to do this?" The president acceded to the student's request, and asked for permission to open the discussion.

Then the president asked, in turn, about Wellhausen's Documentary Hypothesis concerning the authorship of the Pentateuch, the Aramaic element in the Hebrew Bible, and other matters known to Biblical scholars. Last of all the president asked the young man whether he was a post-millennarian, an a-millennarian, or a pre-millennarian. In no case could the young man give a satisfactory answer; he did not even understand any of the questions.

Looking the lad in the face, the Christian leader said, "Did you ever tell a lie?" The young fellow confessed, "Just a few white ones." "In the eyes of God," said the president, "there are no white lies; they are all black." "Son, did you ever hate anyone?" "Just one or two," answered the student. The president continued, "According to the Bible, hatred is tantamount to murder." "Did you ever steal?" "Well, I have cheated on examinations." "Then," said the older man, "in the eyes of God you are a thief.

"Now let us consider what God sees when He looks at you. He sees a liar, a murderer, and a thief. Do you still think that the Bible teaching about sin is outmoded? Don't you feel that you should get down on your knees and confess your sins, asking God for Christ's sake to forgive you?" The young man dropped to his knees as if he had been shot. He uttered the prayer of a penitent, and thus gave the grace of God a chance to operate in his life. By grace he became a new creation in Christ Jesus. Today he is a strong Christian leader in his home church. He knows that the function of God's grace is to bring salvation.

III. THE FORCE OF GOD'S GRACE

In the third place, the Apostle testifies to Titus about the force of God's grace: "Teaching us that denying ungodliness and worldly lusts, we should live soberly, righteously, and godly, in this present world." Here the stress on God's grace is didactic; it comes through teaching. The Apostle Paul declares to Titus that the grace of God has didactic force. It instructs, or trains, Christian people, both negatively and positively. Negatively, it teaches all who name the name of Christ Jesus as Saviour and Lord that they are to deny, denounce, and separate themselves from all dishonest practices and lustful indulgences. Positively, it teaches the redeemed children of God to live sanely, quietly, and worshipfully in the busy world of which they are a part. Needless to say, if every Christian would allow the Spirit of God to implement this two-fold instruction about the meaning of God's grace in his life, the world would begin to be turned upside down for Christ as King.

Apart from the power of God, the mightiest force known to man is teaching. During World War II, when our armed forces were struck in the back at Pearl Harbor, the Army, the Navy, and the Marine Corps were at minimum strength, unready to meet the challenge of the onrushing Axis hosts. A call went out for young men and women to enter military services. They responded in amazing numbers, and by the end of that war our country had developed the mightiest fighting force the world had ever seen.

Why did hosts of American youth take up arms, and help to win that victory? Largely because they had been taught that freedom was worth fighting for, and if need be, worth dying for. From childhood they had learned about Valley Forge, where their forefathers had suffered unto death that posterity might enjoy the basic freedoms. On a far loftier plane the Apostle Paul would have his young friend Titus, and every soldier of the Cross today, instructed in the facts about the force of God's irresistible grace. Solely because of this force we Christians can face the future unafraid.

IV. THE FUTURE OF GOD'S GRACE

Last of all, and most assuring to the discerning Christian, the Apostle witnesses to Titus about the future of God's grace. "Looking for that blessed hope, and the glorious appearing of the great God and our Saviour Jesus Christ, who gave himself for us, that he might redeem us from all iniquity, and purify unto himself a peculiar people, zealous of good works."

The future of God's grace is definitely connected with that coming event when the clouds shall be rolled back like a scroll, and Jesus Christ shall return to earth as the King of kings and Lord of lords. Paul anticipated that some persons would scoff at this doctrine of the Second Coming. So he enjoined Titus to speak out the truth: "These things speak, and exhort, and rebuke with all authority. Let no one despise thee" (Titus 2:15). For the greatest of all missionaries to the Gentiles, the teaching about the Lord's Second Advent was of paramount importance.

In a syllabus entitled *Christian Theology,* E. H. Bancroft calls attention to the repeated emphasis that the New Testament places upon the glorious future of God's grace: "More space is given to the doctrine of the Second Coming, it is said, than to that of the Atonement. Where the Atonement is mentioned once, the Second Coming is referred to twice. Where the First Coming of Christ is mentioned once, the Second Coming is referred to eight times. One out of every twenty-five verses in the New Testament makes mention of His Final Advent.

"Of the twenty-seven books in the New Testament, all but four refer to it. Fifty times or more in the New Testament we are exhorted to readiness for the realization of this blessed hope. Entire chapters, such as Matthew 24 and 25, Luke 21, and Mark 13, are devoted to this subject, as well as whole books, such as First and Second Thessalonians and the Book of Revelation. It is an interesting fact that each chapter of the First Epistle to the Thessalonians closes with a reference to the Second Coming. In the 216 chapters of the New Testament, it is said that there are 318 references to this doctrine."

On a Sunday morning Queen Victoria's chaplain preached a very moving sermon about the Second Advent of our Lord. Immediately after the service, the chaplain asked her whether he had said anything offensive. The gracious lady replied, "O no, my Chaplain. I was thrilled by your message. I was weeping because I was apprehensive lest I might not live until my Lord returns."

Quickly the clergyman assured her that as far as her salvation was concerned it did not make any difference whether or not she still lived. He pointed out that if she lived she would be translated to meet her Lord in the air. If she did not live that long, she would be absent from the body and present with the Lord. In order to substantiate his statements he quoted I Thessalonians 4:13-18, that mountain-peak passage concerning the doctrine of the Second Coming.

When he had finished, the Queen responded: "I know all of this, but I want to live until He comes again in order that I may take from my head the crown of England and place it at His feet, for He is the King of kings and Lord of lords."

Every Christian as he waits for the Second Coming should do

away with selfishness, egotism, prayerlessness, and indolence, that he may put the crown of his life's influence at the feet of the One who is altogether lovely, the Lord Jesus Christ.

God grant that every believer, as he looks for the Lord's Final Return, may sing with his life as well as his lips:

All hail the power of Jesus' Name!
Let angels prostrate fall;
Bring forth the royal diadem,
And crown Him Lord of all.

30. John R. Richardson

John Robert Richardson, Presbyterian, U. S. ("Southern"). Born, Centerville, Miss., Nov. 24, 1901. Educated, Louisiana State University (A.B.); Louisville
Presbyterian Seminary (B.D.). Winner, Humphrey Fellowship (1926). Graduate study, University of Edinburgh (1928-29); Pastorates (1926-49); Westminster
Presbyterian Church, Atlanta, Ga., since 1949. Book
review editor, Southern Presbyterian Journal. Numerous articles, religious journals.

*The message about Paul as "The Superlative Christian" shows
that the Christian life calls for the blending and fusing of all
a man's intellectual, emotional, and volitional powers. Without
any direct reference to the psychology of religion, the author
shows a love for philosophy, and a tendency to expect from the
hearers ability to reason together about the deep things of Christian thought and life. He also insists that intelligent, informed
Christianity issues in stalwart character and in fruitful service.*

*Homiletically, the same three elements enter prominently into
almost every sermon. In any man's pulpit work, if one of the three
predominates, so as practically to exclude one or both of the
other two, his pulpit work becomes lopsided, and eccentric. Would
that every young minister could learn from Paul as a preacher
(in the Acts) to give a worthy place to powers of thought; a still
larger place to the sort of Christian emotion that transforms
knowledge into zeal; and perhaps the largest place to the urgency
and passion that once caused a godless ruler to cry out that as a
preacher the Apostle was beside himself, because his learning
had made him mad.*

*In some denominations the place of honor formerly went to
the intellect; in others, to the emotions; and in still other bodies,
to the will. Let us hope that in the evangelical pulpit of the mor-*

row the elements will all appear in apostolic proportions—and, further, that they will be fused together with a burning zeal like that of Paul, the superlative Christian preacher.

Behold what an inner fire this sermon has kindled!

THE SUPERLATIVE CHRISTIAN

"I know whom I have believed, and am persuaded that he is able to keep that which I have committed to him against that day."   II TIM. 1:12

LET US THINK about Paul as the superlative Christian. However exalted and exacting our standards of greatness, he must be classified as the noblest example of what a Christian ought to be and become. For a while Peter may have been the top man among the followers of Christ. If so, the time came when he yielded the primacy to the later Apostle. Since those early days no one has arisen to compare with Paul as an all-round Christian. Who can wonder that John Crysostom was moved to exclaim, "Three cubits in stature, Paul touched the sky!"

Better than anyone else in history the Apostle shows how "the truth that is in Jesus" ought to work out in character and conduct. In Second Timothy, the final product of his inspired pen, he opens up his heart and lets us see the factors that contributed most largely to his character and career. Especially does our text throw a flood of light on the determining influences that made him the superlative Christian of all the ages. In this brief autobiographical sentence three elements stand out. Like Ariadne's magic thread, they should lead us to understand the superlative Christian, and then, one by one, to seek much the same kind of equipment for our own Christian service.

I. CHRISTIAN KNOWLEDGE

"I know whom I have believed." The Apostle here uses a strong Greek verb, *oida,* which means "assured knowledge," beyond the peradventure of a doubt. Such enlightened understanding comes to a believer through his own Christian experience of revealed truth. Our superlative Christian was not afflicted with the mental disease of chronic uncertainty. To him Christianity was a final and ultimate body of truth, not a collection of provisional hypotheses. He believed that Christ came into the world to be known, and that Christianity rests on a definite supernatural revelation.

Distrust of Christian knowledge always works havoc. In the study of philosophy what is called "epistomology" has a place of prominence. It has to do with the origin and the ground of knowledge, the structure and the method, the validity and the limits. On these subjects learned men have written ponderous volumes. Every philosopher raises the question, "What can I know?" "How can I know?" To any such inquiry Paul gives a Christian answer. Unlike some philosophers, he looks at all these matters as they relate to God, the supreme Person, who makes Himself known in Christ, the living Word.

Such Christian knowledge is real. It all has to do with the conscious apprehension of facts, the conscious perception of truth, as it appears supremely in Christ. Any such knowledge has three elements: first, the mind that comprehends; second, the fact that is understood; third, the awareness of this knowledge. In the experience of Paul as the superlative Christian, all three of these factors led him to say with glad assurance, "I know whom I have believed."

In this note of exultation he shows the inseparable connection between knowledge and belief. This is the way every believer in Christ has to start. It would be vain for anyone to accept Christ unless he knew Christ. It would be fatuous to exhort a person to love Christ unless he knew Christ. It would be useless to ask anyone to obey Christ unless he knew Christ. Even among church members He is not likely to get much from us in the way of service unless we can say, one by one, "I know whom I have believed."

As Christians we dare not gamble on uncertainties. When we make our investments for eternity we must look for heavenly securities based on sound knowledge about Christ.

My friend, do not settle for anything less than Christian knowledge. Be an intelligent believer. In a sense there can be no other kind. In matters of the soul to know Christ means the difference between growth and decay, between life and death. In many lives the lack of such an intellectual foundation is responsible for haunting anxieties, debilitating fears, and baffling frustrations. On the contrary, last Easter I received a letter from a friend almost ninety years of age. In one brief sentence she voiced the glory of the Easter hope, "For we know" (II Cor. 5:1)!

II. CHRISTIAN PERSUASION

In our text the superlative Christian gives the central place to a certain feeling, "I am persuaded that he is able to keep." Such a persuasion grows out of knowing Christ as the supreme Person. The word translated *keep*, "phulasso," is a military term that means "to guard, defend, keep watch." Such constant watch is no easy undertaking. Today as of old ten thousand foes arise to beset the soul of a believer. But Christ is superior to all our foes, who are likewise His foes. From Him alone comes the persuasion that one is secure.

When Paul wrote that he was persuaded he meant that he not only knew, but that he knew that he knew. He was fixed in an immovable position, from which no one could dislodge him. Unlike those whom he described as "forever learning and never able to come to a knowledge of the truth," he did not hesitate to feel certain of any truth about Christ. The Apostle gladly took his stand on the basis of his Christian convictions. In the right sense of an abused term, he dared to seem dogmatic.

As a believer Paul was persuaded that Christ is the only Saviour from sin. On this assurance he based everything else. In his own experience sin had become so hard and unyielding that he had felt his need of the Saviour. In a spirit of desperation he had confessed, "What I hate I do." In a time of anguish he had cried, "O wretched man that I am! Who shall deliver me from the body of this death?" Then through divine grace came the answer, out of a heart overflowing with gratitude, "I thank God through Jesus Christ our Lord!"

Even to the Apostle sin stood out at the most mysterious fact of life, more mysterious than pain, or even death. But one thing he knew about sin. He was persuaded that Christ came into the world to break the power of sin and to set its captives free. So persuaded was he about Christ as the only Redeemer from sin that he spent his life in sacrificial service, everywhere telling men what he himself had experienced of Christ's power to save. Throughout the Roman Empire he proclaimed this message: "I was such a sinner that evil had the mastery over me. It gripped me and manacled me. But in His mercy God sent His Son into my heart, and now Christ has broken the power of reigning sin. I am persuaded that He is able to save unto the uttermost."

When Christ once takes into His hands the keeping and defense of a trusting soul, He will never let it go. He promises that His care and protection will be perpetual. "They shall never perish, neither shall anyone pluck them out of my hand." "The Lord is faithful, and He shall establish you, and keep you from evil." The old doctrine about "the perseverance of the saints" does not refer to our holding on to Christ, but to His way of holding us, with the omnipotence of God. "We have Christ's own promise, and that cannot fail." To rely upon Him for security of soul is Christian persuasion, not foolish presumption. If we recognize and accept the power of gravity, which holds the earth in its orbit round the sun, how much more should we rejoice in the grace of the Lord Jesus Christ, which binds us close to the heart of God.

Such a persuasion of Christ's protection puts iron into a man's blood, and sets him free from fear. You may recall how David Livingstone, working his way through the swamps of Africa, began to fear, and how he found courage to cross a certain stream on the morrow, to face what seemed to be certain death. At the age of forty-two he wrote one night in the *Journal*:

> Felt much turmoil of spirit in view of having all my plans for this great region and teeming population knocked in the head by savages tomorrow. But I read that Jesus came and said, "All power is given unto me in heaven and

earth; go and teach all nations, and lo, I am with you alway, even unto the end of the world." It is the word of a Gentleman [sic] of the most sacred and strictest honor, and there's an end on't. I will not cross furtively by night, as I had intended. It would appear as flight, and should such a man as I flee?

III. CHRISTIAN COMMITMENT

"He is able to keep that which I have committed unto him against that day." Here the Apostle voices the sort of personal commitment that figures powerfully in the make-up of the superlative Christian. On the basis of Christian knowledge, and with the warmth of Christian assurance, he pushed onward to practical commitment. On the basis of what he knew and felt, he acted. Among men who know much and think hard there is a perilous temptation to let knowledge become an end in itself. In "A Grammarian's Funeral" Robert Browning gives a suitable epitaph for an impractical pedant: "This man decided not to live but know." "Before living, he'd learn how to live." On the other hand, says Browning, the low man "throws himself on God, and unperplexed, seeking shall find him."

The Apostle affirmed that he knew Christ, believed Christ, and was persuaded about what He could do. Therefore he was committed to Christ forever. Paul had nothing to do with the sort of intellectualism that paralyzes action. He would have no patience now with the man who declares that he is "a student of all religions, but gives himself to no one in particular." To the Apostle commitment meant decision plus. As someone puts it, decision with depth! This kind of commitment appears everywhere in the New Testament, and nowhere else so clearly and strongly as in Paul. This is perhaps the chief reason why we look on him as the superlative Christian.

At the beginning his commitment was private. In the depths of his soul Paul was confronted with Christ as the Son of God. On the Damascus road when Saul of Tarsus met the Living Christ he faced this question of commitment, "Lord, what wilt thou have me to do?" When Christ gave His answer the future Apostle responded with the sort of commitment that determined all of his later Christian service. From that time onward he took as his motto, "For me to live is Christ." "I live, yet not I, but Christ liveth in me." This commitment for life was full and complete. When from the heart Paul received Christ as "Lord," he accepted all the implications of the holy title. From that time onward he held nothing back from his Lord.

At once this private commitment moved forward to a public avowal of Christ as Saviour and Lord. From the very beginning of his discipleship, people might love the Apostle or they might hate him, but they could never doubt that he was committed to Christ, and that his commitment was passionate. Before his conversion Saul of Tarsus had been a vehement personality. After he became a Christian his heart was full of holy fire that burned more and more strongly until the very end. From him John Calvin may have got the idea of his crest, which shows an open hand that holds a burning heart.

Today we all recognize the need for a commitment even more intense than that of Communists. In Paul as the superlative Christian we behold such superior devotion to Christ as Redeemer and King. Under the leadership of the Apostle and others, the early Christians "out-thought, out-lived, and out-died" their non-believing neighbors. From us who believe in Christ today surely our God expects no less in the way of wholehearted and passionate commitment.

We have been thinking about these factors separately, but really all three belong together. In Paul we can see how they blended so as to make him the superlative Christian. But let us never rest content merely with admiring and praising Paul. Sorely do we church folk of today need to know the Lord Christ, as we find Him in Holy Scripture. So let us beseech the Holy Spirit to shine upon the open page and bring the truth to light in His blessed face. Then we shall be changed into His likeness.

And how urgent it is that our lives be undergirded with Christian conviction. It stabilizes. It fortifies. It gives us light in all our darkness. It brings us calmness in every storm. When we feel persuaded that Christ is ready and able to keep His own in the midst of this hazardous world, we have in Him the faith that expels every unworthy fear.

If we are to make our lives count for the most, we need Pauline commitment. It will enable us to distinguish between what is central and what is peripheral. It enables every believer to single out a lofty goal, like that of the Apostle. "This one thing I do. . . . I press toward the mark for the prize of the high calling of God in Christ Jesus." Any such goal calls for a life full of dynamic power, and that too comes through commitment to Christ.

It is easy for any of us to be satisfied with living as "an average Christian." But God forbid that any of us should rest content with that sort of spiritual mediocrity. Surely the example of Paul as the superlative Christian should inspire and nerve every one of us to strive for maturity in Christ, "that measure of development which is meant by 'the fullness of Christ.'" So let each of us take the words of Paul and make them his own. "I know whom I have believed and am persuaded that he is able to keep that which I have committed to him against that day."

31. Harold J. Ockenga

Harold John Ockenga, Congregationalist. Born, Chicago, July 6, 1905. Educated, Taylor University, Ind. (A.B.); Princeton Seminary; Westminster Seminary, Philadelphia (Th.B.); University of Pittsburgh (A.M., Ph.D.) Many honorary degrees. Pastorates (1930-36); Park Street Church, Boston, since 1936. President, Fuller Seminary, Pasadena (1947-54). President, National Association of Evangelicals (1952-54). Summer supply preacher, Westminster Chapel, London (1946, '48, '51, '57). Many books and articles. Recent volumes: Our Evangelical Faith (1946); The Spirit of the Living God (1947); Faithful to Jesus Christ (1948); The Church in God (1955); Protestant Preaching in Lent (1957).

Under the present extended pastorate at "Brimstone Corner" the annual budget has increased from $20,000 to over $450,000, most of it for Missions. The missionary program is said to be the largest in the States. The preacher draws hearers from all over Greater Boston, and by radio reaches many others. Often he stresses pulpit evangelism. In the message about taking Christ as our Example he brings out the truth of his passage, and also throws light on other parts of Scripture. He enlists a large and ardent following of orthodox folk who on the Lord's Day wish to enjoy a sort of Bible conference in their church home downtown.

Every city needs at least one such intellectual preacher, perhaps downtown, to explain, defend, and promote the evangelical understanding of Christianity today. Though the two men differ in many ways, Donald G. Barnhouse renders such a service to people from all sections of Greater Philadelphia. In more than one city almost as large as Boston laymen have complained to me because they could not find such a church home, where they could take their brains to church every Sunday, and then keep *them busy all week digesting the pulpit food from the pre-ceding Lord's Day.*

In many another field local conditions may call for a different sort of pulpit work. If the young minister took this Boston preacher as his model, his difficult kind of pulpit work might not suit the capacities of ordinary people in a community with only one Protestant church. Even if the young man did his part superbly, he might not meet the heart needs of many people in the parish.

After all, is it wise to take any minister as a model? In the past many a young man of promise fizzled out because he had chosen Brooks or somebody else as a model. After a while his people concluded that with him the model meant "a small imitation of the real thing." Instead of desiring to become an Ockenga, a Barnhouse, or a Clarence E. Macartney—who in a fashion all his own excelled as a downtown preacher—let every young evangelical minister determine that by the grace of God he will in the pulpit dare to be himself.

JESUS, THE CHRISTIAN'S EXAMPLE

"Even hereunto were ye called: because Christ also suffered for us, leaving us an example, that ye should follow his steps."   I PET. 2:21

CHRISTIANS are called to follow Jesus Christ. When we worship Him as the God-man, the Mediator, the Saviour, and the eternal King, there is a tendency to forget His human nature. Some years ago a sermon was published under the title, "The

Peril of Worshiping Jesus." It was by a leading modernist. His argument was that the worship of Jesus removed Him from us as an example, a standard, and a companion. We who worship Him as God should recognize the danger of putting Him on a pedestal, elevating Him far above human experience, and thus removing Him as our Example.

The following of Jesus is as essential to the Christian life as is the worshiping of Christ. We should take Him as God to worship and as Man to follow. This is the implication of His dual nature. His human nature leads us to follow Him in self-denial, in sacrifice, and in service. It is folly to leave this aspect of following to a modernist, who believes only in the moral influence of the Cross, not in its nature as the substitutionary Atonement; who accepts Jesus only as a man who appropriated God rather than as the unique Son of God, whom we worship.

THE THREEFOLD COMMANDMENT OF JESUS

Peter wrote these words to Christians scattered abroad through Asia Minor. His injunction to follow Jesus was stimulated by his own memory of the thrice repeated commandment of the Lord to him. The first was given while he was engaged in the labor of fishing in the lake of Galilee. Jesus walked by the sea, saw Simon and his brother casting a net into the sea, and said unto them: "Come ye after me, and I will make you to become fishers of men" (Mark 1:16,17).

The next occasion was at Caesarea Philippi when Peter made his great confession of Christ's Deity, the confession that was followed by the revelation from Jesus about the inevitability of His Cross. Then Jesus said to His disciples, particularly Peter, "If any man will come after me, let him deny himself, and take up his cross, and follow me" (Matt. 16:24).

The third time was by the lake of Galilee, following the Resurrection of Jesus. He had appeared to His disciples, shared with them a post-resurrection meal, and elicited from Peter his confessions of love and faithfulness. When He was leaving, Peter followed Him. When Peter turned and saw John also following Him, Peter said to the Lord, "What shall this man do?" Jesus said to Simon, "If I will that he tarry until I come, what is that to thee? Follow thou me" (John 21:21,22). As Peter grew older the command "Follow me" lingered definitely in his mind.

The Jesus we are to follow is the Jesus who walked among men. This truth is illustrated in John 1:29 and the verses following. When John the Baptist and two of his disciples saw Jesus as He walked in their midst, John declared, "Behold the Lamb of God," and the disciples who heard him speak followed Jesus. It was as Jesus walked this way and that way in human circumstances that we are now to follow Him. We must follow Him in our business deals, in our social relationships, and at the points of stress in life. The daily walk of those who follow Jesus should be higher, nobler, and far better than that of the world. Jesus Himself asked His disciples, "What do ye more than others?" Are you more courteous, more honest, more pure, more kind, more generous, more useful, more helpful?

In years gone by children learned to write by following a copyhead placed either in a written display or on a blackboard. Laboriously we pupils learned how to imitate those letters of the alphabet. When my boy was five years of age he received several birthday gifts. Therefore he dictated a letter that his mother wrote, and he copied it laboriously in order to send it to those whom he wished to thank. This is the sort of copyhead that God has given us in the Person of Jesus Christ. His holiness, meekness, calmness, courtesy, and humility set an example that we should follow. Peter says that we should follow His steps. What then are the steps that we are to follow?

THE PURITY OF HIS CHARACTER

The first step that Peter singles out is the purity of the sinlessness of Christ. The Apostle says, "who did no sin, neither was guile to be found in his mouth." The sinlessness of Christ is a doctrine plainly taught in the Bible and also affirmed in Christian teaching. He possessed a nature like unto ours. He did not take upon Him the nature of angels, but He took upon Him the seed of Abraham. "Wherefore in all things it behooved him to be made like unto his brethren." Thus He was tempted in all points like as we are, apart from sin. Having been so tempted,

He is able to succor us when we are tempted (Heb. 2:17,18; 4:15,16).

The temptations, testings, and trials of Christ exhaust everything that befalls the believer. At the beginning of His ministry a great series of temptations occurred. First came the temptation to pride. After His fasting forty days in the wilderness, Satan said, "If thou be the Son of God, command that these stones be made bread." This was the temptation to use His power and authority selfishly. What politician, businessman, or leader has not met this temptation to pride?

The second was the temptation to presumption. The devil took Him to the Holy City and set Him on a pinnacle of the temple, and said, "If thou be the Son of God, cast thyself down: for it is written, 'He shall give His angels charge concerning thee: and in their hands they shall bear thee up, lest at any time thou dash thy foot against a stone.'" This was a quotation from the ninety-first psalm, which was a Messianic passage containing the promise given of God directly to the Messiah. And yet, if Jesus had used His power for personal display, He would have presumed on the goodness and the grace of God. Presumption is a sin from which we all need to be preserved. So let each of us pray with David, "Keep back thy servant from presumptuous sins."

The third temptation was to position. Satan took him to an exceeding high mountain and showed him all the kingdoms of the world and the glory of them, and said, "All these things will I give thee if thou wilt fall down and worship me." In a moment of time, in kaleidoscopic fashion, the vision of the great kingdoms of the world passed before the mind of the Messiah. As the prince of this world Satan offered Him the Kingdom that was to be His rightfully, but only after He had obtained it through the sufferings and the humiliation of the Cross. For some such power and fame men have surrendered virtue, integrity, and life itself.

In addition to this series of temptations, Jesus endured the grim demands made upon Him by hunger, weariness, sleeplessness, misunderstanding, mockery, hatred, and every other trial that can possibly come to a human being in a world of sin. Finally, in Gethsemane He faced the temptation of refusing to drink the cup that not only contained every human sorrow, but also the curse of the broken law, the guilt of sin, and the wrath of God. It was the facing of this temptation and trial that caused Him to agonize with sweat like drops of blood. That was a dark trial which demanded all His powers.

In all these temptations, trials, and testings Jesus was triumphant. He did not fall. In every form of human temptation all hell assailed Him, so that the inspired writer could say that He "was in all points tempted like as we are, yet without sin." Whatever your temptation, whatever your trial, whatever your tribulation, whatever your testing, remember that the Lord Jesus has met it before you and has triumphed over it all.

THE SINLESSNESS OF OUR SAVIOUR

Hence the testimony that Jesus had before men was one of sinlessness. In the Scriptures He is declared to be "holy, harmless, undefiled, separate from sinners" (Heb. 7:26). Peter declares, "Neither was guile found in his mouth." Thus Jesus announced, "The prince of this world cometh and findeth nothing in me." Pilate declared, "I find no fault in this man." The thief on the cross said, "He hath done nothing amiss." The centurion who watched Him die exclaimed, "Surely this was the Son of God!" Christ's own challenge to His generation was this, "Which of you convinceth me of sin?" What a life He led! He came to do the will of God (Heb. 10:7), and when Christ came to the end of His days He could declare, "I have finished the work thou gavest me to do." Yes, Jesus lived a life without sin.

What was the source of such a character? The answer is threefold. First, His knowledge of the Word. In the midst of His great temptations it was by the Word that He repulsed Satan. His quotations from the Bible came from the Book of Deuteronomy, which He accepted as the Word of God. In answer to the first temptation He declared, "Man shall not live by bread alone" (8:8). To the second, "Thou shalt not tempt the Lord thy God" (6:16). To the third, "Thou shalt worship the Lord thy God, and him only shalt thou serve" (6:13). If the Lord Jesus was able to vanquish the devil by quotations from the Word of God, then the security of the believer must rest in the degree to which he has saturated his mind with the Word of God, and has it ready for use as the sword of the Spirit. Such a mastery can come only by constant reading, by memorization, and by meditation upon the Bible.

The second source of His sinless life was prayer. It is interesting to study the way that Jesus prayed. The Gospels tell us that He arose a great while before day and went out to commune with God; that He prayed at His meals; and that He uttered ejaculatory prayers. We read of seasons that He devoted to prayer, such as His forty days in the wilderness. We learn about nights that He spent in prayer, such as the night before He chose His disciples, the night following the day when people tried to make Him king, and the night in Gethsemane. What then shall we conclude about our need of prayer? If the Lord Jesus, while still the Second Person of the Trinity, as the incarnate and perfect Man needed prayer for strength and help, for fellowship and victory, how much more do we as His followers need to pray without ceasing!

The third secret of victory in Jesus' life was the Holy Spirit. We read that the Father gave Him the Spirit without measure (John 3:34). When He began His public ministry it was with the quotation of a text from Isaiah 61: "The Spirit of the Lord is upon me, for he hath anointed me to preach the Gospel." Jesus needed the Holy Spirit in order to live in a way acceptable to God. How much more do we! In these days of our pilgrimage we stand desperately in need of what the Spirit did for Him in the days of His flesh. We need enlightenment and guidance, grace and empowering, all of which are mediated through the Holy Spirit.

If we are to follow in the steps of our Lord Jesus, there should be in us a similitude to His purity. Such purity we may obtain through the forgiveness of our sins and the cleansing from their guilt. Faith in the atoning Sacrifice of our Lord Jesus Christ upon the Cross brings the believer a declarative righteousness. The regeneration wrought by the Holy Spirit initiates a pure life. As a result there is lodged in the heart and mind of the believer a longing for purity and a hatred of anything that is impure.

Purity demands obedience to God, a walking in the light as

God reveals to us His truth and way. "If we walk in the light as He is in the light we have fellowship one with another, and the blood of Jesus Christ His Son cleanseth us from all sin." Whether it be in sport, in music, or in work, a parent does not give a child new lessons until he walks in the ones that he already has in hand. The same holds true in our spiritual lives. By observing the means of grace, by attention and heed to the Word of God, by the practice of prayer, by engaging in worship, by bearing testimony, we can achieve purity more and more like that of our Lord.

II. THE PATIENCE UNDER TRIAL

The second step Peter here declares we are to follow is that of Christ's patience under trial. This He first revealed in His attitude toward others. Said Peter, "Who when he was reviled, reviled not again." No man was ever more reviled than the Lord Jesus Christ. Before Caiaphas, Herod, and Pilate they mocked Him, they set Him at naught, they examined Him, and they accused Him; but He bore it all meekly and patiently. In all this Peter had to learn that he was to follow the example of Christ.

Let us remember that the Lord Jesus had respect for men. He always treated an individual as an end in himself, and never as a means to an end. He conferred dignity, honor, and value upon the individual. Moreover, He always ministered to men in love, seeking to help them and heal them, one by one. He demonstrated a permanent concern in teaching, as in the Sermon on the Mount; in exhorting, as in His Parables, and in admonishing. Those who would follow Him now must develop His kind of patience in all sorts of human relations.

This is the antithesis of the world's attitude. As Peter said, "When he suffered he threatened not." The world's view is that we ought to stand upon our rights, and claim our legal privileges; that we should endure nothing with patience, but return evil for evil, and blow for blow. In the *Merchant of Venice* Shakespeare expresses this point of view. In the famous speech of Shylock about the pound of flesh he says, "If it will do nothing else it will bait my revenge." But the world's attitude is not that of our Lord or of the Christian who follows His steps. He must be willing to bear evil rather than inflict it. He must be ready to forgive rather than seek revenge.

This truth is aptly expressed by our Lord in the Sermon on the Mount (Matt. 5:45-48). However, some declare that the Sermon on the Mount is not for this present age. Interestingly enough, in paraphrasing the Sermon on the Mount, Paul expresses the same truth as applicable to the Christian in his system of ethics now. Peter pronounces an encomium upon the servant who endures grief, suffering wrongfully. This is thankworthy, because it goes beyond the powers of the natural man (I Pet. 2:19,20).

Such patience under trial is the achievement of faith. Peter declared that Christ "committed himself to Him that judgeth righteously." No one can take this attitude toward life unless He has committed himself to God. Such a committed life is dependent upon faith. One must believe in God as omnipotent and omniscient, as sovereign and holy. Only such a faith can undergird a committed life. It is because we believe in God that we are able to express our faith by a definite act of self-commitment to His goodness and control. This attitude of life expresses trust. It is submission to His working out of our problem, His answering our need, His undertaking on our behalf. This is the hardest lesson for faith to learn. It implies a sense of rest. He who commits a matter to God leaves it there. Such faith believes that in due time God will fully vindicate the Christian. Many times the vindication will come in this world, and again it may not come until the Judgment. God is righteous, and we may leave our vindication with Him.

This sort of life is courageous. On the basis of such a philosophy, it is a life with ability to face with patience any kind of suffering, as Peter later expresses it, "If we suffer with Him, we shall reign with him." This is a conquering life. To such a life the Lord imparts a quality of peace and internal tranquility. It manifests power, and gains the victory over external obstacles. Look at the example of Jesus, with His calm acceptance of every emergency and every other situation in life. He never hurried. He was always in possession of Himself and in control of the situation.

III. HIS PURPOSE IN REDEMPTION

As an illustration of the third step we are to follow in the life of our Lord, Peter now introduces one of the greatest truths in all his writings. Here is one of the noblest statements about the vicarious Atonement of our Lord Jesus Christ, and yet it is introduced as an illustration of how we are to live. This corresponds with Paul's introduction of the Incarnation to illustrate our call to humility (Phil. 2:5-11). Peter said, "Who his own self bare our sins in his own body on the tree, that we, being dead to sin, should live unto righteousness."

This describes the redemptive work of Christ. It places Peter squarely with Isaiah (53), with Paul (II Cor. 5:21), with John (1:29; Rev. 1:7), and with the other Bible writers about His death on the Cross. That it was substitutionary was declared by the saying, "He bare our sins." That His Death on the Cross was a satisfaction for sin, and not a mere example for exhortation, is self-evident. Peter believed in the declarative expiation and propitiation of Christ; and as he here explained, it was sufficient to make the sinner righteous through faith. Peter here pictures the sufferings of Christ on Calvary as far more than a physical death. The Apostle shows that the sufferings constituted His taking of our sins in His own body, as the bearing of the penalty of judgment upon them. He was the Victim offered on the altar for sin.

Peter also revealed that such redemptive work bore regenerative fruit. "We being dead to sins should live unto righteousness." Moral influence over the life of the believer flows from Calvary. Nothing so moves his heart and life as this loving sacrifice of Christ. It is the strongest impetus we have for the termination of the old life in sin, and the initiation of the new life in righteousness. Peter here suggests the mystical union of the believer with Christ in life and in death, all through faith. Christ not only died for us; we also died with Him. The result is that we should bear much fruit in righteousness; we should live the life of the Spirit who bears His fruit in us.

The Apostle then refers to the soundness, or healing, of the individual through this suffering of Christ. "By his stripes ye are healed." Our healing is directly connected with the suffering of Christ. There is a possible connection between the healing of men and the undeserved suffering that the believer accepts in his redemptive living. In the proportion that he voluntarily identifies himself with the Cross of Christ he contributes to the healing of others (Cf. Col. 1:24-27). We may not be able to understand the full implications of this truth, but it has a bearing upon the lives of others. The perfection of the saints, like the perfection of their Leader, comes through suffering (Heb. 2:10). Therefore we ought not to despise suffering, but we should follow Christ in this step also. We are not greater than our Lord. There is a corresponding relationship between our suffering for Christ and our being glorified.

Peter then concludes with a look at Jesus as our Chief Shepherd. "For ye were as sheep going astray, but are now returned unto the Shepherd and Bishop of your souls." There is a definition of sin as "going astray." So Isaiah describes it: "everyone turned to his own way" (53:6). Whether in matters great or little, sin is the seeking of my will rather than God's. It is disobedience to law, asserting independence, revolt against authority. While we are in this condition, following the example of Jesus is futile. No one can become a Christian merely by following Christ's example. Far more than that is needed. First there must be reconciliation with God through acceptance of Christ's Death for us, and through our identity with Christ in life and in death.

Next, Peter describes conversion. "Ye . . . are now returned to the Shepherd and Bishop of your souls." This is a picture of repentance and returning, of faith and obedience, all of which is postulated upon the redemptive work of Christ in taking our sins in His body on the tree. Past sin must be dealt with before present following is possible.

Then Peter speaks about the direction of one's life by the "Shepherd and Bishop of your souls." Thus we may follow, obey, and conform to the life of Jesus (Heb. 12:1,2). Let us therefore be followers of Christ.

32. Frank E. Gaebelein

*Frank Ely Gaebelein, Reformed Episcopal Church.
Born in the home of the well-known leader, the Rev.
Dr. A. C. Gaebelein, Mt. Vernon, N. Y., Mar. 31, 1899.
Educated, New York University (B.A.); Harvard Uni-
versity (M.A.); D.D., Reformed Episcopal Seminary;
Litt.D. Wheaton College, Ill. Headmaster, Stony Brook
School, L. I., since 1922. Deacon, R. E. Church (1940);
presbyter, 1941. Chairman, Board of Evangelical
Books, Inc. Special lecturer, Dallas Seminary, 1944-
1952. Bible Conference speaker and guest preacher in
colleges and universities. Consulting editor, Eternity,
Christianity Today. Many volumes. Recent: The Christian Use of the Bible (1946); The Servant and the
Dove (1946); Christian Education in a Democracy
(1951); The Pattern of God's Truth (1954); The Practical Epistle of James (1955).*

*The message about "Liberty in Christ" comes from a man who
knows and loves the Bible and teen-age boys. He wishes every
boy to love the Bible and accept Christ. He delivered this sermon
on Sunday in the Chapel of the large and famous Lawrenceville
School, near Princeton, N.J. Note the following:*

*1. The sermon consists largely of facts, facts about persons of
interest to a lad preparing for Princeton or Yale.*

*2. The minister respects the intelligence of these boys. He
expects them to feel concerned about the present world struggle
between freedom and totalitarianism.*

*3. The element of interest comes and increases through care
in marshaling facts, so as to foster a feeling of suspense.*

*4. Soon every lad can see that the visiting preacher is no mere
entertainer. He is trying to teach something important.*

*5. Most amazing of all, the visitor preaches to boys about a book
of the Bible. Of course he takes one of the simplest books, to
encourage lifelong reading of the Bible, "as if increase of appetite
had grown by what it fed on."*

6. At heart the sermon impresses one as being expository, in the main. As such it escapes the pitfalls of much expository preaching.

7. Would that every minister had the courage to preach sermons largely expository, and the ability to adapt every one of them to the interests and the needs of teen-age lads.

8. Would also that every evangelical preacher could learn how not to misrepresent a Bible book or passage by making it seem abstract and impersonal, uninteresting and irrelevant to lads the age of Jesus of Nazareth when He "increased in wisdom and stature, and in favor with God and man."

LIBERTY IN CHRIST

"If he hath wronged thee, or owest thee ought, put that to mine account. I Paul have written it with mine own hand, and will repay it, albeit it I do not say to thee how thou owest unto me even thine own self besides." PHILEMON 18,19

IF THERE IS any issue before the world today that overshadows all others, it is that of liberty versus totalitarianism, a conflict that, if translated into personal terms, consists of the inner struggle against everything that enslaves the spirit of man.

Among the earlier books of the British novelist, W. Somerset Maugham, there is one entitled *Of Human Bondage*. It is probably his best book, and certainly it is one of the most distinguished novels of the twentieth century. The title itself is eloquent in its incompleteness. Yes, the world today knows plenty about human bondage. The trouble is that the knowledge and the practice of liberty are lagging behind the need for freedom. But the Bible is different. It deals with human bondage frankly and fearlessly. And then, with an authority all its own, it goes on to set forth the truth that makes man free.

Hence we open the New Testament at such a place as the fifth chapter of Galatians, and hear Paul say, "Stand fast in the liberty wherewith Christ has made us free." Or we turn to the Gospel according to John and read the words of the Lord Jesus, "You shall know the truth and the truth shall make you free. . . . if the Son [meaning Himself] therefore shall make you free, you shall be free indeed."

I. AN EXAMPLE OF CHRISTIAN FREEDOM

By way of an example of these words, I take you to the Scripture reading of a few minutes ago, the letter of Paul to Philemon. This letter, by the way, is the only purely personal note that we have from the great Apostle. Behind the brief letter there is a story that speaks directly to our need of inner freedom today.

Suppose that you were to step up to a piano. There you might try a simple experiment in acoustics. You might strike the simple C major triad, consisting of the three notes, C, E, and G. Then the three tones would sound together. Or you might strike the chord again, with your foot on the pedal, releasing the dampers from the strings, and along with the three basic notes there would sound a whole series of overtones, caused by the other strings vibrating in sympathy with the chord. So with great books, and above all with the Bible; there are, as it were, overtones between the lines. When we use our imagination, as we ought to do whenever we read the Bible, we may hear the overtones of truth.

We come, then, to this letter from long ago. First of all, we must take a moment to sketch in the background. And the background is nothing less than one of the most horrible institutions known to man, the institution of human slavery. In a country like ours today it is difficult to realize what slavery was really like in ancient Rome. But history leaves no doubt concerning the character of that slavery. In *The Decline and Fall of the Roman Empire,* Gibbon estimates that half the population, or 60,000,000 people, were slaves. Other historians tell us that the proportion was even higher, probably two out of three.

It follows, then, that in ancient Rome life was appallingly cheap. In some parts of the Empire you could buy a human being for seventy-five cents. Such a situation could lead only to a terribly callous disregard of human life. For example, one writer tells how the Emperor Augustus interfered with a citizen named Pollio, who threw an offending slave into a pool of flesh-eating lampreys. But lest we call the Emperor Augustus a humanitarian, we must remember that on one of his ships the same Augustus had a slave crucified at the mast for killing a quail. The satirist Juvenal tells of a "lady" who ordered one of her slaves to be crucified just for the perverted thrill—the "kick," as we might say—of watching his agony on the cross. Someone remonstrated. She replied: "So then slave man, is he? He has done nothing, you say? Granted! I command it. Let my pleasure stand for a reason."

Just about the time when Paul wrote this letter to Philemon, Pedanius Secundus, a rich Roman, was assassinated by one of his four hundred slaves. During the trial, which was reported by the historian Tacitus, the counsel for the prosecution, Cassius, argued for the execution of all the four hundred slaves. He won the case, and all four hundred were led out to death as a public spectacle. With their lives they paid for the crime of one man.

It is not difficult to see that in ancient Rome a slave had no rights. Indeed that was what Roman law declared: that a slave was a chattel, like a beast or a wagon. If a slave committed a crime, such as stealing, or if he ran away, he was subject to a terrible penalty. If caught, he might be given double labor, or have branded on his forehead the letters "C.F.," which stood for *Cave furem,* "Beware of the thief!" Or else he might be thrown to lions in the arena, according to his master's whim. But notice this one fact, for it is a leading clue to our story. According to Roman law, there was but one hope for a fugitive slave: to find a friend of his master, who would intercede for the slave to be forgiven and reinstated.

II. THE CONTENTS OF THE EPISTLE

So much for the background. Now for the story written between the lines of this letter, the overtones of the epistle, if you will. There was in Colosse, a town of Asia Minor, a wealthy Christian, Philemon by name. He had a slave called Onesimus. This slave, who may well have occupied a place of trust in Philemon's household, stole money from his master and then ran away. In our mind's eye we can see him, a fugitive, fearful of being denounced as a runaway slave and a thief. Going from place to place, at last he comes to Rome, where, as Tacitus said, "All things horrible and disgraceful find their way."

One day, while the runaway slave is walking the streets, afraid and unhappy, he sees a crowd gathered at a certain house. Impelled by curiosity, he investigates. A man is speaking, and Onesimus listens. The speaker, who is chained to a Roman soldier, is a rather small man, not young, but with a powerful personality and commanding gestures. And how he can speak! So Onesimus, the fugitive, hears the Gospel truth that makes men free. And, as has happened through the ages, wherever that story has been told, he lingers to talk with the preacher. Thus Paul, the prisoner, brings Onesimus, the fugitive slave, to faith in the Lord Jesus Christ, whereby Onesimus becomes the spiritual son of Paul.

It is not hard to imagine that Onesimus returned for further talks with Paul, and that one day he opened up his heart to tell the story of his life. I think that we can hear Paul saying something like this: "Onesimus, there's just one thing for you to do. You'll have to go back to your master, and make everything right." Then Paul must have gone on to ask where Onesimus came from, and who was his master. When Onesimus replied, "Philemon of Colosse," Paul smiled and said: "Why, I know Philemon. I met him once when I was in Ephesus. Don't be afraid. Just come back tomorrow, and I'll have something for you." So Onesimus came back, and Paul gave him the very same letter that we heard read this morning, and told him to take it to his master.

III. THE SPIRIT OF THE APOSTLE

Do you know that this is one of the greatest personal letters in world literature? Even the skeptical French critic, Ernest Renan, called it "a true little masterpiece of letter writing." It has only one rival of its kind, a letter that Pliny the Younger wrote to his friend, Sabinianus. Pliny also was interceding for a fugitive slave. The other day I reread Pliny's letter, and I can assure you that, polished and persuasive though it is, Paul's epistle far surpasses it in tactful and powerful appeal. Indeed, this letter to Philemon is a primary source for our knowledge

of human relations. Believe me, from this one page of the New
Testament you can learn more regarding how to win friends
and influence people than you can learn from a whole shelf of
Dale Carnegie.

With exquisite tact, Paul greets Philemon and his family;
compliments Philemon on his reputation for hospitality; speaks
of himself as the prisoner of the Lord; and then with quiet humor
refers to Onesimus, whose name means "useful." Making a gentle
pun, the Apostle writes, "Formerly he was useless to you, but
now he is useful to you and to me." "Perhaps," he goes on, "this
is why he was parted from you for a while, that you might have
him back forever, no longer a slave but more than a slave, now
as a beloved brother." Here between the lines there sounds the
note of emancipation. Indeed, the letter to Philemon is the
first of the great anti-slavery documents. When Christianity got
to work in the Roman Empire, slavery was doomed.

"So if you consider me your partner, receive him as you
would receive me." Do you know what Paul did at this point? He
took the pen from the scribe and actually wrote what was, in the
eyes of the Roman law, a promissory note, obligating himself
to pay the debt of Onesimus: "If he has wronged you at all, or
owed you anything, charge that to my account. I, Paul, write this
with my own hand. I will repay it."

IV. THE LIBERTY IN CHRIST

So we come to the heart of the matter. Now the overtones
of deep inner freedom sound with compelling force. For we miss
the chief point of the story if we fail to see that what Paul did so
nobly for Onesimus is like what Christ has done to make us free.
As Martin Luther said, "We are all God's Onesimi, to my
thinking." Just as Onesimus sinned against his master, so have
we all sinned against God. Just as Onesimus was overwhelmingly
in debt to Philemon, so our trespasses place us in debt to God.
This we acknowledge when we say in the Lord's Prayer, "Forgive
us our debts."

"But where," someone asks, "is slavery today? Slavery in our
country was abolished almost a century ago." The answer is:
"Slavery may have been abolished politically. Yet it is still here,

inside men's hearts and lives." Says Solomon: "His own iniquity shall take the wicked himself, and he shall be held with the cords of his sins." There is a story of a famous smith in the Middle Ages who boasted that he could forge chains so strong that no one could break them. Then he committed a crime. When he came to himself in the dungeon, he knew that his case was hopeless, for there on his wrists were manacles with his own hallmark. As St. Peter says, "A man is a slave of anything of which he has been overcome." Yes, slavery is here today. Men are bound by a multitude of things: by habits they cannot break, by overt sins of the flesh, or by more respectable but equally enslaving frustrations, as well as by other evils. And by themselves men cannot free themselves.

In a book about Beethoven, *The Man Who Freed Music,* Robert Haven Schauffler says of the great composer: "He freed music. Himself he could not free from the bondage of his own absent-mindedness, his lack of practical common sense, and his dangerous temperament." What was true of Beethoven holds true with the rest of us: by ourselves we cannot free ourselves. Said Christ: "Whosoever commits sin is the slave of sin." There is not one of us here this morning who has not in the past been in bondage to sin, or is not now in bondage of one kind or another.

But Christ also said: "Ye shall know the truth, and the truth shall make you free. . . . If therefore the Son shall make you free, you shall be free indeed." Then He went on to die to make us free. Behind what Paul did for Onesimus there is the infinitely greater deed of Jesus Christ for us. So we may hear Him saying to God His Father something like this about us: "If he has wronged you at all, or if he owes you anything, charge that to my account. With the blood of my Cross I paid all his debt. I died to make him free."

How then do we secure this freedom, this payment of our debt, this emancipation from all that binds our lives and our spirits? The answer is the same now as in Paul's day, and in every other day: We have this freedom through faith in Christ as our only Lord and Saviour, through personal trust in Him whose service is perfect freedom.

At the close of the *Divine Comedy,* Dante is asked by St. Peter whether he has faith. Says Peter: "Good Christian, speak and manifest thyself; what thing is faith?"

Dante answers: " 'Faith is the substance of things hoped for, and the argument of things which are not seen,' and this I take to be its essence."

Then Peter says, likening real faith to a coin that rings completely true: "Right well hath now been traversed this coin's alloy and weight; but tell me if thou hast it in thy purse."

And the dialogue goes on in the words of the poet: "Whereupon I, 'Yea, so bright and round I have it that for me there is no perhaps in its impression.' "

When you and I come to the point of trusting to the Lord Jesus Christ all that we are and have and hope to be, without any "perhaps," then in our lives we shall know the meaning of His freedom.

VI. With Christ in the Unknown Future

33. Peter H. Eldersveld

Peter Herman Eldersveld, Christian Reformed Church.
Born in a manse, Kalamazoo, Mich., Jan. 18, 1911.
Educated, Calvin College, Grand Rapids, Mich. (B.A.);
Calvin Seminary (B.D.); University of Michigan
(M.A.); University of Chicago Divinity School. Pasto-
rates (1936-46). Radio minister, Christian Reformed
Church, "Back to God Hour" (estimated weekly hear-
ers, 3,000,000), since 1946. Editor, The Family Altar.
Books: Getting the Right Pitch (1949); That Ye May
Believe (1950); Of Law and Love (1954).

*This radio sermon about "A Time for the Truth of God" con-
sists in a survey and a critique of the current scene in our land,
theologically. Without any mention of names, the author shows a
sound working knowledge of recent times, when leading professors
of theology wrote about how often and how much they had
changed their doctrinal outlook and beliefs during the preceding
ten years. More recently, such conditions have become more stable,
and apparently, more nearly evangelical. But this preacher warns
his lay hearers that many ministers who count themselves orthodox do not yet accept what the Bible teaches and assumes about
its own inspiration and authority. To Protestants as followers
of the Reformers, the matter ought to seem crucial.*

*It would be difficult to question this interpreter's diagnosis.
The wide appeal of his radio ministry throughout the States and
Canada, as well as in other lands, shows that radio preaching
to laymen in our time need not be semi-secular, inspirational,
and entertaining. A message of this kind has strength rather than
charm. It belongs with literature of realism, not romance. Hence
it shows clarity and force, but with no fleeting glimpses of shift-
ing mists over distant unseen mountains. This latter kind of
"nature worship" some of us have heard occasionally, and in a*

sense enjoyed, at Lake Chautauqua and other semi-religious centers of entertainment for jaded oldsters. In fact, we may at times have attempted something of the sort ourselves.

Someone may wonder if the sterner kind of preaching would appeal to his home people. Let him ask himself two questions: first, "Why do I keep on reading?" and second, "How do I feel at the end?" Then let him hand the sermon to a succession of his strongest men and women, later asking each of them much the same two questions. He will find that they think it a pastor's duty at times to make people feel uncomfortable.

Many lay readers wish from the home pulpit stronger fare than they usually receive. But they wish it to be well cooked and served warm.

A TIME FOR THE TRUTH OF GOD

"The time will come when they will not endure sound doctrine; but after their own lusts shall they heap to themselves teachers, having itching ears; . . . and they shall turn away their ears from the truth, and shall be turned to fables." II TIMOTHY 4:3,4

WHEN PAUL WROTE the words of our text he was undoubtedly thinking of some time near at hand. But he has aptly described the religious condition of the day in which we live, an age of religious confusion, a time of "loose tongues and itching ears." In their search for peace of mind, people have fallen victims to every kind of cult and fad. Men now have more religion than in most previous generations, but amid all the tensions of our time their religion leaves them feeling bewildered and insecure.

One reason for this confusion is that people today are caught between two theological extremes, both of them in conflict with historic Biblical Christianity, as it is set forth in the historic Creeds of the Church. In order to understand what our text says about this matter, let us try to set it in the modern scene.

A DOCTOR WITH NO DOCTRINE

Not long ago it was fashionable for a minister to start his sermon by saying something like this: "I am no theologian, I am no dogmatist, I have no doctrine. I merely want to talk about a practical problem in your life, and you don't need any doctrine for that." He was not apologizing for such words. Indeed, he said them proudly, with a smile of sophistication. He thought that he was being clever. Of course the members of the congregation were delighted. That's why they came to church every Sunday! Strangely enough, they called him "Doctor," a title that comes from the same Latin root as the word "doctrine." Imagine a doctor with no doctrine! That would be like a physician with no science, a lawyer with no law, or a politician with no principles.

Nevertheless, it used to be popular in America to be a preacher without theology. In fact, many students prepared for the ministry by getting an education that carefully omitted doctrine almost completely. Except for the purpose of making historical surveys, they were not concerned about the Creeds of the Church. They were "liberals," and to them that meant being "liberated" from all dogmas. Students for the ministry were trained, not to be theologians, but to be public servants, who could talk on a variety of social themes, and engage in all sorts of social tasks.

That was the older liberalism as it came to expression in many American churches. It said that man's mind was the measure of all things; that we had progressed far beyond the historic Creeds of Christendom; that we had broken the shackles of ancient dogmas; and that the supernaturalism of Biblical theology had been discredited by modern science. The older liberalism insisted that the idea of God was simply the sum of the highest human virtues; that the only true religion was one of ethical values and of social action for the common good; that salvation was merely a matter of gradually improving ourselves and our world by our own efforts, after the example of Jesus; and that ultimately man would emerge from the long process of evolution, to find himself in a beautiful heaven right here on earth. So why bother about the doctrines of a pre-scientific past?

Isn't it amazing how naïve that sounds today! But it is not a caricature. That is what people in their right minds actually believed. They were serious about it, and thought that it made good sense. Now it seems that they are somewhat embarrassed, for today this older liberalism is being called a fool's paradise, even by those who once lived in it. To them has come a tragic disillusionment. In our dreadful time of world-crisis they have discovered that if man's mind is the measure of all things, it has given us mortals small dimensions; that if science is better than Scripture, science can also be destructive; that if the idea of God is only the sum of the highest human virtues, that sort of God doesn't amount to much; and that if we are to be saved by our own ethical efforts, we are both doomed and damned.

A RETURN TO THEOLOGY

Of late things religious have certainly changed! Theological doctrines have suddenly become somewhat popular again. The names of theologians appear in our newspapers and magazines. On their front pages leading periodicals have pictures of theologians. New books on theology are being published and old ones reprinted. Once more it has become quite fashionable to be theological!

In their pulpits some ministers now tackle the problems of theology, and people listen attentively. In the process of theological reconstruction seminaries and divinity schools have become centers of doctrinal ferment. Students for the ministry are no longer chiefly concerned with the social sciences, but they are probing the mysteries of faith and reason, sin and grace, transcendence and immanence, creation and redemption. Dogmas that were said to be archaic are now being re-examined and re-interpreted. Many of the old doctrinal terms are being revived, and much of the old liturgical language is to be found in this theological renaissance.

It is no longer a mark of intellectual servitude to have a

creed, even though it rests on divine revelation as well as on human reason. Once again, God is thought to be not only in man, but above him, and beyond him. Sin is a term that has come back into sermons, and in connection with sin there is much talk about the grace of God, instead of the works of men. Yes, there has been a decided change, both in the pulpit and in the pew, a change that has attracted public attention, no doubt because it reflects tremendous changes that have been taking place in our world.

However, a change is not necessarily a good thing. In the case of contemporary religion the change represents a reaction, and reactions are not always improvements. Often they lead to opposite extremes, which are usually no better, and essentially are no different. Opposite extremes may have the same point of departure, and may exist within the same framework. They may be poles apart, but only because they travel the same road, though in opposite directions. The north pole and the south pole are but the opposite ends of the same axis in the same earth, and at both poles the climate is much the same. Both are incredibly cold, because they are equidistant from the same equator.

This may not be an ideal analogy, but still it may help to indicate that the reaction against the older liberalism is only another kind of liberalism. Even though one has often been called modernism, and the other one orthodoxy, the two are not essentially different. They stem from the same roots, and they stand in the same tradition. This has often been pointed out by spokesmen for both sides. The two groups may be critical of each other, but only as members of the same household differ with each other. Despite the differences between the older and the newer liberalism, they show many signs of real kinship. Opposite poles attract, of course, because they are under the compulsion of the same magnetism.

A CURRENT BELIEF ABOUT THE BIBLE

From the viewpoint of our historic Christian faith, one basic fact proves the essential affinity of these two apparent opposites. They both have the same point of departure. They both reject the doctrine that the Bible is the only inspired and infallible

Word of God. From this point of departure they may go in opposite directions, but only to opposite ends of the same axis. The one group may be more concerned with ethics, and the other with theology; the one may depend primarily upon reason, the other upon revelation; the one may stress the immanence of God, the other His transcendence; but these differences are only superficial.

Both parties are fundamentally agreed about the Bible. Whatever may be its values, it cannot be regarded as God's only inspired and infallible revelation of Himself to man. Though in different ways, both parties call it "myth." They do not mean to say that it is altogether false. Neither do they say that it is altogether true. Rather, they say that it has many historical and moral and cultural values, and that it may even be a somewhat poetic or fictional approximation to what lies beyond the limits of human reason. It's a good Book, of course, but it isn't the redemptive self-revelation of God, upon which our thinking must be founded, by which our lives must be governed, and, above all, in which we may find the way of salvation for our souls.

This is the point at which the older and the newer liberalism join hands, and mutually take their leave of historic Biblical Christianity, as it is expounded in the great Creeds of the Church. Afterwards the two groups may go their own separate ways, but here at the start they are basically one. To strain the analogy just a bit, when you begin by denying that the Bible is the only inspired and infallible Word of God, you can go either toward the north pole or the south pole, but you cannot go round the world and over the face of the earth with the Gospel of our historic Christian faith.

To put the same truth in terms of our text, we are seeing today a modern fulfillment of the Apostle's words: "The time will come when they will not endure sound doctrine; but after their own lusts shall they heap to themselves teachers, having itching ears; and they shall turn away their ears from the truth, and shall be turned unto fables." What a description of the contemporary scene!

A PEOPLE IN PERPLEXITY

Because men have turned away from the authority of God's Written Word, we are now living in a time of great spiritual confusion. There is now going on an almost feverish theological activity, a frantic search for some sort of belief to replace the sound doctrines of historic Biblical Christianity. We now have a wide variety of theological thinking, which is represented by a multitude of teachers. Some of them still cling to the older liberalism, others go all the way with the newer forms, and still others are struggling somewhere between the two extremes. Many today call this an era of theological reconstruction. The Bible terms it a time of turning away from truth to fables. Men may have doctrine, but is it the sound doctrine of Holy Scripture?

People in general are feeling the effects of this theological confusion. They keep on searching for spiritual security, but they are not finding it in the fables that men have substituted for God's truth. In many ways the newer theology seems to appeal to them, but obviously it does not satisfy their heart hunger. Eventually they become suspicious of its paradoxes; for sometimes it sounds like a new kind of theological double talk. It uses the old Biblical language, but often with un-Biblical meanings. It criticizes modernism, but will not go back to historic orthodoxy, which would be the logical alternative. And so it leaves many people more confused than they were before.

According to a recent survey, ninety-eight per cent of our people believe in God, but only thirty-two per cent of them come to church regularly. That's like saying that you believe in liberty, but not in celebrating Independence Day, or in going to vote at the polls, or in singing the national anthem. What kind of God do these people have? Certainly not the God of Holy Scripture! Evidently they don't know much about Him. That they demonstrated clearly by their answers to other questions in the same survey. And what they do "know" is sadly confused. Indeed, this is the most disturbing fact about our day: the appalling ignorance of God's Word, and the mighty truths of historic Christianity, which it teaches. Of course you can hardly

expect anything else in a culture where theologians declare that
the Holy Bible is only "myth."

A PROGRAM FOR THE PREACHER

What shall we say to people who live amid such confusion?
This question confronts the Church of Jesus Christ with a new
seriousness today. The answer, of course, is always the same, and
it lies here at hand: "Preach the Word." This is what Paul told
young Timothy to do, because the Apostle knew that men would
turn away from sound doctrine to follow fables. Preach the
Word, for it gives men salvation through faith in the incarnate,
crucified, risen, and coming Christ. Preach the Word, for it is
the only antidote to the fables of both the older and the newer
liberalism. Preach the Word, for this is a time of spiritual confusion, and therefore a time for the truth of God.

In the eighth century before Christ the prophet Amos told
the people of his generation, which was much like our own:
" 'Behold the days come,' saith the Lord God, 'that I will send a
famine in the land, not a famine of bread, nor a thirst for water,
but of hearing the words of the Lord: and they shall wander from
sea to sea, and from the north even to the east; they shall run to
and fro to seek the word of the Lord, and shall not find it' "
(8:11,12).

In later Hebrew history that prophecy was literally fulfilled.
The four hundred years before Christ are properly called "the
silent years." There was little to record, for God had nothing
more to say to the people in those times. He sent them no
prophets, no revelations, no promises, no warnings. Nothing!
What could be worse than to exist in a world where God keeps
silent? Such silence may help to show why at the end of those
four hundred years a later generation did not even recognize
the Son of God, the Word made flesh. They even called Him a
devil! They crucified Him!

There comes a time when God takes away His Word from
those who do not want it. And then, even if they begin to
seek it, they may not find it. No, it hasn't gone this far with us
as yet. We can still preach the Word to the modern man. But
the silence of God may be nearer than we think. If we turn

away from His Word, and in its stead listen to fables, we cannot expect Him to continue speaking forever.

We of today have an abundance of Bibles, but unless we take the Bible seriously, it may have nothing to say to us. Try to imagine living in a world where the Bible was a closed book! Already it has become that to a growing number of our fellow men. And look at them! As Amos said, they are wandering from sea to sea, running to and fro. They dash from one psychiatrist to another; they read all manner of religious books; they consult the spirits of superstition. But nothing satisfies the deepest longings of their hearts. They have turned their ears away from the truth, and so the truth has turned away from them.

A MESSAGE FROM MARTYRS

About four hundred years ago, in what is now Belgium, people of the Protestant faith suffered the most horrible persecutions. Why? Because they believed the Bible to be the Word of God, and refused to submit to any government or Church that tried to make them renounce their faith. For reasons both religious and political they were brutally murdered by foreign overlords. Those people loved the Word of God so much that they were willing to die for it rather than give it up. To that little country belongs the honor of giving to the Reformation its first martyrs. According to Philip Schaff, historian of the Church, the number of those martyrs exceeded that of any Church in the sixteenth century, and perhaps that of the Early Christian Church under the tyranny of Rome. Belgium was bathed in the blood of those who believed in the Bible!

What if we could go back to reread such pages from the records of the past, and thus relearn our rich heritage? What if we could recapture the spirit of those who would rather lose their lives than lose their Bibles? Certainly we of today need that martyr spirit. We Protestants are supposed to be the spiritual descendants of those martyrs. Are we worthy heirs of that glorious heritage? Look at what we have done to the Bible for which they died! What does the blood of those martyrs say to our time of confusion, when theologians call the Word of God "myth," when churches prefer the words of men to the Word of

God, and when people turn away from the truth of God to follow the fables of men?

We know what those martyrs would say, the same thing that they did say four hundred years ago with their blood. If it were possible, they would say it again, and in the same way, especially in an age like our own. If they could speak in our time, with its modern means of communication, such as radio and television, what an impact they would make on this generation!

We are living in a time of crisis, when the truth of God's Word must be brought to bear upon the souls of men and upon the world in which we live. In some places the opposition is blatant, and in others it is subtle. To all those who take the Bible seriously, as the Word of God, there comes a tremendous responsibility. In this age of doctrinal confusion God is calling on us to speak out boldly. He would have us speak from the Bible the truth, the whole truth, and nothing but the truth, in the saving name of Him who alone is the Way, the Truth, and the Life.

So help us God!

34. Ralph L. Keiper

Ralph Lester Keiper. Baptist. Born, Easton, Pa., Mar. 29, 1912. Educated, Overbrook School for the Blind, Philadelphia; Moody Bible Institute; Lafayette College (A.B.); Eastern Baptist Seminary (B.D.); Columbia University (accepted candidate for Ph.D. in philosophy). Pastorates (1943-49). Instructor, Philadelphia School of the Bible (1949-57). Director of Research, Evangelical Foundation, Inc., Philadelphia, since 1957. Conference speaker, Mt. Hermon, Cal.; Winona Lake, Ind., et al. Guest preacher, Tremont Temple, Boston; First Baptist Church, New York; Tenth Presbyterian Church, Philadelphia, et al. Contributing Editor, Eternity.

The accompanying sermon illustrates what John A. Broadus recommended about "Preaching on Bible Books," one book to a sermon. Many of us have dealt with this "prison epistle" in terms of the Indwelling Christ, the Christian secret of joy, or an ideal church in the making. All of this is there, but so are "leads" toward a practical understanding of how to live in the light of the promised Second Coming.

The sermon grew out of notes jotted down during devotional readings. The minister found that his mind often wandered, because he was not reading with any special purpose. So he started through the Bible seeking to learn anew what each book teaches about the Final Return of our Lord. There was no conscious search for meaty sermon texts, or materials for the pulpit. But as a good householder the devotional reader jotted down from each Bible book every reference to the truth he had in view.

In the resulting homemade thesaurus of Bible passages, arranged textually according to Bible books, he now finds an unfailing source of fascinating materials for sermons, addresses, and articles. What comes to a minister devotionally, with a sense of newness, will later go to lay people helpfully, with no sense of sameness. As for "leads" toward an understanding of how to live in light of the Final Return, they appear in the sermon. Like Paul's love letter from prison, the following message breathes a spirit of "sweet reasonableness" (a rendering of Phil. 4:5).

HOW TO LIVE BEFORE CHRIST'S COMING

"Being confident of this very thing, that he which hath begun a good work in you will perform it until the day of Jesus Christ." PHILIPPIANS 1:6

IN THE EPISTLE to the Philippians the Apostle Paul sets forth most appealingly the precious truth of the Second Coming. In this letter he does not concern himself with the nature of Christ's Coming, nor has he anything to say about the time or the place of His Appearing. But he does write much about the way we are to live before the Lord comes again.

The Apostle here uses two expressions with reference to our Lord's Return. One of them points to "the day of Jesus Christ," or "the day of Christ" (1:6, 1:10, 2:16). The other tells about our spirit of expectation. The Apostle has been speaking about heaven. Then he says: "From whence we also look for the Saviour" (3:20). Each of these phrases bears on the Final Return of our Lord, and in a way that emphasizes our holy living in this present hour. It is as though the saints at Philippi had asked the Apostle, "What shall we do before the Lord returns?" The letter to the Philippians gives his inspired answer: "Until He comes live in a holy manner."

To one who knows the Apostle Paul it is no surprise to find

this "servant of the Lord Jesus Christ" setting forth the practical implications of our Lord's Return. "For me to live is Christ"— this is the theme of the epistle. "Let this mind be in you which was also in Christ Jesus"—this is the practical appeal. In looking forward to "the day of Jesus Christ," Paul sets forth the power for holy living, the pattern, the motive, and the reward.

I. THE POWER FOR HOLY LIVING

In our first passage the Apostle shows the power that enables us to lead holy lives. "Being confident of this very thing, that he which hath begun a good work in you will perform it until the day of Jesus Christ" (1:6). In characteristic fashion Paul has no doubt concerning the possibility of the believer's leading a sanctified life. His word "confident" comes from a Greek term that means "having been persuaded, and still remaining so." He can speak from personal experience, knowing how the Lord has enabled him to live righteously in the midst of a sinful world.

He appeals, also, to the readers' own experiences. The Lord has begun in them a good work. What is this good work? It is the work of faith through which we accept Christ as Saviour and Lord, and thus surrender to the will and good pleasure of God. You remember that on one occasion the people asked our Lord: " 'What shall we do, that we might work the works of God?' Jesus answered and said unto them, 'This is the work of God, that ye believe on him whom he hath sent' " (John 6:28,29).

The initial work of God is faith in the Lord Jesus Christ. This is the good work that God has begun in us. "For by grace are ye saved through faith, and that not of yourselves; it is the gift of God, not of works, lest any man should boast" (Eph. 2:8,9). Faith is the work that God has begun in us. The Greek word "begun" has a prefix equivalent to our word "in." Paul's emphasis here is on a faith worked into us of God, not on a faith that any man can regard as his contribution to his own salvation.

What is the nature of the good work that God has begun in us? In the term "work" we have the idea of activity. This inworked faith will ever afterward manifest itself in outward conduct. The standard of this conduct will ever be the will

and good pleasure of God. "Work out your own salvation with
fear and trembling, for it is God which worketh in you both to
will and to do of his good pleasure" (2:12b,13). Literally, the
Apostle here says "in the interests of the good pleasure." He
means that the child of God should ever have foremost in his
heart the interests of his Heavenly Father.

Is it always possible to do the will of God? Is there on earth no
condition in which we can fail our Heavenly Father? There is
only one such condition; that is, our self-will. According to the
original Greek, our text says, "He who has begun a good work . . .
will bring it to completion up to [even up to] Jesus Christ's
day." From the moment of regeneration to the time of our appearance in the very presence of the Father, moment by moment
He will continue His good work in us. What a provision, what
power, what a possibility for holy living in a sinful world! This is
our privilege, for this is His promise.

II. THE PATTERN FOR HOLY LIVING

In this first chapter verses ten and eleven set forth the pattern
for our holy living. According to the Apostle, three things are to
characterize our conduct. We are to approve things that are
excellent, we are to be sincere, and we are not to become an
offense to others. In the first of these statements Paul actually says,
"Keep testing the differing things." Evidently Christian discernment is a gift of grace. Not only are we to possess this gift; we
are also to use it daily.

We live in a complex world. Each day brings us its own
varied experiences. Some are of the Lord, and some of the world.
Some appeal to the spirit, and some to the flesh. Some are of
His grace, and others lead to disgrace. What are we to do? We
are to keep on "approving the excellent things." It would be
better to use the term prove, for Paul here employs the word of
the miner or the chemist who takes ore and tests it for purity.
Through study of the Word, by the witness of the Spirit, being
energized by the work of God from within, we are in a position
to make proper choices, which will enable us to live as saintly
children of God.

Then too we are to be sincere. In its English form this word comes from the Latin *sine cera,* which means "without wax." To a Roman this term had a story. Let us suppose that one of the believers in Philippi is on a visit to the Imperial City, and that he wants to take home a gift for his wife. He goes to one of the big "department stores." He approaches a counter with vases of various size, and finds one that appeals to him. Forgetting its fragility, he presses his finger against it, so that it falls to the floor, and is cracked.

What is to be done? In consternation he tells the clerk what has happened. Soon all seems right again. Nothing has happened that a little wax will not remedy. Retouched with glaze, and still cracked, to be sure, the vase looks as beautiful as before. But it is not so with the Christian life. We are to be "vessels fit for the Master's use" (II Tim. 2:21), vessels for the honor of our King. There must be no cracks, no need of "touching up." Our God requires perfection, nothing less.

The Greek term for "sincere" suggests another line of thought. The word means "to submit to the sun." "Bring your conduct out into the sunlight, and see if your ways of living stand the test of the brightest rays." Not only does the sunlight of God's presence here and now reveal in us defects that otherwise remain hidden. The Greek term for sincere suggests that at the coming of the Lord Jesus, the Sun of Righteousness, we are not to be ashamed in His Presence.

Not only are we to be sincere. We are also "not to be an offense." Here Paul is saying that we are so to live before the world that there will be nothing to injure or ruin our testimony. The root idea of the word "offense" has in it the picture of a stone of stumbling. True believers are "living stones." They are useful where they belong, according to the plan of the Master Builder. But other stones are out of place. They cause passers-by to stumble and fall.

Is it possible in all things to have spiritual discernment, ever to be sincere, and continually to live without offense? Paul replies that the secret of good conduct consists in "being filled with the fruits of righteousness" (1:11). This is a moment-by-moment process. It means that God expects us to show the fact of our salvation by the manner of our daily living. The term righteous ness has in it the idea of our being on a level with God. When we determine within our hearts to be honest with Him, we shall have no insuperable difficulty in pleasing Him.

Can we be thus righteous? Paul answers in the affirmative. This righteousness is not of ourselves, but of the Lord. It is the righteousness provided for us in Jesus Christ. It is made operative by His risen life. The Holy Spirit makes it possible for us to attain the righteousness of Christ as He takes the Word and speaks to our hearts, for it is His office to "convict us of righteousness."

Why are we to be righteous? Paul says, "Unto the praise and glory of God." Only those who believe are in a position to commend the goodness of God. Only Christians are in a position to become Lordlike. We alone can adorn the doctrine of the written Word. The Gospel according to us is the Gospel that the world reads. When we abound in the fruits of righteousness we adorn the doctrine acceptably to God, and at the same time we bear a good testimony to those who know not the Lord. Here again, the Apostle tells us about the time, "till the day of Christ." Our living in the present is ever to be a looking unto the future for His Return. The hope of seeing Him will encourage us to live in a holy manner until He comes in glory.

III. THE MOTIVE FOR HOLY LIVING

The second chapter of Philippians gives the motive for holy living. In a world full of darkness we are to be missionaries, holding forth the Word of life. Often we think of a missionary solely as one who preaches the Word of God in a foreign land. In verse fourteen Paul's suggestion is somewhat startling. He begins by saying that as missionaries our first task is not to "gripe" here at home. "Do all things without murmurings and disputings, that ye may be blameless and harmless, the sons of God without rebuke, in the midst of a crooked and perverse nation, among whom ye shine as lights in the world, holding forth the word of life" (2:14-16a).

It is difficult to think that the life of a missionary is so practical. Whether we serve God across the sea, or across the street, we are to be Christians without a "gripe," not given to quarreling.

We are not to live as men, but as sons of God, without rebuke. In a world of sin, our lives must shine as lamps for God. We must be more than men; we must be like God. Only then can our preaching and our other testimony be effective. Today we need men to live for Christ. When we live for Him we have in our grasp the mightiest defense of the Gospel. Perhaps the greatest foe of the Christian faith today is the professed follower who does not live for his Lord.

As we live for Him we can hold forth the Word of life; literally, hold it up. The strongest argument in support of the Gospel is a Christian life. As we shine for Him we shall have no difficulty in giving forth a testimony to which our part of the world will listen. All the while the fact of the Second Coming affords a powerful motive for holy living, and for constant service.

IV. THE REWARD FOR HOLY LIVING

In the last passage of our study Paul sets forth the promised reward for our holy living. He reminds us that our conversation, or citizenship, is in heaven. "We are a colony of heaven, and we wait for the Saviour who comes from heaven, even the Lord Jesus Christ" (3:20). Because of this blessed hope we can live out of the abundance of faith that is ours in Christ Jesus. This is why our lives ought to be different, not in the sense of being peculiar, but in the way of being holy in a world full of sin. Whether we act or speak, we are to have ever with us a sense of Christ's Presence, and a hope of His Final Advent. How wonderful it would be if people about us could hear in our words the voice of the Lord Jesus, and see in our walk the tokens of His Presence!

On that wonderful day when we shall see our Lord face to face, it will be in bodies fashioned like His own glorious body. No longer shall we have bodies with marks of sin and death. We shall be like Him, and we shall have bodies like unto the body of His glory. How wonderful for us now to contemplate that day. How important for us now to live in the light of His Second Coming!

35. Frederick C. Fowler

Frederick Curtis Fowler, II, United Presbyterian. Born, Denver, Colo., Dec. 2, 1901. Educated, Princeton University (A.B., A.M.); Princeton Seminary (Th.B.) D.D., Burton College; LL.D., Colorado College. Pastorates (1927-54); First Church, Duluth, Minn., since 1954. Chaplain, U. S. Navy (1944-46). President, National Association of Evangelicals (1950-52). Vice Chairman, All-American Association to Combat Communism (1950-53). Other religious, patriotic, television and radio responsibilities.

The accompanying message to believers takes up in turn three parts of a golden text. This textual method should help the listener to carry home the gist of the sermon, and associate these truths with the text. The phrasing of the three heads, with assonance that almost rhymes, tends to bring out the salient points. There is much to be said for textual sermons at times, especially in messages of assurance and hope for those who already love and serve the Lord.

The element of variety and human interest comes through the use of examples, most of which differ from the ordinary. The sermon begins with God's way of preparing to bless people in a vast city, and later beholds the glory of morning light on mountain peaks before the sun appears to have arisen. Thus it seems that preaching from a familiar golden text calls for a careful blending of old truths and new experiences. Ideally this would mean what John Morley said about the budget addresses of Gladstone: "The noble and imaginative use of the commonplace."

THE PROMISE OF BEING LIKE JESUS

"Beloved, now are we the sons of God, and it doth not yet appear what we shall be: but we know that, when he shall appear, we shall be like him; for we shall see him as he is."
                                                                    I JOHN 3:2

THESE WORDS tell of the Gospel that transforms us sinners. I have read that the great city of London is built over a bed of chalk. If you could sink a shaft down anywhere within its wide areas, you would have a spring of water, clear, cool, and pure. Should you go to the wealthier districts, or the poorer ones, and sink your shaft down where honorable, clean-living people dwell, or where crime, squalor, and sin abound, it matters not where, there would gush forth a spring of water, clean, and sparkling.

This is a picture of our human nature and the effects of the Gospel. It matters not whether there is honorable respectability or the foulest type of degeneration, let Jesus enter that life, sink the shafts of His love down into the depths of that soul, change the heart of stone into one of gentleness. Immediately, being born again, being given a new and different life and nature, from that heart will flow streams of living water, clear, pure, and sparkling. "In the wilderness shall waters break out, and streams in the desert" (Isa. 35:6).

What is the future, the end, for one who is born again? Paul states it clearly: "to be conformed to the image of his Son." John states it more fully: "Beloved, now are we the sons of God, and it doth not yet appear what we shall be: but we know that, when he shall appear, we shall be like him; for we shall see him as he is." What a marvelous truth! No matter how degraded the persons, how unlikely in outward seeming, there lies the divine possibility: we may be like Jesus. You can change that "may" to a "shall" simply by giving yourself into the keeping of Jesus Christ. What love this promise reveals! What encouragement this promise yields! What hope this promise seals!

I. WHAT LOVE THIS PROMISE REVEALS!

"Beloved, now are we the sons of God." The Scripture speaks of believers in the most exalted terms. According to the Bible, we are not merely servants, but "sons of God." We became His sons by adoption. By nature each of us was once "a child of wrath." But God takes into His family whom He will. He has adopted us, and made us heirs of His glory: "For ye have not received the spirit of bondage again to fear; but ye have received the Spirit of adoption, whereby we cry, 'Abba, Father.' The Spirit itself beareth witness with our spirit, that we are the children of God: and if children, then heirs; heirs of God, and joint-heirs with Christ" (Rom. 8:15-17a).

Then too we become sons of God by regeneration. Once we had only a carnal mind, which was at enmity with God. Then we were born again of the Holy Spirit, and thus renewed after the image of the Heavenly Father. "The carnal mind is enmity against God; for it is not subject to the law of God, neither indeed can be" (Rom. 8:7). "But as many as received him, to them he gave power to become the sons of God, even to them that believe on his name: which were born, not of blood, nor of the will of the flesh, nor of the will of man, but of God" (John 1:12,13). "And we have put on the new man, which is renewed in knowledge after the image of Him that created him" (Col. 3:10).

We who believe enjoy this blessed state here and now. It matters not whether we are rich or poor, learned or unlearned, we all share in this honor, here and now. Those who are not yet believers, whether they are rich or poor, learned or unlearned, are children of wrath, carnally minded, sons of Satan. To be carnally minded is death, "because the carnal mind is enmity against God." Thus they are not now sons of God. "But to be spiritually minded is life and peace."

Now as believers we are the sons of God. Such a relationship is not natural; it is supernatural. It was not wrought by us men; it was wrought of God. It came neither through our will, our deeds, nor our merits, but by the blessing of God on our faith in Christ. We became children of God by "being born again, not of corruptible seed, but of incorruptible, by the word of God, which liveth and abideth forever" (I Pet. 1:23).

We have been born anew, entirely by grace, through the agency of Christ who on the Cross bore the just desert of our sins and thus redeemed us with His precious blood; and through the agency of the Holy Spirit, who prepared our hearts to receive the Gospel.

"Now are we the sons of God"! What an unspeakably blessed state! God once showed His power in making us living creatures, and He revealed His love in making us sons. Plato gave thanks to God that He had made him a man and not a beast. But what cause have we to adore God's love, who hath made us children! The apostle puts into the text an *Ecce,* "Behold!"

What love the words of our text reveal! They embody the Lord's answer to the cry in a blessed old hymn, "Rock of Ages": "Foul, I to the fountain fly; wash me, Saviour, or I die." Notwithstanding all his imperfections, the present condition of the believer is one of joy and honor. As redeemed children of God we all are sheltered, protected, and bountifully supplied.

Nevertheless, we should not wish this life to be prolonged forever. It is like a tourist's pilgrimage, a sailor's voyage, a soldier's campaign. As God's redeemed children we should look forward to the end of our pilgrimage with joyful anticipation, and await the glorious future with increasing delight. "We know that, when he shall appear, we shall be like him; for we shall see him as he is."

II. WHAT ENCOURAGEMENT THIS PROMISE YIELDS!

"It doth not yet appear what we shall be, but we know"! When we consider our lives, we are apt to become discouraged. There is in us so little to display as evidence of the glory that is to be. Despite all our strivings after goodness, there is in our lives little evidence of His sweetness, gentleness, and purity. Perhaps the difficulty lies in the fact that we have been relying on our own efforts to make ourselves better.

According to an old tradition an angel assigned Nicodemus the task of making an image of the Lord. In pursuance of the angel's bidding, Nicodemus went into the forest, hewed down a cedar of Lebanon, and began to make the image. But despite all his skill he felt baffled. At last, unable to accomplish his task, and weary with ineffectual labor, he fell asleep. When he awoke, he saw that the work had been done. It had been carved by angel hands. Thus are we transformed from glory to glory, not by our own hands, but by those that were pierced, and through the work of the Holy Spirit. "We all, with open face beholding as in a glass the glory of the Lord, are changed into the same image from glory to glory, even as by the Spirit of the Lord" (II Cor. 3:18).

In order that you may become like Jesus, you need to know Him. In order to know Him, you have to see Him. He is no longer here in the flesh; He is in the Father's house. How, then, can you see Him? With the eye of faith, and through the appointed means of grace. Note what the Apostle says about the secret of being transformed: we are to behold the glory of the Lord in a glass, or mirror. There are two mirrors in which you can behold the likeness of the Lord.

The written Word of God reflects His glory. In the Bible you can behold Him. Read the Holy Scriptures, for they testify of Him. There is also the mirror of a consecrated life. In the lives of those who are truly His own, you can see reflections of His goodness. Let any child of God by faith live close to Him, and the goodness of the Lord will be reflected in that person's face, manner, and disposition. Any minister can tell of more than one saint of God, thrown on an invalid's couch, unable to leave the room for years, and yet through constant communion with her Lord, sending forth a fragrance not to be found elsewhere on earth.

Everyone of you has witnessed the transforming power of love. You have seen an aged pair, married over a period of four or five decades, loving and living together, and becoming more like each other. The resemblance is not merely in habits and ways of thinking, but in their very appearance, as though some gentle angelic hand had been fashioning their faces into the same image. Love has wrought such a transformation that it almost startles us: the light of eyes full of love, the expression of a dear face, and the tone of voice speaking words of cheer.

The same principle appears in a storied form. In "The Old Stone Face" Nathaniel Hawthorne tells of a lad who grew to manhood, and then became old, inconspicuously, in a valley where everyone awaited the advent of a person resembling "the man in the mountain." At last to their amazement they discovered that constant thought and communion with the Great Stone Face had transformed their humble neighbor into the very same likeness.

Look, then, unto Jesus! It is the vision of the Lord Jesus in all His glory that brings the transformation. By constant communion with Him you will become like Him. Do not let any church or creed, any priest or ordinance, come between your soul and your Lord. He alone is the light of the world and the bread of life, the true manna from heaven. Constant fellowship with Him will mean that your growth into His likeness will be normal and wholesome.

III. WHAT HOPE THIS PROMISE SEALS!

"When He shall appear we shall be like him, for we shall see him as he is." When our Lord was here in the flesh, His glory was largely veiled. His Deity was concealed in infirmity. His power was ofttimes hidden in sorrow and weakness. His riches were buried under poverty and shame. But when He shall appear in glory, then we shall see Him as He really is. We are not worthy to appear in His presence, but still we need not despair. When at last we behold Him we shall become like Him. Yes, what a hope this promise seals!

God's promises are certain to be fulfilled. He promises that we who are His children shall be like the Lord Jesus. Little by little, here and now, we are being transformed into the perfect likeness of our blessed Redeemer. What a hope this promise seals!

Do not wonder that I can not describe the glorious transforma tion. Remember that John, the beloved disciple, walked and talked with Jesus in the days of His flesh, inquired into His secrets, and received His revelations. On the Mount of Transfiguration John beheld Moses and Elijah in glory from heaven, and witnessed the glorified form of the Lord Jesus Christ. Afterward the beloved disciple often communed with the Risen Lord, not yet the Ascended Saviour. In visions not of earth he later beheld the new heavens and the new Jerusalem, in all the glory of God. If John, I say, did not attempt to describe the transformation of the saints, except in the most general terms, how can I portray such splendor?

But one thing I know. I know that the promise is given and that the hope is sealed. I know that I shall have a body like unto His body, sinless and incorruptible, spiritual and free from disease, clothed with beauty and power, yet real and true. I also know that this can come to pass only through my being made progressively like Him now, so that when He shall appear I shall be found perfectly like Him forevermore.

Sometimes here on earth the Lord gives one of His children a vision of the glory that is to be in heaven. Such an experience He granted to Moses on Mount Sinai, and so great was the glory shining from his face after communing with God that he had to put on a veil before he returned to be with men. The Lord granted some such vision to Peter, James, and John on the Mount of Transfiguration. Stephen, also, when dying, saw "the heavens opened, and the Son of man standing on the right hand of God." Then the bystanders saw that his face shone like the face of an angel.

Many an aged saint, like my mother and my father, has looked on the face of the Lord long and lovingly, and then has mirrored the glory that is to be. One morning in boyhood my mother awakened me early so that I could see the foreglow of the coming dawn. We were in Paradise Valley at the base of Mount Rainier, whose summit was covered with ice and snow. The sun had not yet risen, but before it reached the horizon, the peak reached up so high into the heavens as to catch and reflect rays of the sun while it was still unseen. That mountain peak was shedding abroad a foreglow of the splendor yet to be. So does many a saint mirror to others the foregleams of the Son of Righteousness at His coming glory, when we shall all be changed, at the twinkling of an eye, and made like unto His own glorious majesty.

What a hope His promise seals! "Now we see through a glass, darkly, but then face to face." Knowing what we are now, having the encouragement of what Christ is doing for us, realizing the assurance of the hope that He has sealed, what faces us? Our expectancy ought to issue in responsibility. "Every man that hath this hope in Him, purifieth himself, even as he is pure." He who does not seek to live out his inbred hope fails his Lord. Watching and waiting, hoping and longing, all mean that we cannot forget our debt to Him who has called us out of darkness into His marvelous light, adopted us into His redeemed family, and made us joint-heirs with Christ in the glory that is to be.

On every hand we ought to hear the call today: "O ye who bear the image of God, while on your way to share the glory of Christ, be sure to lead a Godlike, Christlike life!"

There is an old legend that a huge black stone statue of the king in Ethiopia sat upon the throne. The feet were close together, and the hands were pressed on the arms of the chair. The king was ready to arise. The face of the statue looked wistfully toward the East, awaiting the morning sun. With the first glimmer of dawn, the face lighted up, and a strain of music came from the parted lips. To him the dawn must have meant the beginning of a new and glorious day.

This is the ideal attitude for the Christian today. Amid the darkness keep your face toward the rising sun. Ere long the trumpet will sound, the dead in Christ will rise, and in the twinkling of an eye you will be transformed into the glorious image of your Lord. At last you shall see Him as He is. What a glory His promise seals!

36. Howard O. Jones

Howard Olean Jones, Christian and Missionary Alliance. Born, Cleveland, O., Apr. 21, 1921. Educated, Oberlin High School; Nyack Missionary College (1944). Pastorates (1944-52); Smoot Memorial Church, Cleveland, O., (1952-58). Staff worker, Billy Graham New York Crusade. With Mrs. Wanda Jones, an evangelistic mission, Liberia, Ghana, and Nigeria (1957). Full-time associate evangelist, Billy Graham Team, since 1958. Plans removal to Liberia as headquarters for radio and television ministry by husband and wife; also help in preparing for the Graham Crusade in Africa (1960), and elsewhere later.

This young Negro evangelist feels that in the States, as in Africa, his people most need Christ, and that believers need a personal experience of His indwelling. In keeping with First John, which appeals to the heart, most simply, the sermon speaks to the heart, with every evidence of sincerity and spirituality. Often we think of such pulpit work in terms of Pietism. The preacher here would have us look on it with reference to the indwelling Christ.

With all our proper emphasis on making it seem intellectually respectable to believe in Christ today, do we not as evangelicals also need to learn with Pascal that "we know the truth, not only with the reason, but also with the heart"? Structurally the message follows the two parts of the text, in the original order. The sermon exalts the living Christ, and seeks to bring Him into our hearts as the heavenly Guest. Is not this the most immediate and pressing need of every minister and layman?

O come to my heart, Lord Jesus;
There is room in my heart for Thee.

THE INDWELLING CHRIST

"Hereby we know that he [Christ] abideth in us, by the Spirit which he has given us." I JOHN 3:24b

CHRIST LIVES in us as our Heavenly Guest! What a wonderful and precious truth for the Christian to meditate upon! What a blessed and glorious spiritual reality and experience for every child of God to have here on the earth, and to know in this life! As we undertake this study, therefore, may God bless this truth to our hearts and lives. According to the text, our study ought to consist of two main parts.

I. THE FACT OF CHRIST'S INDWELLING PRESENCE

First let us consider the Apostle John's assurance that Christ now dwells in the hearts and lives of true believers. "We [who accept him as Saviour] know that he abideth in us." This precious truth of Christ's Indwelling was once a mystery, hidden from the ages. The word mystery here means a truth known only by revelation. The mystery of His being our Heavenly Guest appears in Paul's Epistle to the Colossians:

"Even the mystery which hath been hid from the ages and generations, but now is made manifest to his saints: to whom God would make known what is the riches of the glory of this mystery among the Gentiles; which is Christ in you, the hope of glory: whom we preach, warning every man in all wisdom; that we may present every man perfect in Christ Jesus: whereunto I also labor, striving according to his working, which worketh in me mightily" (1:26-29).

Christ lives in us! Exactly what do these words mean to us

now? For the answer let us turn to Alexander Maclaren, noble preacher and "prince of expositors." What he once said in Manchester, England, can be of untold help to us now:

It is not to be weakened into any notion of participation in His likeness, sympathy with His character, submission to His influence, following His example, listening to His instruction, or the like. A dead Plato may so influence his followers, but that is not how a living Christ influences His disciples. What is meant is no mere influence derived but separable from Him, however blessed and gracious that influence might be, but it is the Presence of His own Self, exercising influences which are inseparable from his Presence, and only to be realized when He dwells in us.

Beloved, we who know the Lord as our Saviour rejoice that we have as our daily Guest the Christ who died on Calvary, the Christ who has arisen and ascended, the Christ who is now seated at the right hand of God the Father, making intercession for us. But listen! We must not stop here. Instead, we must tell the world that this same Jesus who is both Lord and Christ is also desirous of dwelling within the hearts and lives of believers right here on this earth.

This is one truth that makes Christianity unique and distinctive in its preëminence over all the other religions of the world today. Consider any of them, whichever one you choose, and you will discover that since the founder or founders of that religion have died none of the followers have had any experiential knowledge of such indwelling on the part of their leader, or leaders. Any such continued presence, or experience, would be utterly impossible. It would be unthinkable. All of those other religious leaders and would-be prophets are now dead, and in their graves are awaiting the judgment of God.

But not so with Christianity! Christianity lives because Christ lives. My friend, Christianity is Christ, and Christ is Christianity. You cannot separate the two, not even in thought. The teachings and the doctrines of Christianity all center in the Living Christ. On the Cross He once gave His precious and sinless life for the redemption of sinful men and women everywhere. But His death was not the end. According to the authority of God's written

Word, on the third day He came forth from the grave as the Victor over death. Now He lives in the heart of every true believer.

In a book entitled *Sanctification* Charles G. Finney further expounds this blessed truth: "The Spirit of Christ, then, or the real Deity of Christ, dwells in the truly spiritual believer. But this fact needs to be spiritually apprehended, and kept distinctly and continually in view. Christ not only in heaven, but Christ within us, as really and truly inhabiting our bodies as we do, as really in us as we are in ourselves, [this] is the teaching of the Bible, and must be spiritually apprehended by a divine, personal, and inward revelation, to secure our abiding in Him.

"We not only need the real presence of Christ within us, but we need His manifested presence to sustain us in hours of conflict. Christ may be really present within us as He is without us, without our apprehending His presence. His manifesting Himself to us, as with us and in us, is by Himself conditioned upon our faith and obedience. His manifesting Himself within us, and thus assuring us of His constant and real presence, confirms and establishes the confidence and obedience of the soul."

Yes, it is wonderful to have within our hearts as Christians the personal and abiding presence of Jesus Christ, the Son of the Living God. Let us, therefore, testify to this truth with all assurance and boldness. With the Apostle may we ever feel ready and glad to bear our witness: "We know that he abideth in us."

II. THE SECRET OF HIS INDWELLING PRESENCE

In the second place the Apostle tells us how the Indwelling of Christ as our Heavenly Guest actually takes place in the hearts of true believers. "Hereby we know that he abideth in us, by the Spirit which he hath given us." Through the work of the Holy Spirit Christ now dwells in the hearts of Christians. In the "days of His flesh," when He lived in a human body, He chose to be limited in the scope of His ministry. In other words, practically, it was out of the question for Him to be in more than one place at a given time. But after our Lord ascended into heaven, the Holy Spirit came to earth at Pentecost and filled the hearts of all the believers gathered together in prayer for His coming.

Because of Infilling by the Holy Spirit, the lives of those early believers were transformed, so that they had personal piety and power such as they had never known before. Also, the Scriptures clearly reveal, when they experienced this blessed Infilling, they became conscious of Christ's Indwelling Presence. This experience, too, seemed to them new, strange, and glorious. Christ became more than merely their Saviour and Friend, who walked by their side, bringing them inspiration and comfort by His words full of grace. Through the Incoming of the Holy Spirit this same Christ also became their Heavenly Guest, dwelling within their hearts and lives. He alone became the Lord and Master of their entire being. Henceforth they lived to glorify Christ, not themselves. In Him they found new power over the forces that formerly had defeated them. At last their preaching was full of power. Consequently, their ministry for God became effective in winning souls to Christ, and in furthering the cause of righteousness here upon earth.

Today many professing Christians are living without power, victory, and joy. The reason seems to be simply this: they have not yet fully yielded themselves to God in glad obedience to His will. They have not yet admitted the living Christ to their hearts through the Infilling of the Spirit. These persons know Christ as their Saviour. They accept the assurance that their sins have been covered by the Blood, and that their Lord will take them to heaven when they die. But these same persons do not yet know Christ as their Indwelling Guest. Since they do not by personal experience know the presence and power of the Indwelling Christ, who would enable them to prevail over the world, the flesh, and the devil, their lives seem to be shallow, weak, and largely devoid of joy. Surely they cannot testify with the Apostle Paul:

> I am crucified with Christ; nevertheless I live; yet not I, but Christ liveth in me: and the life which I now live in the flesh I live by the faith of the Son of God, who loved me, and gave Himself for me (Gal. 2:20).

Today we need desperately to rediscover the difference between these two stages in Christian experience. If we are ever going to produce the sort of believers for our day and time, we all need to realize that there is a vast difference between accepting Jesus as our Saviour and knowing Him as our Indwelling Guest. Today as almost never before we need a generation of believers with spiritual dynamic: believers with Christlike purity, power, and passion. Unless we rediscover the revealed truth that only through the Holy Spirit does Christ dwell in the hearts and lives of believers, we can not begin effectively to meet the challenge of this critical hour. Hence we must not only teach our new converts that they should accept Jesus Christ as their personal Saviour. We must also carefully lead them to allow the Christ of God through the Holy Spirit to come into their hearts as their Heavenly Guest. Unless the believer acknowledges this ministry of the Spirit within his heart and life, how can he ever rightfully call Christ Jesus his Lord?

Dear Christian friend, in this present evil world do you enjoy a life of power and victory? Or in the home, the school, and the shop are you often a weak and defeated follower of the Lord? If so, you need not remain in this pitiful condition, with only enough religion to make you feel restless and wretched. In the Living Christ a new and transforming experience awaits you. You need only surrender your entire being to God, so that the Holy Spirit may reveal in you the presence and glory of the Indwelling Christ. When you allow Him to become your Heavenly Guest, and thus make your heart His home, He will give you victory. He will give you power for every weakness and solace for every sorrow. Then you will know why the Apostle says:

> Being confident of this very thing, that he which hath begun a good work in you will perform it until the day of Jesus Christ (Phil. 1:6).

Dear Christian, open your heart to Him now, that He may come in. Behold, the Living Christ stands at the door of your heart, and knocks, with the hand that was pierced on the Cross. If by faith you open the door and let Him come in, He will become your Heavenly Guest, and ever henceforth make His home in your heart. By His Indwelling He will give you victory and peace, with many blessed foretastes of heaven's joy. Then you will want to sing and pray with Frances R. Havergal:

Live out Thy life within me,
  O Jesus, King of kings;
Be Thou Thyself the answer
  To all my questionings.

Live out Thy life within me;
  In all things have Thy way;
I, the transparent medium,
  Thy glory to display.

37. Oswald C. J. Hoffmann

Oswald Carl Julius Hoffmann, Lutheran Church, Missouri Synod. Born in a parsonage, Snyder, Neb., Dec. 6, 1913. Educated, Concordia College, St. Paul (A.B.); Concordia Seminary, St. Louis (B.D.); University of Minnesota (A.M.); D.D., Concordia Seminary; LL.D., Valparaiso University, Valparaiso, Ind. Instructor, Bethany College, Mankato, Minn. (1936-40); University of Minnesota (1940-41). Professor and director of public relations, Concordia Collegiate Institute, Bronxville, N. Y. (1941-48). National director of public relations, Missouri Synod, since 1948. Past President, National Religious Publicity Council. Secretary, Lutheran Church Productions, (Martin Luther, et al). Various other activities and honors. Speaker, National Lutheran Radio Hour, since 1955.

This radio preacher has found that hearers desire preaching about heaven. So do hosts of other laymen. In a recent article a prominent lay editor discussed reasons why the modern man comes to church. Apart from the main reason, which is that it is a worthy habit, the editor insisted, the average man comes to church to find out if it is still possible for an educated person to believe in the life hereafter. Often, alas, he quits coming, partly because the man in the pulpit concerns himself with secondary things.

The sermon evinces a pleasing spirit. Clearly and simply, without apology, dogmatism, or any surmises, the speaker sets forth what the Lord Jesus tells about heaven as the home of God's redeemed children, and about the possibility of a sincere person's failing to find the way home to the Heavenly Father. The words from the Lord Jesus come with all the more appeal to the heart because He spoke them in the Upper Room, on the evening before the "day of the Cross."

The present volume began with a simple Gospel message about "The Grace of God." The closing sermon has to do with "Heaven As Your Home." So ought it to be with all of a man's preaching. As with the golden text of the Bible (John 3:16), the message of the evangelical pulpit bases everything on the love of God in action to redeem and transform us sinners and our world. The action all centers in the Cross of Christ, and issues in heaven, with the fulfillment of all our hopes for the Kingdom of God.

HEAVEN AS YOUR HOME

"There are many rooms in my Father's house."
—ST. JOHN 14:2a
(Goodspeed)

MANY PEOPLE who listen to this broadcast have written in asking us to tell them more about heaven. In answer to their questions, and because the subject comes to mind naturally in the season when the Christian Church celebrates the Resurrection of our Lord, we are going to talk today about heaven.

THE ASSURANCE OF A PLACE

Heaven is a place like home. From the dawn of history believers in God have looked upon heaven as a place. There they will some day be received with the cheery cries of greeting that welcome a man home after a long trip or a hard day at the office. When the doors of home close behind him, the strident noises of the world are shut out and forgotten. As eager faces look for his smile, and little arms entwine themselves about his neck, he finds himself enveloped in a warmth of love and understanding. This is home, the way a home should be. And this is heaven, the way heaven is home.

Small wonder that with glad anticipation the faithful who have trusted in God have looked forward to their homegoing. Indeed, the Death and the Resurrection of Christ have made this homegoing still more vivid, and, if anything, have made those who know Christ more eager to experience it.

Someone has pointed out that the Old Testament prophets, when they spoke of heaven, evidenced their belief in God by their willingness to go, even when they wanted to stay. With the Resurrection of Jesus Christ, Paul could give expression to an even greater anticipation, which may be described as willingness to stay, but wanting to go. Listen to what he has to say in this epistle of joy: "To me to live is Christ, and to die is gain. If it is to be life in the flesh, that means fruitful labor for me. Yet which I shall choose I cannot tell. I am hard pressed between the two. My desire is to depart and to be with Christ, for that is very far better" (Phil. 1:21-23).

The Apostle, of course, had a special insight into the glories of eternal life, because of the personal experience that he described in Second Corinthians. He said that he was caught up into heaven, and into paradise itself. Moved by this experience, he was set on fire with a longing to depart and be with Christ. He had found heaven completely indescribable, and he noted that he had heard unspeakable words. These ineffabilities will not be for us today, but we shall simply recount what the Bible tells us about heaven.

THE DWELLING PLACE OF GOD

The Bible speaks continually about heaven as the dwelling place of God. The Second Book of Chronicles tells us that the Temple priests prayed, and that "their prayers came up to his holy dwelling place, even unto heaven." The Psalmist asked, "Whom have I in heaven but thee?" In another place he affirmed, "Unto thee do I lift up mine eyes, O thou that dwellest in the heavens." Isaiah prophesied, "Thus saith the Lord, the heaven is my throne, and the earth is my footstool." Heaven is God's place, God's palace, God's home.

In the sixteenth chapter of St. Luke Jesus tells the story of a rich man and a beggar named Lazarus. The beggar died and was carried by the angels into Abraham's bosom, a common Hebrew expression for heaven. The rich man also died and was buried. Finding himself in hell, the rich man looked across a deep gulf. There he saw Father Abraham, and Lazarus in his company. In the ensuing conversation it becomes apparent that there is a vast deal of difference between heaven and hell.

The rich man felt his fate deeply, for he was in torment. Lazarus felt his destiny deeply, for he was comforted. The rich man was so disturbed over the outcome of his life that he begged Father Abraham to send someone to earth, in order that his five brothers might be warned, and avoid his fate. Father Abraham replied that the brothers had warning enough in the Word of God, and that if they did not believe the Word of God as it was preached to them, they would not be changed if someone would wave a red flag at them after having risen from the dead.

It is not pressing the story too far to say that heaven is a real place, just as earth is a real place. The main difference is that earth is a place spoiled by sin and corruption while heaven is a place holy and pure. This world shall pass away, but that place shall not vanish, for it is a city that hath foundations, whose Builder and Maker is God.

That place will be different from this place. In heaven there will be no unhappiness or sorrow. There will be no sin, or any of its consequences. "God shall wipe away all tears from their eyes; and there shall be no more death, neither sorrow, nor crying, and there shall be no more death, for the former things are passed away" (Rev. 21:4).

There will be people in heaven, for heaven will be their home. They will be gathered round their real and only Father, who created them. It would be strange indeed if the children of the same heavenly Father did not recognize each other. They will all be one loving, happy, and heavenly family.

In heaven people will be people, just as they are here. They will not be angels, but they will be like angels, completely happy to do God's will, and completely ready to serve Him. They will be at home, for heaven is home to those who have come to God through great tribulation and have washed their robes in the blood of the Lamb.

THE PLACE NOT FOR EVERYBODY

All of this raises an important question. "How do I get to heaven?" The question is not irrelevant, and it is not superfluous. One of the tragic facts about heaven is that not everybody is going to get there. Some of those who do not get there will be victims of the popular idea that the way to reach heaven is simply to be sincere. Sincerity is a mighty good quality, but it will not be enough to get anybody into heaven.

You can be sincerely mistaken. Common sense tells us that this is true. Several years ago a doctor issued a prescription calling for a certain quantity of barium sulphate. The druggist used barium sulphite. There is very little difference between the names of the two drugs. Any layman might think that the one is another form of the other. However, one is used for curative purposes, and the other is a deadly poison. So the druggist was arrested and tried. He was found guilty, and was given a three-year sentence. In this case the druggist was obviously sincere, but his sincerity did not save him. It is necessary to be sincere, and at the same time, to be right.

No one is right who thinks that he is going to get into heaven simply by being good. All men know that they ought to be good. They have an instinctive feeling that they ought to be holy. What many fail to reckon with is that their unholiness makes all their good works, no matter how well intentioned, useless and purposeless when it comes to getting into heaven. The Bible is very clear about this matter. It says bluntly: "By grace are ye saved, through faith, and that not of yourselves: it is the gift of God: not of works, lest any man should boast." Dwight L. Moody once commented that if a man could work his way into heaven you would never hear the last of it! He went on to say: "I'm glad that through all eternity in heaven we will never hear anyone bragging about how he worked his way to get there."

There is not a man alive who by his own efforts can earn his way into the dwelling place of God. In the history of the world only One has constantly looked upon the face of God, and has never had to turn away in shame. He lived His life, and died His death, not in His own behalf, but in the place of each of us. When we recognize that anyone who tries to earn God's favor by his own efforts will fail by virtue of the fact that he thinks he can do it simply by trying, then the real import of what Christ did on the Cross begins to dawn upon us. No one has ever reached heaven, or ever will reach heaven, by his own efforts, or by his own worth.

In St. Paul's Epistle to the Romans the eighth chapter holds the key that must be inserted into the doors of heaven before they will swing open wide: "God hath done what the law could not do." God has seen to our eternal salvation and our residence in heaven. That is the whole point of the Cross of Jesus Christ. God has done for us what none of us can do for ourselves. By our good works, by our observance of the Law, we cannot win our way through to heaven, but God has won through for us.

THE PLACE FOR YOU IN CHRIST

There is only one way to heaven. Christ says, "I am the way; . . . no man cometh unto the Father but by me." He also says, "He that believeth on the Son hath everlasting life; he that believeth not shall not see life, but the wrath of God abideth on him." Jesus Christ alone is the Way, the Way that leads to the Father, and to the mansions that the Lord has prepared for those who love Him. Once again, our Lord says, "If it were not so, I would have told you."

When you put full confidence and trust in Jesus Christ for your salvation, you are walking in the way to heaven. It is not enough to try your best. It is not enough to learn to repeat by heart a Scripture passage or two. It is not enough even to know the right way. You must go in that way, the way of complete dependence upon Jesus Christ, of whom the Bible says that His blood cleanses us from all sin.

The Lord Jesus issues this stern warning: "Not everyone that saith to me, 'Lord, Lord,' shall enter into the kingdom of heaven, but he that doeth the will of my Father which is in heaven." It is not enough that you confess Christ while your heart is far from Him. It is not enough to join the church, and then neglect to do God's will; to be indifferent to His praise; to reject the privilege of prayer. In other words, it is not enough to go your own way.

This is a personal matter. You cannot claim, "Heaven is my home," until your heart says, "Christ is my Lord." Take Jesus Christ into your heart as Saviour and Lord, and He will take you to His home in heaven. When the doors of His house open to you, and then close behind you, you will begin to understand that you have come home, to your home as well as His. And suddenly the whole glorious reality will unfold before you, the reality that is as yet only a promise and an eternal prospect. "We shall be like Him, for we shall see Him as He is."

❧

"O Lord, support us all the day long of this our troublous life, until the shadows lengthen and the evening comes, and the busy world is hushed, and the fever of life is over, and our work is done. Then in thy mercy grant us a safe lodging and a holy rest, and peace at the last; through Jesus Christ our Lord. Amen." (John Henry Newman).

❧

"The God of peace, who brought again from the dead our Lord Jesus, the great Shepherd of the sheep, by the blood of the eternal covenant, equip you with everything good, that you may do his will, working in you that which is pleasing in his sight, through Jesus Christ; to whom be glory for ever and ever. Amen" (Heb. 13:20,21).